Recreation and the Law

Valerie Collins
Senior Lecturer in Law
Nottingham Trent University
UK

E & FN SPON
An Imprint of Chapman & Hall

London · Glasgow · New York · Tokyo · Melbourne · Madras

Published by E & FN Spon, an imprint of Chapman & Hall, 2-6 Boundary Row, London SE1 8HN

Chapman & Hall, 2–6 Boundary Row, London SE1 8HN, UK

Blackie Academic & Professional, Wester Cleddens Road, Bishopbriggs Glasgow G64 2NZ, UK

Van Nostrand Reinhold Inc., 115 5th Avenue, New York NY10003, USA

Chapman & Hall Japan, Thomson Publishing Japan, Hirakawacho Nemoto Building, 7F. 1–7–11 Hirakawa-cho. Chiyoda-ku, Tokyo 102, Japan

Chapman & Hall Australia, Thomas Nelson Australia, 102 Dodds Street, South Melbourne, Victoria 3205, Australia

Chapman & Hall India. R. Seshadri. 32 Second Main Road. CIT East. Madras 600 035, India

First edition 1984
Second edition 1993

© 1984, 1993 Valerie Collins

Typeset in 10/12 Times by Fox Design, Bramley, Surrey
Printed in Great Britain by Page Brothers, Norwich

ISBN 0 419 18240 3

The publisher makes no representation, express or implied, with regard to the accuracy of the information contained in this book and cannot accept any legal responsibility or liability for any errors or omissions that may be made.

A catalogue record for this book is available from the British Library

Library of Congress Cataloging-in-Publication data
Collins, Valerie.
Recreation and the law / Valerie Collins. – 2nd ed.
  p. cm.
Includes index.
ISBN 0–419–18240–3
1. Recreation–Law and legislation–Great Britain. 2. Sports–Law and legislation–Great Britain. I. Title.
KD3521.C65 1993
344.41'099–dc20
[344.10499]
                                                          93-17601
                                                          CIP

∞Printed on permanent acid-free paper, manufactured in accordance with the proposed ANSI/NISO Z 39.48–199X and ANSI Z 39. 48–1984

Contents

Acknowledgements

I would like to thank Terry Hanstock, law librarian at Nottingham Trent University, for his help in researching the information for this new edition, and my colleague Janet Ulph for her support and humour.

The role of law in recreation | 1

The increasing scale of recreation and leisure facilities has required the law to intervene in a greater number of situations and for a greater variety of reasons.

In most cases, this intervention has simply taken the form of the application of an existing law to a new, recreational situation. Typical of this process is the use of the *Occupier's Liability Act 1957* to make financial compensation available to anyone injured while on sports premises (Chapter 4) and the application of the ordinary law of contract to agreements under which patrons make use of leisure facilities (Chapter 2). These aspects of 'recreation and the law' are described in the chapters which follow.

Of equal importance to the operators of leisure facilities are those laws which govern the use to which they put their premises (Chapter 4), the operation of governing bodies in sport (Chapter 5) and the raising of funds for sporting activity (Chapter 6). In more recent years local authorities have been given powers to make land available for recreational use (Chapter 8) and to protect from pollution those areas of land already in such use (Chapter 9). All this is of primary importance to 'leisure managers', and is therefore dealt with in this book.

Neither can any manager, whatever the product that is managed, afford to ignore the laws relating to employment, which are given appropriate treatment in Chapter 7. At the same time, we must take note of the specific application of certain areas of the criminal law to sporting activity, and this is done in Chapter 3.

Occasionally, the existing law cannot deal with a particular situation, and it becomes necessary to introduce new legislation. Such legislation tends to concentrate on safety aspects of particular activities, for example in 1990 the *Horses (Protective Headgear for Young Riders) Act* was passed making it an offence to allow a child under 14 years of age to ride a horse on a road unless the child is wearing protective headgear. Another example of this was the passing of the *Safety of Sports Grounds Act 1975*, in an attempt to secure the safety of sports stadia housing crowds of spectators. It was passed following the tragic deaths of several spectators as the result of the collapse of a stand at the Ibrox Park Football Stadium in Glasgow, which reflected the fact that the existing law had no adequate way of preventing a recurrence. Unfortunately the measures introduced by this Act were not sufficient to prevent the tragedies that occurred at Bradford Football Club in 1985 when fire broke out in one of the stands and at Hillsborough in 1989 when people were crushed to death by a sudden, uncontrollable influx of spectators arriving at the stadium. Further measures were therefore introduced and these are dealt with in Chapter 4.

It is, in fact, as the result of such well-publicized excursions by the law into the field of recreation that those primarily interested in the latter became aware of the importance of the former.

Publicity attaching to the celebrated *Packer* case of 1978[1] for example, drew attention to the fact that recreation and the law are now inextricably linked. Kerry Packer was able, through recourse to the law, to prevent the governing bodies of cricket from interfering with contracts he had signed with top professional cricketers (page 18).

Cardiff City Football Club may not have achieved fame for their football in 1979, but they did earn a reputation for their involvement with the law, being at one time included in five separate legal actions! Their ex-chairman was suing their present chairman and their present vice-chairman was suing their ex-chairman for damages for libel. The club itself was involved in an action for damages brought by their former manager who claimed that his dismissal, less than half-way through a four-year contract, was breach of contract. Meanwhile, a lottery run by the club resulted in a charge being brought under the *Gaming Act 1968*, while the club was the first to face charges brought under the *Safety of Sports Grounds Act 1975*. Finally, summonses had been issued against the club concerning an incident at the end of a home match in which three spectators were injured. Such experiences by just one club illustrate the diversity of potential legal intervention in recreational activity.

Sportspersons themselves have recognized the increasing importance of law in recreation. Examples of this were the use of lawyers by the cricketer Geoff Boycott in his post-suspension negotiations with Yorkshire County Cricket Club and by tennis star John McEnroe in his dealings with the international governing bodies of tennis. In the latter case McEnroe's lawyers were able to use the rules of the relevant association to his benefit by rendering his suspension from tennis meaningless and delaying the imposition of fines for his misbehaviour.

Offending participants in recreational activities are liable to punishment not only by the governing body of those activities, but also by the law. In 1981, for example, a footballer who was banned for life by the Football Association was also fined and ordered to pay compensation by a magistrates' court following his conviction for causing actual bodily harm to a referee when he punched him during a football match. This aspect of the application of the ordinary law of the land is further examined in Chapter 4.

The problem of violence in sport is not, of course, confined simply to the players themselves, and 'football hooliganism' has become an unhappily common media catchphrase. During the 1980s this problem became so acute that special legislation was introduced to deal with the problem of spectator 'control' and, although these measures were initially introduced to deal with football spectators, they can be extended to any other sport. These measures are also described in Chapter 4. A suggestion that legislation should be introduced empowering the Foreign Office to withdraw passports from Britons convicted of violence abroad has not been implemented because of the practical difficulties of enforcing it. This suggestion was made following incidents involving English football supporters in Switzerland, two of whom were subsequently banned from Switzerland for five years following their arrest during the disturbances. Following a riot leading to deaths at the Heysel Stadium in Brussels in 1985 several British fans were extradited, and some were charged with manslaughter and given prison sentences. Another consequence of the riot was that English football clubs were banned from European football competitions (a ban that was unsuccessfully challenged in an English court) until they satisfied the authorities that their fans would behave. This ban was not lifted until 1990.

Football hooliganism is an international problem and computer records of British football hooligans are kept at the Football Unit at the National Intelligence Service and names of British football hooligans can be circulated when British teams play abroad. In November 1992 a Welsh football fan was stopped at Brussels central railway station by Belgian police while on his way to watch Wales play Belgium. His name was checked against a computer print out and although he had no record of football hooliganism his name was on the list. He was taken to a police station and then deported for being a football hooligan. It subsequently transpired that his name had been added to the records following a routine check although his name was subsequently removed. This was not an isolated incident. The passing of information on an international basis and the establishment of a European database to which all European police forces have access mean that the accuracy of such information is vital and individuals should use their right of access under the Data Protection Act 1984 to check the accuracy of any personal information on a computer record.

Using police officers dressed as football fans to patrol and instigate arrests was suggested by a chief inspector following four years' research into the problem. This was done in the late 1980s and the first prosecutions were brought in 1991.

The Football Association has also suggested that the government should intervene to control football hooliganism through special legislation or increased police powers. This was done in the *Public Order Act 1986*, which gave police powers to limit the numbers at a 'public meeting' (this includes events like football matches) and introduced exclusion orders. It also urged the provision of better facilities by football clubs. These suggestions were made because the Football Association felt it had done as much as it possibly could to control crowd behaviour during football matches, but has no power to control hooliganism both before and after matches. The difficult question of spectator control by the law is dealt with more fully in Chapter 4.

The strict application of the law to recreation has, on occasions, had unexpected results. One of those concerns 'discrimination', which is considered more fully in various contexts throughout this book. Generally speaking, it is illegal to practise discrimination on the grounds of either race or sex in relation to any activity, business or social, and there are only a few strictly defined exceptions. One of these arises under the *Race Relations Act 1976*. Whereas it is generally unlawful to discriminate against a person on the basis of their nationality or place of birth, or period of residence in a particular place, it was necessary for Parliament to exclude the operation of the Act where a person is selected to represent their country, place or area, or any related association, in any sport or game, or in relation to eligibility to compete in any sport or game.

To discriminate against anyone on racial grounds in other matters is un-lawful anywhere in Britain. However, the Scottish division of the National Federation of Football Supporters Clubs failed in their efforts to prove that a ban imposed by the Football Association on the general sale of tickets in Scotland for an England-Scotland international match at Wembly constitu-ted racial discrimination. The court felt the ban was necessary to prevent a recurrence of the violence that erupted at a previous Scotland–England international and in English law the keeping of the peace is of paramount importance.

Discrimination on the grounds of race has also, in recent years, drawn together sport, law and politics in the sensitive area of apartheid: in particular, it has resulted in the Commonwealth Statement on Apartheid in Sport, known more popularly as the Gleneagles Agreement. The aim of this agreement by the countries which were party to it was to 'discourage contact or competition by their nationals with sporting organizations, teams or sportsmen from South Africa or from any other country where sports are organized on the basis of race, colour or ethnic origin'. It seems that the underlying policy of this agreement was to provide guidelines by which every national and sporting governing body could assess the facts of each case and then direct its conscience to the question of whether or not apartheid had been applied to any particular sport in South Africa.

During 1981 the Irish, New Zealand and American courts all refused to grant injunctions to stop the all-Ireland rugby team tour of South Africa and the South African Springboks tour of New Zealand and America. In the same year, and after much deliberation, Mrs Gandhi agreed to allow England's test cricket tour of India, following objections based on connections between South Africa and individual members of the English team. These decisions prevented minorities who opposed apartheid generally from imposing their views on the majority in the field of sport. In New Zealand unlawful attempts to prevent the 1981 tour were punished as simple crimes, as in the case of the three-month prison sentence imposed on the pilot whose unlawful use of an aeroplane resulted in the cancellation of one of the fixtures on the tour.

Decisions to organize such tours to or from South Africa were made by governing bodies of sport in the Commonwealth in the light of the Gleneagles Agreement, and on the basis that the body concerned was satisfied that on the relevant facts relating to the degree or extent of multi-racialism in their particular sport the decision was being taken within the spirit of the agreement, and was one which they were legally entitled to take. It is outside the powers of national governments to intervene with any decisions made under the Gleneagles Agreement.

The Gleneagles Agreement was an agreement involving only members of the Commonwealth. The United Nations also took steps against racial discrimination in sport, but its so-called 'blacklist' of sportspersons having connections with South Africa had no legal significance and could have resulted in legal action should it interfere with sporting contracts or profit-making activities. This point is taken up again in Chapter 2.

South Africa participated in the Olympic Games in 1960; it was not allowed to compete in 1964 and was formally expelled from the International Olympic Committee (IOC) in 1970 because of its apartheid policies. South Africa did not take part in the Olympics again until 1992, when the IOC judged that reforms in South Africa justified their inclusion.

In September 1981 South Africa had challenged their expulsion from the International Amateur Athletics Federation (IAAF), but the IAAF decided that this expulsion should stand because the progress made towards multi-racial athletics in South Africa still did not warrant their return as a member, even with the same status they had before expulsion in 1976, namely that of a suspended country whose athletes may still compete internationally as individuals. The IAAF did not consider that athletics or sport in general could be isolated from existing laws in South Africa which discriminated generally on the basis of colour.

Some individuals were caught in the 'crossfire' in their attempts to compete internationally, particularly the young South African middle-distance runner, Zola Budd. In 1984, as the result of having a British grandparent (and being a very good middle-distance runner), Zola Budd was granted a British passport with the minimum of formalities. However, there followed a series of challenges regarding her eligibility as it was felt that she did not satisfy the residential qualifications for most major international athletics events, even though she had bought a house in Britain. In 1988 the IAAF passed a resolution that the British Amateur Athletics Board (BAAB) should suspend Miss Budd on the grounds that she had 'taken part' in an athletics event (without actually competing) in which there were competitors who were themselves ineligible to compete under IAAF rules. Originally the IAAF stated that if the BAAB did not take action they could use their suspensory powers to ban British athletes from the Olympics. The IAAF subsequently withdrew this threat, but while the BAAB were investigating the charges Miss Budd returned to South Africa permanently and the BAAB adjourned its inquiry indefinitely.

In February 1991 South Africa decided to remove all remaining apartheid legislation from the statute books and this decision paved the way for its return to international sport and the lifting of sanctions concerning those who had taken part in sporting events in South Africa. South Africa was formally welcomed back to the IAAF in May 1992. Holding the Unity Games in their country was one of the conditions imposed for their return to the world field. Readmission to world sport for South Africa has been dependent on those sports with two governing bodies (black and white) achieving unity. South Africa has now been 'officially' welcomed back to the international scene by most sports including cricket, golf, rugby union and tennis.

Legislation relating to sexual discrimination has also thrown into doubt the legality of all-male preserves in certain areas of sport, and has even led some braver souls to challenge the traditional division of sport into 'men's' and 'women's' events. This fascinating application of a law which was primarily intended for other purposes is explored in Chapter 2.

A by-product of sex discrimination is 'sex determination', which has arisen many times in the context of athletics, especially in the Olympic Games. There is in fact no common law or statutory definition of what constitutes a 'male' or a 'female', as the variation of types may make it difficult to classify some persons as male or female. Most governing bodies have regulations relating to sex determination and the eligibility of persons failing to satisfy these regulations. In 1991 the IAAF adopted a new system of gender verification for the World Championships. Under this new procedure every athlete had to undergo a medical health check and physical examination to verify gender, and this included competitors already listed as women on the register. Doctors recognized by national federations are required to carry out the examination, and complete a health and gender certificate. This test was intended to replace the old sex chromatin test which could have led to certain men with chromosomal abnormalities qualifying as women. In fact, in 1985 a female Spanish sprint hurdler was banned after failing the chromatin test, but reinstated after it was shown that her abnormality did not give her a competitive advantage.

The legality of sex tests has, however, not yet been tested in any court of law, although in theory such a test could amount to an 'assault'. Promoters of sports competitions may be entitled to insist on a 'sex test' as a term of the contract under which participants are invited to take part, but the matter remains unresolved, and is a further illustration of the limits which the law suffers when dealing, or attempting to deal, with a new problem. If Parliament will not introduce legislation, and if no one will raise a 'test case', there is no vehicle through which the law can regulate the situation.

The current problem of coping with Aids has been 'tested' in the sense that a ban by a football club preventing a homosexual Aids carrier from refereeing its Sunday matches because it feared players might catch the disease was upheld by the club's county football association. Generally it is accepted that Aids carriers should be able to take part in sport and that the following simple precautions, if taken, provide adequate protection:

1. keep recent cuts or abrasions covered with a waterproof plaster;
2. wash hands after giving any first aid;
3. if blood, semen or other body fluids have to be mopped up, use disposable gloves. These must now be kept in first aid boxes.

In some areas the 'law' affecting recreational activities may be a mixture of the legislation of the country, and the rules and regulations of both the national and international governing bodies of the activity concerned. One such area concerns the use of drugs such as steroids to build up strength to improve performance, and another involves the use of stimulants. Although the use of drugs is apparently widespread and is universally condemned by governing bodies in sport, the detection of offenders has been the main stumbling block to the imposition of a total ban. The leniency of governing bodies in relation to sportspersons who are caught using drugs is also seen as a problem. In the 1988 Olympics the Canadian sprinter, Ben Johnson was stripped of his 100 metres gold medal and banned for life. However, he was reinstated after only two years. The ineffectiveness of English law in the control of drug abuse in sport is further considered in Chapter 3.

'Amateur status' is an area of controversy in sport which should perhaps be left to national and international governing bodies to determine without recourse to the law in order to avoid inconsistencies between competing countries. This was illustrated by the controversy surrounding the status of the rugby player J.P.R. Williams who, following the publication of his autobiography, announced his retirement from the game. He later expressed a desire to play again and was selected to represent Wales against a New Zealand touring team. The provisions of the International Rugby Football Board (IRFB) stated that any person involved in rugby union football, wishing to retain amateur status after writing a book, must dispose of the money earned by the book in a manner acceptable to the board. This must be done through the 'Member union', in this case the Welsh Rugby Union, who announced they were holding all the money due to J.P.R. Williams, pending the negotiation of a sports medicine charity which they felt fulfilled the requirements of the IRFB. However, if a member union does not fulfil its obligations in a manner satisfactory to other member unions there were no means of enforcement, except to decline to fulfil fixtures. McLauchlan, a Scottish rugby player, had a lifetime ban from playing or coaching rugby union imposed on him for keeping the earnings from his autobiography.

In 1990 the IRFB decided to change its rules to allow players to become fee-earning amateurs. Players will be allowed to be paid for off-the-field engagements, including opening supermarkets, making after-dinner speeches, and writing books and newspaper articles. But there will still be restrictions, for example no rugby-related clothing and shoe endorsements will be allowed. The aim of the IRFB was stated as determining and safeguarding the principles relating to amateurism in rugby football, and preserving the game as an amateur game. It has been predicted that these new rules will be open to very wide interpretation, particularly as the IRFB is allowing different sets of laws for different countries. An addition to the rugby bureaucracy are regulations officers, who will try and enforce the new code of conduct on the basis of a book of case law establishing precedents to be built up by a solicitor 'because precedents are a basis of law'. The English Rugby Football Union decided to set up a sponsorship deal whereby eight sponsors would pay £250 000 each to associate their company with the England squad. Half of the expected total of £2 million raised will go to the grass-roots level of the game and the other half will go to the players, who will in return undertake promotional activities on behalf of rugby and the sponsors. Such schemes are seen as a way of preserving amateur status, yet allowing financial reward for the players. Sceptics suggest that it will not be long before rugby union follows other 'open' sports with the best players being concentrated in a small number of teams. Rugby union's hitherto unique claim as an amateur sport was recognized by a High Court judge who ruled against a club challenging their removal to a lower league for disciplinary reasons on the basis that rugby union was an amateur game and the livings of players were not at stake.

Legislation would not clarify this confusing issue. Belgium, for example, defines a 'professional' sportsperson as one earning more than a fixed annual amount for the purpose of legislation relating to employment law. Most countries, however, leave this matter to the international governing bodies of sport; as the concept of an amateur varies from one country to another, it should perhaps be left to governing bodies to apply a universal standard and impose sanctions for non-adherence.

In 1981 the IAAF decided to remove some of the restrictions on financial rewards for amateur athletes although the sport is still not completely 'open'. Athletes may now negotiate contracts with commercial concerns for advertising and sponsorship. Money earned in this manner, in Britain, goes to the governing body of athletics, now the British Athletic Federation, which will take a small percentage. Athletes will be able to draw expenses from this money while they are still competing and the remainder will be put into a trust from which they will be given their share when they retire. Until retirement they will remain 'amateurs' within the terms laid down by the IAAF.

The law may also be asked to intervene when an activity is felt to be particularly dangerous and against public policy. This occurred in a test case at the turn of the century involving boxing, in which an attempt was made to declare boxing contests criminal[2]; the 'knock-out' rule made them very similar to prize-fights, which are illegal. However, the court decided that the rules governing boxing contests did not make these fights illegal. Boxing continues to be an emotive subject and in July 1992 the British Medical Association announced their intention to publish evidence of long-term brain damage to young boxers and sponsor a Private Member's Bill in Parliament prohibiting boxing by anyone under 16 years of age. Where other dangerous activities are concerned, participants and organizers take the view that these risks are freely accepted. Although deaths occur in sport (for example, the Fastnet yacht race tragedy in 1979, when several lives were lost in severe storms; the death of Johnny Owen the boxer, in 1980; and the death, in 1981, of a karate competitor after a blow in the stomach resulted in a heart attack), it is usually left to the governing bodies responsible to remedy the situation by the introduction of stricter rules. New rules were implemented, for example, in the Fastnet yacht race, introducing higher qualification standards. The law does not seek to punish people for partaking in dangerous activities, but will intervene where an activity is against the law or likely to harm the public as a whole, as in the case of prize-fighting. One aspect of this intervention takes the form of 'spectator protection' in sport, which is considered more fully in Chapter 4.

The law may intervene on grounds other than the dangerous nature of an activity, as illustrated by an attempt in 1992 to pass a Private Member's Bill, the Wild Mammals (Protection) Bill, which would have outlawed all hunting to hounds. As the bill was only defeated by 12 votes, it is likely that there will be further attempts to ban hunting with hounds.

In many ways, therefore, the law is important to recreation. It may control, restrict or encourage such activities. The attitude of each country to the importance of recreation, whether it is seen as being for the public good or giving international prestige, is reflected in legislation, or the lack of legislation, relating to recreation. In England and Wales very few laws relate specifically to recreational activities, such activities being brought within the ordinary law where this is applicable. Where new problems arise it is usually possible to deal with them within the existing framework of the law. This occurred during the skateboard craze of the late 1970s. Over-zealous use of public roads and footpaths by skateboarders, a potential danger to other users and the cause of several accidents, was controlled through the use of miscellaneous provisions in various statutes including the *Highways Act 1835*, the *Town Police Clauses Act 1847* and the *Offences Against the Person Act 1861*.

The popularity of roller-skating resulted in the imposition of a £10 fine upon a roller-skater for 'playing a game of skating to the annoyance of inhabitants or passengers on the highway'. He was also found guilty of assaulting the police constable who tried to stop him skating. A jetskier was fined for 'speeding' at 33 m.p.h. in the harbour at a Devon resort, as a result of invoking a local by-law. In October 1991 gas-powered paint guns used in war games were declared illegal under the *Firearms Act 1968* by the Crown Court at Swansea. The European Paintball Sports Federation declared its intention to fight this ruling as it will affect all war games centres using these paint guns. The two perpetrators of the 'crime' of possessing a firearm without a certificate were given unconditional discharges, but their business for which the paint guns were purchased collapsed after the guns were confiscated by the police. These examples illustrate the application of the ordinary law of the land to recreational activities.

Some bizarre prosecutions have also been brought in an attempt to bring recreational activities within the ordinary law. In 1991 three appeal judges in Scotland effectively ruled street soccer 'on-side' by quashing convictions of seven men who had been found guilty of conducting themselves in a disorderly manner by playing street soccer. A parachutist who leapt from the Whispering Gallery of St Paul's cathedral was charged with riotous behaviour in church and the vexing of preachers under the *Ecclesiastical Courts Jurisdiction Act 1860*. When the case was heard in October 1992 the magistrates ruled that it was out of time. However, another skydiver who parachuted from Tower Bridge was not so lucky, and was fined £50 with £102 costs and bound over in the sum of £500.

Britain became a member of the European Community (EC) when it signed the Treaty of Accession in 1972. Membership was ratified by the *European Communities Act 1972*, whereby Community law became directly applicable in Britain. Community law may therefore directly affect recreational activities and will be referred to where relevant. This is a continually changing area of the law, and is affecting more and more diverse activities. Detailed discussion of Community law is beyond the scope of this book, but anyone involved in recreation should be aware that such legislation exists and could have far-reaching consequences for some activities. The European Court of Justice deals, *inter alia*, with problems of interpreting conflicts between national law and Community law. This court has already made it clear that professional sport is subject to Community law and that no exceptions will be made when the laws come into effect. Indeed the Rugby League has already been told by the Advisory Conciliation and Arbitration Service (ACAS) that they must amend their restrictions on overseas signings because there can be no restriction on the movement of players from EC countries.

There have been many legal arguments concerning Britain's obligation to accept the supremacy of Community law, and in cases referred to the European Court concerning employment the English courts have accepted the ruling of that court, even though it was contrary to their own decision. Certainty concerning the application of Community law in Britain in some areas, therefore, awaits judicial decisions. The English Football Association has, however, anticipated events by changing its domestic rules to accommodate more foreign players than have previously been allowed in England, in accordance with Community law in relation to freedom of movement and employment between member countries. From 1 January 1993 there has been a single European market, when all workers are free to find employment in any one of the Member States and this is expected to cause problems in professional sport, especially football, because it is feared that it will strengthen the good teams and destroy the weaker teams. The Union of European Football Associations (UEFA) has been warning of the dangers of such a policy and in an attempt to rationalize the situation has decreed that from the start of the 1991/2 season clubs participating in the three major European club competitions will be restricted to four non-national players.

In November 1990 a proposed European Directive was put forward that the supplier of a service should be liable for damage to health and physical integrity, or the physical integrity of movable or immovable property, caused by a fault committed by that person in the performance of the service. Such a Directive was felt to be necessary to take account of legal developments and case law in Member States which could create an atmosphere of uncertainty to consumers and to the forthcoming single market in services. Discussions concerning this Directive have resulted in a lot of opposition, as many Member States resent this interference with existing laws relating to civil liability. There has also been a lot of opposition to the inclusion of all services, except medical services, which means the Directive may extend to recreational activities.

The principal aim of the Service Liability Directive[3] is to reverse the burden of proof so that the onus is on the supplier to prove he was not negligent when a consumer suffers because of poor or defective service. The Directive was debated and commented on by the European Council during 1992 and after this the Commission was to amend the draft.

This, then, is the role of law in recreation. Sometimes it is employed to deal with a specific problem unique to the area, while on other occasions it is found that the existing law, originally designed for a totally different task, is quite adequate. There are, as has already been indicated, yet more areas in which common sense, agreement and co-operation are to be preferred to legal intervention.

Against this interesting background, we may now examine the specific application of the law to recreation.

NOTES

1. *Greig v Insole* [1978] 1 WLR 302
2. *R v Roberts, Sporting Life,* 20 June 1901
3. COM (90) 482

The participants

Without the participants, there would be no sport, and it is therefore logical that we should begin our examination of law and recreation by considering the various ways in which the law protects, controls and otherwise affects participants of all descriptions.

If they are professionals, then they will be intimately involved with the law of contract in its application to contracts of employment, sponsorships, promotions and so on. But even amateur sportspersons cannot avoid some contact with this area of the law, if only when they enter a competition and agree 'to be bound by the rules' of that competition.

In addition, all sportspersons, whether amateur or professional, are entitled to some protection against the consequences of unjustified and unexpected injury, either on the field of play or to their reputation as athletes. They are also both protected and bound by the normal criminal law of the land, and may not use the cover of a sporting event to commit crimes against the person which would not be tolerated off the field.

At the same time, they are only partly protected by those laws against sexual and racial discrimination which the rest of us now take for granted.

PROFESSIONALS AND THEIR CONTRACTS

Professionals may 'come under contract' in a variety of ways. They may, like the professional footballer, be retained under a permanent contract of employment which dictates that they must devote their talents exclusively to the one club. Alternatively, they may be 'freelance' in the sense that, each season, they seek the best return, and the best management backing they can, from an available range of sponsors (a process best exemplified by the 'team' system in professional motor racing). Yet again, they may 'sign up' for a particular sporting event, such as a professional golf tournament player who competes for prize money, or a cricketer for a cricket touring series. They may even agree to lend their names to a commercial product such as a snooker cue or a tennis racket, or they may be persuaded, for a fee, to constitute the star attraction at the opening of some business venture such as a supermarket or a nightclub. The possibilities are numerous, but they all require the professional to engage in and, therefore, to be aware of, the law surrounding a contract.

A book of this nature cannot deal with all the numerous considerations of the law of contract with which a lawyer might be concerned, and any serious professional should, in any case, seek legal advice before entering into contractual obligations. There are more detailed works on the law of contract which the reader may consult in order to pursue the subject in more depth, and we may concentrate instead on some of the more common pitfalls which have been revealed over the years, as generations of sportspersons have sought to make a career out of their talents.

Perhaps the most vulnerable group are the starry-eyed youngsters eager to break into professional sport at almost any price, and stories of exploitation of 'groundstaff' and 'schoolboy' entrants by commercial football clubs have become almost as numerous as tales of similar exploitations by managers of teenage pop groups.

If these youngsters are still under 18 (but not otherwise), such hopefuls are protected by the law in the sense that any contract which they sign is voidable, unless it was, at the time of signing, 'on the whole' for their benefit. Such contracts will be examined in their entirety, so that even if one or two clauses may be regarded as harsh, they may be offset by other terms, notably those which enable the young person concerned to develop and progress in their chosen career. It should be noted in this context also that the law no longer regards apprenticeships as being any different from any other type of contract of employment - they are all subject to the same rules.

Doyle v White City Stadium Ltd (1953)[1] is a good example of a contract made by an 'infant' (someone under 18). Here Doyle, an infant, was disqualified in the second round of a 15-round contest for the heavyweight championship of Great Britain. His purse contract was £3000, win, draw or lose, subject to the rules of the British Boxing Board of Control. Under these rules a boxer who was disqualified forfeited his 'purse', but Doyle claimed he was entitled to the money on the basis that the contract, being with an infant and not for his benefit, was not enforceable. The court decided that he was bound by the contract including this clause, as the contract as whole was similar to an apprenticeship and therefore beneficial to him, and the forfeiture clause encouraged clean fighting.

Adult superstars may also be vulnerable in relation to the terms of a contract which they should read with great care. Bo Jackson, a baseball and American football superstar, was released from his contract in 1991 by the Kansas City Royals by invoking a clause in the contract that stated he 'failed to exhibit sufficient skill or competitive ability' to justify his place in the training squad. In fact this lack of ability was due to a serious injury during an American football match which seemed likely to end his career. By invoking the clause Kansas City Royals saved themselves the equivalent of about £2 million.

Not all professional sporting contracts, of course, are contracts of employment, and although in the case of employment contracts the employee is entitled to 'something in writing' after the first 13 weeks (a requirement considered in more detail at page 124), no other form of professional contract need be in writing before it will be valid. In the great majority of cases of course, for obvious reasons, it will be, and from now on we will assume that it is. Once an adult, in full possession of their faculties, has signed a contract, that person will normally be bound by it, warts and all. This is because everyone is expected to take good care of their own business interests, and explains why lawyers always advise their clients to 'read the small print'. Only when there has been a misrepresentation by one of the parties prior to the signing of the contract will the courts normally step in and either set it aside or award damages by way of compensation to the injured party.

The issue of misrepresentation in a sporting context arose in the case of *Queen's Park Rangers Football Club v Sheffield Wednesday Football Club* in 1977.[2] In this case Queen's Park Rangers claimed damages from Sheffield Wednesday for selling them a 'lame duck'. The London club claimed that the former England under-23 star, Vic Mobley, must have had osteoarthritis of the knees when transferred, since after only one year he was forced into early retirement, at the age of 27, because of the knee condition. Allegations of fraud and misrepresentations were rejected by the judge as Mobley had no symptoms at the time of the transfer, and the statement by Sheffield Wednesday's manager the day before the transfer that Mobley was fit was not a false statement.

A contract may not, in fact, include all the terms which govern the relationship between the two parties, so it may be necessary for the courts to make commercial sense of the agreement by 'implying' certain terms into it.

Implied terms are terms implied by the courts to cover certain situations which the parties have not themselves covered or they are terms implied in particular types of contract by an Act of Parliament. In the former case the courts will impose terms which they would have expected the parties to have agreed, had they considered the matter. Such assumption of additional terms occurs in order to make a contract workable, which was presumably the original intention of the parties. In *Bournemouth and Boscombe Athletic Football Club Co. Ltd v Manchester United Football Club Ltd* (1980),[3] for example, a player had been transferred from the plaintiff club to the defendant club for an agreed fee, with an additional agreed sum to be paid when he had scored 20 goals for the first team in competitive football. The player was transferred to another club after three months, having scored only four goals. The court ruled that there was an implied term in the contract that the player was to be given a reasonable length of time in which to score the required goals, and consequently that the plaintiff club was entitled to damages.

Another problem encountered in contracts signed by professional sportspersons results from the 'exclusive services' clause which the other party frequently seeks to secure from the sportsperson concerned. Such clauses may be unenforceable in the courts because they are deemed to be 'in restraint of trade', and therefore contrary to public policy in that they interfere with the free operation of market forces.

In a sporting context, such attempts at restraint can consist of unreasonable attempts to control entry into professions, unreasonable restrictions on competition and unreasonable restraints on the movement of individuals from one enterprise or club to another. Rules have been formulated by the courts to ensure, as far as possible, free competition and freedom of employment. These rules are applicable to all areas of sport and recreation, since control by governing bodies of recreation can adversely affect an individual's freedom. Such controls include licensing systems, registration with a particular authority, transfer fees, rules ensuring performance only for 'official' organizations and the sharing of broadcasting revenues.

Some of these controls have arisen from the desire of promoters to retain spectator interest by ensuring that the result of an event is uncertain, due to evenly matched opponents. Restrictions have therefore been imposed to prevent one organization in any particular activity from attracting all the 'superstars', resulting in unequal competition. The success of such restrictions, however, is dubious, as consideration of past results in professional football and cricket illustrates. Between 1960 and 1978, 10 of the 18 football league championships decided went to the four teams in Liverpool and Manchester; in cricket the county cricket championship has in the past been dominated by Yorkshire and Surrey.

The doctrine of restraint of trade provides that no person or organization should prevent a person from earning a living as that person wishes, or to work for whom that person chooses. This doctrine applies to contracts concerning recreational activities, including contracts made between sporting associations, contracts made between such associations and their members, and also to the constitutions and administrative rules of the governing bodies which control these associations and their members. Restraints in a contract may be deemed justifiable if it can be shown that:

1. a legitimate interest is being protected;
2. the restraint is reasonable as it is in the interests of all the parties involved;
3. it is in the public interest.

A 'legitimate' interest does not include freedom from competition between rivals, but a more limited interest such as the long-term health of the particular activity concerned.

Professional footballers' contracts, and the restrictions they have imposed, have been the subject of several law suits. An early example was *Kingaby v Aston Villa Football Club* (1912),[4] in which a professional footballer employed by Aston Villa Football Club was offered employment by another football club, but the offer fell through because of the transfer fee charged by Aston

Villa under the rules of the Football League. The plaintiff claimed damages for loss of employment, alleging that Aston Villa had maliciously charged an excessive transfer fee. However, the court decided that the plaintiff was bound by the terms of his contract and any motive concerning enforcement of the terms of a valid contract was immaterial.

By 1964, however, the attitude of the courts to such contracts had changed, as shown by the decision in *Eastham v Newcastle United Football Club Ltd* (1964).[5] Here, Eastham, a professional football player registered with Newcastle United, had requested, and been refused, a transfer. He had been given notice of retention by Newcastle United, and he sought a declaration that retention and transfer listing at a fixed fee according to the rules of the Football Association were in restraint of trade. The court decided that the then existing retain and transfer system was in restraint of trade.

Decisions such as this have led to major changes in the relationship between professional footballers and their employers. These have been implemented through agreement following discussion between a body representing the players (the Professional Footballers' Association (PFA), the employers and the league clubs represented by the Football League). In 1978, after much discussion, including reference to the Commission on Industrial Relations which led to the setting up of the Professional Footballers' Negotiation Committee, a new system was introduced including standard form contracts, without recourse to the courts.

Standard form contracts for boxing were the issue in the case of *Watson v Prager* (1991),[6] which decided that a contract between the boxer Mike Watson and his promoter Micky Duff on the basis that the latter's dual role as promoter and manager gave him the power unilaterally to fix the terms on which Watson would fight, and gave the boxer no right to negotiate on his own behalf. This decision was followed by the High Court in October 1992 when they released Gary Stretch from his contract with his former manager Frank Warren on the basis that the contract was void and an unreasonable restraint of trade.

Despite this new system problems still arise from the apparent refusal of sporting organizations to accept that they are an industry and should act as responsible employers. The new transfer system for professional footballers has allowed only limited freedom of contract, because although a player may change clubs freely at the end of his contract, the clubs involved are still allowed to agree compensation between themselves with an independent tribunal to arbitrate if there is no agreement. This maintains the idea that a club has a financial interest in a player, even though the contract of employment has expired, and the employer no longer has any rights under it except the enforcement of a 'restraint clause'.

The Commission of Industrial Relations criticized the content of contracts of employment relating to professional footballers, although their criticisms may be equally applicable to other professional sportspersons. Their criticisms were based on the lack of proper disciplinary and grievance procedures, and the failure to make provision in the Football League's standard form contract for sickness pay, severance pay and holiday entitlement. Lack of certain provisions could result in legal complications, particularly in relation to unfair dismissal (page 140).

A further recommendation of the Commission of Industrial Relations was that the PFA should be recognized as a trade union legally representing the players. This would enable them to take advantage of the many legal rights available, such as those embodied in the *Employment Protection (Consolidation) Act 1978*, dealt with more generally in Chapter 7. In 1992 when the new Premier Football League was established the PFA used the threat of a footballers' strike to agree an arrangement whereby a percentage of television income was to be used for benevolent, education and insurance purposes.

Although the transfer system used in professional football has been modified it will always be open to challenge as being in restraint of trade, until no restrictions at all are placed on the movements of players and transfer fees are abolished completely.

Cricket has also had problems concerning professional cricketers' contracts. *Grieg v Insole* (1978),[7] the celebrated *Packer* case, concerned the rules of two of the governing bodies of cricket, the Test and County Cricket Board, and the International Cricket Council. These bodies changed their rules to ban from test and county cricket all those players who had signed contracts to play 'out of season' World Series Cricket in Australia, organized by Australian businessman Kerry Packer. The court decided that the changes in rules were unreasonable and in restraint of trade, and that the contracts with Kerry Packer were not invalid as being in restraint of trade as the two governing bodies claimed. The two governing bodies, by changing their rules, had directly interfered with the cricketers' contracts with Kerry Packer, as they may have induced players to be in breach of these contracts in order to continue playing test and county cricket.

Restrictions as a result of a licensing system for trainers or players in particular recreational activity may be valid, as they may be considered essential to guarantee standards and safety. Refusal of a licence may not be against public policy as being in restraint of trade. In *McInnes v Onslow Fane* (1978),[8] for example, refusal of a boxing trainer's licence was allowed on the basis that governing bodies of sport were entitled to restrict the number of licences issued for the 'good of the sport', provided the body concerned was acting fairly.

Nagle v Fieldon (1966)[9] concerned the rules of the Jockey Club, which controls horse-racing on the flat throughout Great Britain, and would allow no one to train horses to race at their meetings without a licence. The plaintiff was a woman who had trained race-horses for many years, but the Jockey Club, prior to the *Sex Discrimination Act 1975*, had a policy of not granting licences to women. The plaintiff, who had frequently applied for and been refused a licence, brought an action claiming that this refusal was void as it was against public policy. The court ruled that, although there was no contractual relationship, they would intervene to protect a person's right to work, particularly where a governing body has a monopoly over the organization of a professional sport.

Before leaving the specific topic of professional contracts in sport, the possibility of sexual or racial discrimination, both on the field of play and in a contract of employment, should be noted. To avoid duplication of material, the reader is referred to the sections on discrimination which appear in this chapter and in Chapter 7.

Many professional sportspersons, particularly towards the end of their playing careers, seek security in the 'management' of their particular sport or activity. Professional football club managers and trainers, golf professionals and television sports commentators are obvious examples of this process whereby sportspersons become managers and consultants. Although they may always have worked under a contract of employment (as in the case of the professional footballer), their transition to management means that their job security is no longer dependent upon their playing ability, but upon their talents as business managers. It is at this point in their careers that we may look upon them as 'employees' in the more commonly accepted sense of the word, and the law governing them in their new careers is considered more fully in Chapter 7.

AMATEURS AND THEIR AGREEMENTS TO PLAY

Unlike professional sportspersons, who earn a livelihood from their particular game, the amateur sportsperson usually participates purely for the enjoyment derived from the activity, with no thought of personal gain. Because of this difference in motivation there is frequently no legally binding contract involved when an amateur engages in play.

It is easy to see why there should be this important distinction drawn between the two types of competitor, since the professional is engaged in a business enterprise, while the amateur is simply out for relaxation, albeit only mental. The latter is, therefore, involved in what the law terms a mere 'domestic arrangement', and for well over a century the courts have ruled that such arrangements will not be enforced as contracts.

For example, if a man who for years has devoted his talents to playing football for his works or village team suddenly announces that he will, from next season, be playing for another team, even a non-lawyer would recognize that the former team would be wasting its time in attempting to sue him for damages. And yet, in *Fulham Football Club v George Best*,[10] in 1978, the famous football 'star' was ordered to pay damages to a club which he 'left' in a manner inconsistent with the contract he had with them.

Somewhere between the two extremes, the law has to draw a line, enforcing one type of agreement as a 'contract', and refusing to interfere with the other because it is simply a 'domestic arrangement'. In doing so they will examine the intentions of the parties, and ask themselves whether when entering into their agreement, the parties intended to be bound by it. In lawyers' language, was there an 'intention to create legal relations'?

Generally the courts say that business and commercial agreements are intended to be legally binding, whereas social and domestic arrangements are not, although there are exceptions in both cases. A business contract may contain an express clause that it is not entered into as a formal or legal arrangement. An example of this is the situation that occurred in *Jones v Vernons Pools Ltd* (1938)[11] in which the court decided that a clause on a football coupon, stating it was 'binding in honour only', declared an intention not to create legal relations, and therefore there was no legal obligation to pay the winnings on the football coupons.

On the other hand, when the parties, although engaged in what appears to have been an amateur event, seem to have regarded their arrangement as having legal implications, the courts will sometimes uphold it as a contract. This is more likely to occur where there is an entry fee or prize money involved (*Clarke v Dunraven*, below).

In short, it would seem to depend upon the facts of each individual case and, in a sporting event in which amateurs compete with professionals, it may be the case that there is a different contract between the organizers and the professionals than between the organizers and the amateurs.

Decided cases reflect the individuality of each set of facts. In *Lens v Devonshire Club* (1914),[12] for example, it was decided that the winner of a competition organized by a golf club could not sue for his prize because 'no one concerned with that competition ever intended that there should be any legal results flowing from the conditions posted and the acceptance by the competitor of those conditions'. Similarly, in *White v Blackmore* (1972),[13] it was decided that the rules of a competition organized by a 'jalopy' club for charitable purposes did not amount to a contract between the club and the competitors. In both cases it was found that there was no intention to create legal relations.

Informally organized competitions therefore generally do not result in contractual relationships between the organizers and the competitors, or between the competitors themselves. This is not true of formally organized competitions where participants pay an entry fee and, in return for their entry being accepted, 'agree to abide by the rules'. In *Clarke v Dunraven* (1897)[14] two members of a yacht club had each entered a yacht in a club race, each member having given a written undertaking prior to the race that they agreed to be bound by the club sailing rules. One such rule was that any yacht disobeying any of the rules was to be liable for 'all damages arising therefrom'. One yacht, in breach of a sailing rule, ran into and sank another yacht. The court decided that there was a contract between the owners on which the owner of the damaged yacht could sue the other owner.

Once the courts have decided that a particular sporting agreement is enforceable as a contract, they will ignore any attempt by the party or parties to it to eliminate interference by the courts. *Baker v Jones* (1954)[15] concerned an unincorporated association (defined on page 77) formed to promote the sport of weightlifting. The association's rules, which constituted a contract between each member and the other members, stated that its council should be the sole interpreter of the rules, and in all cases the council's decision would be final. A member applied to the court for a declaration that the use of the association's funds for a particular purpose was against the rules. The court held that it did have jurisdiction to entertain the action and consider whether the council's interpretation of the rules was correct at law. The rules purporting to oust the jurisdiction of the court were contrary to public policy and therefore void.

The same would be true of any contractual attempt to limit liability for death or personal injury caused by the organizers' negligence, which is prohibited by statute, and is considered more fully below.

DISCRIMINATION AGAINST PARTICIPANTS

Reference was made in Chapter 1 to the fact that sport has posed certain delicate problems to those concerned with the implementation of statutes designed to eliminate both racial and sexual discrimination in all walks of life. As we have seen, discrimination on the grounds of colour alone is unlawful in sport, and the Commonwealth nations have combined together under the Gleneagles Agreement to oppose apartheid in sport wherever it occurs. Britain's accordance with the spirit of this agreement, and the philosophy underlying it, cannot be doubted when one considers the composition of British international athletics teams.

But it is the basis of international sporting competition that the teams which are fielded by each nation should be 'home grown', and this led to a special section in the *Race Relations Act 1976* which makes it lawful to discriminate, in team selection, against anyone who is not of the required nationality or origins, or who does not satisfy a particular residential qualification. Such discrimination in other areas such as job selection might well be unlawful under the Act.

Legislation relating to sex discrimination has thrown into doubt the legality of all-male preserves in recreational activities. Sex discrimination is dealt with by the *Sex Discrimination Acts 1975* and *1986*, which make it unlawful to discriminate on grounds of sex in employment, training and related matters. It also makes it unlawful for those providing facilities for recreation for the public to discriminate on the grounds of sex by refusing facilities (or providing them on less favourable grounds) for one sex. In 1990 the House of Lords[16] decided that Eastleigh Borough Council had discriminated against a 60-year-old man on the grounds of his sex by refusing to provide him with swimming facilities free of charge when the same facilities were provided free to women of the same age.

However, the sexes can be separated on grounds of 'decency', the reason usually proffered for preserving some facilities for men only. A private, non-profit-making club is exempt from this law and one-sex clubs may therefore be established in this manner.

In relation to recreational activities, section 44 of the Act provides:

> Nothing shall, in relation to any sport, game or other activity of a competitive nature where the physical strength, stamina or physique of the average woman puts her at a disadvantage to the average man, render unlawful any act related to the participation of a person as a competitor in events involving that activity which are confined to competitors of one sex.

Thus, if cricket is a game at which the average woman would be at a disadvantage, she cannot insist on playing in a team of men. The problem which then arises is to ascertain which games fall within this category.

In some American cases, which applied a law similar to that of England, the test was whether the sport was a contact or non-contact sport. In *Brendon v Independent School District* (1973)[17] a refusal to allow high-school girls to take part in tennis, cross-country running and cross-country skiing, for example, was found to be contrary to the law on equality. Later decisions, however, have thrown doubt on the universality of this test. In *Commonwealth v Pennsylvania Interscholastic Association* (1975)[18] the court decided that the only grounds on which a girl could be excluded from athletic competition with boys was that the individual girl was too weak, injury-prone or unskilled, and not merely because she was a girl. *Clinton v Nagy* (1974)[19] decided that a 12-year-old girl must be allowed to compete at American football, perhaps the most violent game in the world, on the basis of evidence given that, at that age, girls almost match boys in size and physical potential. The participation of girls in sport is perhaps more important in America than in most countries, because proficiency in sport plays a vital role in education, and entry into higher education may be denied to women through their inability to compete in sports.

The English courts do not appear to hold such liberal views as their American counterparts. *Bennett v Football Association* (1978)[20] concerned a 12-year-old girl banned by governing bodies of European and world football from playing in league matches, on the basis that it was a sport where the average woman was at a disadvantage to the average man. This ban was upheld by the courts. The test applied by the English courts is the strength and stamina of the average woman, and it would therefore seem that any exceptional qualities of the individual applicant cannot be taken into consideration. This decision was not referred to the European Court of Justice by the Equal Opportunities Commission which had supported the case, as they had originally intended, apparently because by the time a ruling could be given the girl involved, Theresa Bennett, would have been too old to play in the particular league concerned.

In March 1992 a Leeds industrial tribunal ruled that Susan Thompson had been repeatedly refused entry to the male professional pool circuit because she was female. Miss Thompson, the winner of nearly 200 women's titles and five open titles had applications to become Britain's first woman professional rejected four times between 1987 and 1991. Male pool players who had been beaten by Miss Thompson had been admitted to the professional ranks by the Professional Pool Players' Organization (PPPO) during the same period. Although they insisted that the sex of players did not count, an ultimatum to the PPPO gave them three months in which to enlist Miss Thompson into their ranks. Other sports have not been so reluctant to open their doors to females and in September the first female master of ceremonies made her debut in the boxing ring, having obtained her British Boxing Board of Controls licence three months earlier.

PROTECTION FROM PHYSICAL INJURY

Everyone who participates in any form of sport or recreation, be it as an amateur or a professional, runs the risk of injury, and the task which faces lawyers is to distinguish between those injuries which the participant must accept as 'occupational hazards', and those for which the participant may seek financial compensation from the person responsible.

That 'person' may be either a fellow participant (more common in contact sports such as rugby, or inherently hazardous activities such as golf and archery) or an organizer (most likely in activities such as gymnastics where vital equipment has to be kept up to standard). We are concerned in this section solely with injuries in respect of which the victim is seeking financial compensation under civil law - the consequences of an assault arising from criminal behaviour are considered in Chapter 3.

In almost all civil claims for damages arising out of a sporting accident, it is being alleged that someone was 'negligent'. The law of negligence states that damages must be paid by A to B where it is proved that A owed a 'duty of care' to B not to injure B, that A was in breach of that duty of care and that B suffered injury as a result. It is for the court to assess whether or not A does owe a duty of care to B, which is by no means a foregone conclusion in every case.

It is established that participants in recreational activities owe a duty of care to fellow participants and spectators not to be negligent, in the sense that they show a careless disregard for the safety of others: thus, negligently swinging a golf club to demonstrate a stroke or a deliberate foul tackle in football have been held to be situations where a duty of care exists. To establish a duty of care situation a plaintiff must prove the defendant acted recklessly or carelessly. In *Wilks v Cheltenham Homeguard Motor Cycle and Light Car Club* (1971)[21] a rider in a motor-cycle scramble left the course on his motor cycle, for no apparent reason, and injured spectators in the spectators' enclosure. The court decided that the rider had not been negligent, as there was no evidence of reckless disregard for the safety of spectators.

Where a participant has been injured or killed it does not follow that an action for negligence will be brought. Following the death of a 12-year-old boy on his first Scout camp when he slipped and fell down a Welsh mountain, a spokesperson for the Scouts said that all their information showed that the scout leader in charge of the party was 'a well qualified leader, an experienced mountaineer, who did all the right things'. He pointed out that the party was well equipped and well led, and it would appear that it was the sort of accident that can happen occasionally no matter what precautions are taken.

So far as the organizers of sporting and recreational activities are concerned, they owe a duty to participants in their capacity, not only as organizers, but also as occupiers of the premises or facilities concerned. Under the *Occupiers' Liability Act 1957*, an occupier of premises used for recreation must take reasonable care to ensure that there are no hidden dangers, that any apparatus and equipment is fit to use, that there is adequate supervision and that routine safety checks are carried out.

The duty of care includes regular safety checks of any equipment used. Complex or technical equipment should be regularly checked and serviced by the manufacturer. Should a fault have occurred which could not be discovered by a simple safety check, then the manufacturer may be liable to anyone injured using that equipment as they will owe them a duty of care. Following the passing of the *Consumer Protection Act 1987* liability for defective goods produced after the Act came into force in March 1988 will be strict, that is, no fault has to be proved.

Varying standards of care are imposed by the law according to the persons concerned. More care would be expected to be taken with a class of inexperienced gymnasts for example, than a group of Olympic gymnasts. In *Jones v London County Council* (1932)[22] Jones was attending a compulsory physical education course which included the playing of certain games, supervised by an experienced training instructor. Jones fell and was injured during one of these games, but was unsuccessful in his claim for damages for negligence as neither the county council nor the instructor had been negligent, and there was no evidence that the particular game was dangerous. An occupier must show, in such cases, that reasonable care has been taken. In *Gillmore v London County Council* (1938)[23] the council was unable to show it had taken such reasonable care where the plaintiff slipped on a highly-polished floor doing exercises at a physical training class which he had paid a fee to join. The council was found to be liable as it was under a duty to provide a floor that was reasonably safe.

Organizers of recreational activities as occupiers of premises are free to modify the duty of care they owe under the *Occupiers' Liability Act 1957* by either an express term in a contract with a user of those premises or they may purport to exclude any such liability by the prominent display of a notice to that effect. However, occupiers cannot exclude all liability for injury, loss or damage occurring to those using their premises. The *Unfair Contract Terms Act 1977* provides that an occupier of premises used for business purposes cannot, by reference to any contract term or notice, exclude or restrict his liability for death or personal injury resulting from negligence. In the case of other loss or damage an occupier can only exclude his liability for negligence where this is 'reasonable' within the terms of the Act. According to the Act 'in relation to a contract term the requirement of reasonableness ... is that the term shall have been a fair and reasonable one to be included having regard to the circumstances which were, or ought reasonably to have been known or in the contemplation of the parties when the contract was made'. In *Jones v Northampton Borough Council* (1990)[24] it was decided that an indemnity clause in a contract to hire a local authority leisure centre did not satisfy the test of 'reasonableness' because, despite such a clause, the council did not require users to be insured and a reasonable man may therefore infer that insurance was not necessary.

An occupier also owes a duty of care to trespassers, a duty imposed by the *Occupiers' Liability Act 1984*. This duty is to protect trespassers from any 'danger' where the occupier:

1. is aware of the danger or has reasonable grounds to believe it exists;
2. knows or has reasonable grounds to believe that the entrant is in the vicinity of the danger or may come into the vicinity of the danger; and
3. the risk is one against which, in all the circumstances of the case, the occupier may reasonably be expected to offer the entrant some protection.

An occupier is not liable for death or injury where high standards of safety are observed. At the inquest of a jockey who died after being trampled on during a race the coroner said that the safety at the Brighton course, where the incident occurred, was remarkably high. Nothing in the race had contravened safety rules or regulations and he concluded that the accident had been caused by 'one of those entirely unforeseeable hazards which may befall any sportsman'. He recorded a verdict of accidental death. Although coroners cannot decide questions of civil liability, such a verdict may preclude initiation of a civil action.

It should be noted here that many governing bodies in sport produce codes of practice in relation to their particular activity and although these do not have the force of law, following the relevant code may convince a judge that reasonable care was taken because those who drew up the codes will be considered 'experts' in their field. Conversely, alleged breaches of the 'Guide to Safety at Sports Grounds' published by the Home Office formed a substantial part of a successful claim for negligence against Bradford City Football Club, following a fire in one of their stands in 1985, so such guides could also be a useful weapon for plaintiffs in the future.

In relation to the safety of premises occupiers of recreational premises are covered by the *Health and Safety at Work etc. Act 1974*. All recreational facilities come under this Act which aims to ensure the safety of people not only at work (see Chapter 7), but also users of and visitors to such places. The intention of this Act was to replace all existing legislation with a system of regulations and codes of practice to maintain and improve existing standards of health and safety, applicable to all places where people are employed. The Health and Safety Commission may issue draft consultative documents concerning safety in specific places, for example public swimming pools and playgrounds. The Health and Safety Commission and the Health and Safety Executive may also instigate prosecutions for breaches of the Act. They can conduct inquiries into accidents that have occurred at places of employment and can also follow up complaints that a particular facility is dangerous. In 1985 inspectors of the Health and Safety Executive brought an action against Mendip District Council because they did not have enough lifeguards on duty at a pool when an 11-year-old girl drowned. A school was fined £2000 in 1989 after admitting two breaches of the Act which led to the death of its groundsman when a new type of steel rugby post fell on him while staff members and seven boys tried to 'walk' it into an upright position.

Where a person has something potentially dangerous in their charge a high degree of care to prevent mishaps is imposed. In October 1980 proceedings were started against Leeds City Council by an ex-pupil of one of their schools who had been paralysed after an accident in which he was using a trampoline. The trampoline had been left out in a sports hall, unlocked and unattended. Leeds City Council accepted liability, and offered damages of £40 000 before the completion of the case. The extent of the duty to protect a visitor from hazards will depend on the characteristics of the visitors concerned, for example children must be expected to be less careful than adults.

Most of these general principles were brought together in *Harrison v Vincent and Others* (1981).[25] Here an accident had occurred during a motor-cycle-and-side-car combination race, which was partly due to brake failure. The court decided that the rider of the motor cycle owed the side-car passenger, who was injured in the accident, the normal standard of care and not the modified standard applicable to competitors in sport. In this case, the brakes failed as the combination was approaching a hairpin bend and the rider turned off the track on to an escape road where he collided with a recovery vehicle parked on the verge, but projecting into the roadway. The side-car passenger was injured, and brought an action in negligence against the rider, the company that employed the rider (who were responsible for fitting the brakes) and the motor-cycle club. The defendants claimed that no duty of care existed because of the hazardous nature of the sport. This was not accepted by the Court of Appeal, who decided that as the acts complained of in relation to the brake failure did not occur in 'the heat of the moment' during a race, but in the relative calm of the workshop, the normal standard of care applied, and both the company and the rider, who should have checked them, were negligent. The motor club was also found to be negligent in relation to the recovery vehicle parked on the escape road, as this type of accident should have been foreseen by the club who were therefore in breach of their duty of care.

There are, however, several potential defences open to anyone sued for negligence. The first consists of a claim that the injury complained of was a natural and foreseeable outcome of engaging in a hazardous activity, which is a risk all sportspersons are expected to accept for themselves, and are taken by law to have 'volunteered' for (a defence known to lawyers by the Latin tag *volenti non fit injuria*). However, *volenti* cannot be claimed where injury is recklessly or deliberately caused, and is not a risk associated with that particular activity, for example, deliberate fouls in football, 'off-the-ball' incidents in rugby football or negligent actions by the other participants.

In an unreported case[26] a golfer, having hit his ball into the rough, indicated that he would not complete the hole. He then found the ball, by which time the other players were walking towards the green. He played the ball, and it struck one of the other players who had turned round at the defendant's shout of 'fore'. The judge decided the defendant was negligent in showing a complete disregard for the safety of others as his conduct was outside the game, and was not a risk 'accepted' by persons playing golf. Also, in *Cleghorn v Oldham* (1972),[27] where the defendant negligently struck the plaintiff with a golf club while demonstrating how to play a particular stroke, it was decided that the plaintiff had not voluntarily undertaken the risk of being injured in this manner as a result of the defendant's negligence.

To establish the defence of *volenti* the defendant must show that the plaintiff consented to the act complained of, with full knowledge of the risks involved, and that the consent was given voluntarily. Where a plaintiff is subjected to risk in the course of his or her employment then consent has not been given voluntarily. Nor does the defence apply where the plaintiff has no opportunity to consent because the plaintiff became involved after the defendant was negligent. An example of such a situation occurs in 'rescue' cases such as might arise if a bystander were to be injured while attempting to rescue a child trapped in the support cables of a trampoline left unattended.

Where the damage suffered by a plaintiff is partly due to their own fault and only partly due to the conduct of the defendant, the *Law Reform (Contributory Negligence) Act 1945* provides that the damages recoverable for the plaintiff's harm will be reduced by an amount adjudged by the court to cover the plaintiff's share of responsibility for the damage. This defence is known as 'contributory negligence', and where this defence is pleaded the defendant must prove that the plaintiff was careless or negligent, and this carelessness was partly responsible for the harm occurring to the plaintiff.

There are three qualifications relating to this defence: first, that a reasonable person should take into account the possibility of others being careless in relation to that person's own actions; secondly, that, although a child may be careless, the age of the child concerned will always be considered, and this defence is rarely successful against children; and thirdly, that a plaintiff will not be considered to have been careless if the plaintiff acts reasonably in the face of sudden danger, even though that action contributes to the harm done.

In deciding how much responsibility to attribute to each party, the court is under a duty to be fair and just according to the circumstances, and has no set rules to follow.

It is also an acceptable defence to claim that the harm or loss was unforeseeable, or that it would be unreasonable to guard against it happening (for example, because the cost of prevention would be impossibly high when balanced against the chances of the event occurring). *Simms v Leigh Rugby Football Club Ltd* (1969)[27] concerned a claim by a rugby player injured during a rugby match, possibly through contact with a concrete wall 7 feet 3 inches away from the touchline. This complied with the by-laws of the governing body of the Rugby Football League. It was not clear how the player was injured, but it was decided that no liability was incurred by the club whose pitch it was. If the injury had been caused in a tackle it was a risk associated with the game, a risk the player had willingly accepted. Had the injury occurred through contact with the wall, it was so unlikely that injury would occur in this way that there was no duty to guard against it.

In *Clarke v Bethnal Green Borough Council* (1939),[29] the plaintiff had been injured during a women's session at the defendant's swimming baths when she was preparing to dive off the springboard and a child holding on to the under part of the board let go. The attendant on duty did not see the incident. A claim of damages on the grounds of the attendant's negligence failed because she could not be held to be negligent in failing to see an incident involving 2 of the 50 people using the baths. The defendants had complied with their duty to provide a competent attendant. As an accident such as this had not occurred before, and was therefore not anticipated, there had been no negligence. But once such an accident has occurred and been reported it may, henceforward, be deemed foreseeable.

It may be that the injury which the participant suffers is the result of a direct and unjustified attack upon that participant by another participant. This is known in law as a 'battery', and has been the subject of successful claims for damages in 'sporting' circles. In *Lewis v Brookshaw* (1968),[30] £5400 damages plus interest and costs were awarded to the plaintiff for personal injuries suffered as the result of an aggressively vicious tackle the defendant made on him during a football match. The defence that 'the injury arose from the natural hazard that players make *bona fide* errors of judgement in the excitement of the game' was not accepted, as the judge decided the conduct was deliberate and violent. Damages of nearly £4000 were also awarded in *Grundy v Gilbert* (1977)[31] for a foul tackle, again in a football match. Here the plaintiff suffered a badly broken leg, and could not work for 10 months. In this case the judge said: 'Any footballer, amateur or professional, who deliberately breaks the rules of the game, in a way that involves foreseeable risk of injury to an opponent, has no defence to an action for damages'. Thus injury caused in an incident that is not acceptable as being 'part of the game' will be actionable as a civil assault.

The usual outcome of a civil action for either negligent or deliberate injury on the sports field, or in some other area of recreation, is a claim for damages. Although the aim of an award of damages is to compensate a plaintiff for his loss, the plaintiff may not be able to claim for all the losses suffered as a result of the defendant's action. Some losses are felt to be too 'remote', and the defendant is not liable for them because it would be unfair to make a defendant liable for all loss resulting from the defendant's action. A defendant will always be responsible where the results of the defendant's conduct were intentional. Where the conduct of a defendant causes unintentional harm that the defendant will be liable only for the harm that was 'reasonably foreseeable' as a result of the defendant's action.

One harm that the courts consider to be reasonably foreseeable is nervous shock resulting from persons witnessing an accident. This issue is discussed in some detail in Chapter 4, but it is relevant to mention here that in June 1992 a rider who saw a motor bike crash into her pregnant mare, almost severing one of the mare's legs, was awarded damages for 'psychological injury'. Damages agreed by the motor cyclist's insurers covered the value of the horse that was killed, the reduction in value of a second horse present when the accident occurred which subsequently became traffic shy, compensation for the costs of a bloodstock agent engaged to find a replacement for the dead mare, a contribution to the purchase of a lorry to transport the second horse off the road to the nearest bridleway and compensation for the trauma suffered in witnessing the accident. These damages were agreed without recourse to a court of law between the rider's solicitor and the insurers of the motor cyclist. The settlement was much wider than would normally have been expected, which would have simply been the value of the dead horse, and it is expected it will open the way to other riders involved in accidents with motor vehicles who have hitherto been reluctant to pursue their claims because of the costs involved in consulting a solicitor.

A defendant's responsibility may be limited in two ways: first, by proof that the harm would have occurred regardless of the defendant's conduct; and secondly, where another event occurs which breaks the chain of events started by the defendant's conduct. Then the defendant is responsible only for loss occurring prior to the intervention, and not for the whole loss. 'Chain of causation' was discussed in the case of *Hosie v Arbroath Football Club Ltd* (1978).[32] Here a man had been seriously injured when a football crowd surged towards a gate on the football ground and the gate gave way because it had not been properly maintained. The occupiers of the football ground, the club, were found to be liable because they knew or should have known that the gate would give way under pressure from a crowd and that someone could be injured. The occupiers also knew of other similar incidents where crowds had attempted to force gates open. The court decided that such an accident was reasonably foreseeable, and that the behaviour of the crowd did not break the chain of causation and relieve the occupiers of liability.

Once it has been established that the kind of damage occurring was foreseeable by a defendant, then the defendant will be liable for that damage, even though it was more extensive than could have been anticipated. Anyone committing a civil wrong takes their victims as they find them; for example, if someone hits a person on the head, and the result is a fractured skull because that person has an unusually fragile skull, then the assailant will be liable, even though such a blow would normally only cause a slight head wound. However, the plaintiff is under a duty to keep any losses to a minimum, and the defendant is not liable for any loss which could have been avoided by the plaintiff.

Where a negligent action is performed by an employee, for example, a sports coach or a gymnasium manager who fails to conduct regular safety checks on equipment, then not only is that individual liable, but so also is the employee's employer. This arises from a general principle of law known as 'vicarious liability', under which the employer of a person is liable for negligent actions performed by that person in the course of their employment.

To summarize so far, therefore, someone who is unjustifiably injured while taking part in some recreational activity may well be entitled to financial compensation from the person responsible, whether that person is a fellow participant, occupier of the premises or an employee thereof. Whether the injured person will actually receive the compensation to which there is entitlement will depend on the financial resources of the defendant, and whether or not the defendant is insured.

Employers are normally insured against having to pay compensation in respect of vicarious liability, and as occupiers of leisure centres are also normally insured against 'public liability' arising from the use of the premises by the public.

There are two aspects of insurance, compensating a victim for injuries suffered where no negligence is involved and covering anyone who may have to pay compensation as the result of a successful claim of negligence. But by no means all sportspersons are insured against any injuries they may inflict or suffer. It was established in *Van Oppen v Trustees of the Bedford Charity* (1989)[33] that insuring a participant or making sure a participant has insurance is not part of the duty of care even when, as in this case, the participant was a pupil at a school. Van Oppen was severely injured on the rugby football field when he was 16 years old and launched himself in a flying tackle at an opposing player who had the ball. In an action for negligence it was alleged that the school had failed to take reasonable care for Van Oppen's safety on the rugby field because he had not been taught proper tackling techniques. It was also alleged that the school was negligent because it had not advised Van Oppen's father of the inherent risk of serious injury involved in playing rugby and of the consequent need for personal accident insurance for his son; that the school had not arranged such insurance and was negligent in failing to ensure that Van Oppen was insured against accidental injury. The court decided that the school was aware of the risks involved in playing rugby and that Van Oppen had been taught to play the game properly. On the issue of personal accident insurance the court said the question was whether the scope of the duty owed by the school to Van Oppen was wide enough to include having regard for his economic welfare. A school is only under a duty to exercise reasonable care for its pupils' health and safety and this did not include a general duty to insure, even against negligence. A parent is under no duty to insure a child, therefore such a duty could hardly be extended to schools, or indeed to anyone else. However, having adequate insurance could be made a condition of participation in the first place.

This case increased awareness of the necessity of insurance for schoolchildren and the fact that very few were actually covered. Private schemes were available, but the Central Council for Physical Recreation also launched a scheme with an insurance company providing cover for children who suffered sports injuries for a nominal amount per year for each pupil. The scheme is only available if all the children in a school are covered and it must be taken out by the head teacher. Such a scheme ensures compensation without having to get involved in an action for negligence.

Not only is such an insurance beneficial to the person causing injury, but also to the victim, as illustrated by a case decided in March 1981. In this case a 19-year-old amateur table tennis player blinded a spectator, when his bat flew from his hand while he was competing in a tournament. The spectator concerned was awarded over £5000 damages by the High Court, to be paid at £10 per week by the player concerned because he was not insured. It would be 10 years before the victim received the total damages she was awarded. Such cases would seem to indicate the need for compulsory insurance for liability for participants in certain recreational activities, as is currently the case regarding motorists. Insurance schemes specifically related to recreational activities are now being introduced, for example, the Central Council for Physical Recreation has introduced a comprehensive scheme in relation to personal injury and public liability.

As far as recreational activities are concerned, some private insurance companies have agreed to cover participants in recreational activities. This insurance may cover injuries and consequent medical treatment of participants themselves, that is personal insurance, or it may cover compensation payable to a third person as a result of an accident caused by the participant, known as civil liability insurance or simply liability insurance.

There are different attitudes to the question of insurance and compensation throughout the world. In some countries the question of compensation for accidents occurring during recreational activities is treated as distinct from more traditional branches of social security. Other countries include such compensation in their existing branches of social security, because professional athletes are considered to be employees. These countries include France, Great Britain, The Netherlands, Sweden, Belgium and, to a lesser extent, Turkey. Sickness benefit may also be paid where the accident is not within the definition of an employment injury, and such a trend is apparent in the legal systems of Belgium, France, Great Britain, The Netherlands, the Republic of Ireland and Sweden, although in these cases compensation may be lower than that received for employment injury.

The best solution to the problem of insurance would perhaps be a single sports mutual insurance fund in each country, with compulsory membership at law. The aim of such funds would be to provide total compensation for both personal injury and where third-party liability occurs, with the normal insurance provisions of exemptions and ceilings. Such schemes would protect individuals injured by participants in recreational activities who would otherwise have their compensation paid as a small weekly sum, because neither the participant nor the promoters of the activity were insured.

LIABILITY FOR PARTICIPANTS' BELONGINGS

As part of the services and facilities of most sports and leisure complexes the operator makes available an area in which those taking part may change and leave their clothing while they enjoy their sport or pastime. Along with their clothing they will normally wish to leave items such as wallets, purses, handbags, watches and jewellery, and it is hardly surprising that from time to time questions arise as to the liability of the organizer of sporting activities for loss of personal items left in the changing rooms by the participants.

A lot will depend upon the actual circumstances of each case and obviously if a proprietor undertakes express liability for such items the proprietor will be held to it; this can arise, for example, with the provision of some sort of safe-deposit facility, or even staffing the changing rooms with attendants, and makes no reference to the fact that liability is not accepted.

This latter implied undertaking to ensure the safety of property arises from the act of providing an attendant; in the absence of any 'disclaimer', the patron is entitled to assume that the provision of an attendant is some sort of guarantee of the safety of the patron's property. At the same time, the absence of such an attendant does not necessarily imply that no liability is being accepted; if the patron is 'invited' to make use of the changing facilities, particularly if the patron is supplied with a locker and key for which a nominal charge is made, then again, the patron may be entitled to assume that any property left in the changing facilities is being looked after by the management.

Nor does it necessarily matter whether or not there is a 'contract' between the patron and the management; in most cases there will be, since the patron is paying to use the facilities (either as a member of the club, or on a 'one-off' basis as a member of the public), and it may be argued that safe storage for belongings is part of the service for which the patron is paying. But even where it cannot be argued that there is a full contract which contains responsibility for belongings as one of its terms, the law may still hold that there is a 'contract of bailment'. This is simply a form of agreement under which one person agrees to look after the property of another, and there is no need to prove that payment was made in return. Under the terms of such a bailment, the custodian is required to take as much care of the property of that other person as they would of their own property.

Reference was made above to the fact that the management may seek to exclude or limit its liability by means of an 'exemption' clause which is either inserted expressly into the contract or impliedly imposed on the patron by means of notices displayed in relevant parts of the premises. This type of clause is explained further in Chapter 4, where the point is made that, in order to be effective, it must be adequately communicated to the patron before any belongings are left. The display of a notice at the entrance to the changing rooms may not be sufficient, for example, if the patron is already committed to entering the premises by paying an entrance fee at the front desk before there is an opportunity to read the notice. Nor is it necessarily sufficient to make vague reference to 'the terms and conditions of use' of the premises (which may be examined on application) on the back of the entrance ticket. Something much clearer than that is required in every case.

As a result of the *Unfair Contract Terms Act 1977*, such an exemption clause, even if validly communicated, cannot be effective unless it may be regarded by the courts as being 'reasonable' in the circumstances. This will obviously vary from situation to situation, but, for example, while it might be reasonable for the management to exclude liability for loss of property in an unattended changing room in which every patron is given a locker and key without extra charge, it will be a different matter entirely if every patron is required to leave their clothing and belongings in an open changing cubicle (as still happens in some public baths), or in a basket which is handed to an attendant. The courts will also take into account what payment, if any, was made by the patron for the general facilities, the relative 'bargaining strengths' of the two parties and the frequency with which the patron in question used the facilities - the more often he or she uses them in the knowledge that no liability is accepted by the management, the more likely it is that the courts will regard that patron as having accepted such an arrangement.

THE SPORTSPERSON'S REPUTATION

Quite apart from seeking protection from physical injury on the field of play, sportspersons also wish to ensure that no unwarranted slurs are cast on their reputations. This is of particular importance to the professional participant, of course, but amateurs must also protect themselves against unwarranted accusations concerning their honesty, reliability and amateur status. All participants derive this necessary protection from the law of 'defamation'.

Defamation is the communication to one or more persons of a false statement about a person which lessens the character of that person in the eyes of ordinary, reasonable members of society. Proof that a statement is true will avoid an action in defamation. There are two kinds of defamation, 'libel' which is written, and 'slander' which is spoken.

To succeed in an action for defamation, a plaintiff must first prove that the statement was defamatory. This was discussed in the case of *Byrne v Deane* (1937),[34] where an action was brought by a member of a golf club against the proprietors of the club. Automatic gambling machines had been removed from the club as the result of information given to the police. Following the incident, a typewritten verse appeared on the club notice-board which said of the informer 'may he burn in hell and rue the day'. Mr Byrne claimed this was a play on words and a suggestion that he was the informer, and therefore defamatory. The action was brought against the proprietors for allowing the verse to remain on the club notice-board, and therefore publishing it. The court decided, however, that the statement was not defamatory.

In a successful case, *Tolley v J.S. Fry and Sons Ltd* (1931),[35] Tolley, a leading amateur golfer, sued the defendants for issuing an advertisement showing himself playing golf with a packet of their chocolate sticking out of his pocket. The accompanying words suggested that the chocolate was as excellent as Tolley's drive. Tolley's action for libel was based on the implication that he had received money for the publication of this advertisement, which would endanger his amateur status. He was successful.

Words may be defamatory either according to their ordinary meaning or because they have a double meaning. In *Chapman v Lord Ellesmere and Others* (1932),[36] the plaintiff, a horse trainer, had lost his trainer's licence under the rules of racing of the Jockey Club. One of the rules gave the stewards the right to publish withdrawals or suspensions of trainers' licences in the racing calendar. This was done in Chapman's case, but the statement in the calendar could be read in a way that indicated that Chapman was a party to the doping of a horse he trained. The jury decided that there was an innuendo that was defamatory. However, on appeal, the court decided that the publication in the calendar was 'privileged' (explained below), as this was by agreement between the parties, being a condition on which a trainer's licence was granted. There was no evidence of malice to destroy this privilege. Further, since Chapman had agreed to this publication the defence of *volenti non fit injuria* applied, as the possibility of the words having a double meaning was a risk he had elected to take.

In October 1992 the boxing promoter, Frank Warren, lost his libel action against the boxer Terry Marsh which arose from a claim by Marsh that he had been encouraged by Warren to sign a contract to defend his title even though Warren knew that the boxer had been diagnosed as suffering from epilepsy. The jury decided that Marsh's allegations were defamatory, but could not decide which of the two was telling the truth in court in relation to when, exactly, Warren became aware of Marsh's epilepsy. Warren was, however, successful in his claim for damages against two newspapers which had repeated Marsh's allegations and Marsh successfully claimed damages against a magazine that made a 'highly offensive' allegation in an interview with Warren.

The plaintiff in an action for defamation must prove not only that the statement was defamatory, but also that reasonable people would think that the statement referred to the plaintiff. A further aspect of this 'tort' is that the defendant must have 'published' the statement. This involves communication to at least one person other than the plaintiff. In *Byrne v Deane* (above) it was held to be sufficient publication where the proprietor of a golf club, who was responsible for notices on the notice-board, had allowed a notice that was pinned to the board by an unknown person to remain there. Each time there is a communication this amounts to publication, and forms the basis of a separate action.

It is a defence to prove that the statement was a 'fair comment', that is, a matter of opinion, as it is a basic principle of English law that people are free to state their opinions. However, this defence is subject to the following qualifications: it must be a pure statement of opinion based on true facts; it must be made concerning a matter of public interest; and there must be no evidence of 'malice'.

Some communications are 'privileged', which means that certain people are allowed by law to make defamatory statements and are immune from an action in defamation relating to these statements. Privileged situations include Parliamentary proceedings, judicial proceedings, reports of the former and references from past employers to future employers. However, where publication is for malicious reasons this defence will fail in the latter two situations.

The *Defamation Act 1952* provides that an 'offer of amends' may be made which involves an offer to publish a suitable correction and apology. Should such an offer be accepted no action may be brought. Recently it was announced that legislation relating to defamation is to be amended following very high awards of damages by the courts.

Proof that a plaintiff agreed to publication is also a defence, and is an application of the defence *volenti non fit injuria*, as illustrated by the case of *Chapman v Lord Ellesmere and Others* (above). The usual remedy for defamation is an award of damages.

Although such a tort of defamation may not seem relevant to participants in recreational activities, actions have been brought to protect the reputation of well-known participants, as in *Tolley v J.S. Fry and Sons Ltd* (above). Daley Thompson, the decathlete, was also able to claim damages in 1991 from the *Sunday Telegraph* for allegations that he took drugs and in the same year

Arsenal manager George Graham accepted substantial damages from the *Daily Mirror* for reporting that he was so tyrannical he was nicknamed 'Gaddafi'.

This tort has also been used by a governing body to protect its reputation from outspoken comments by sports 'celebrity' Jimmy Hill, a football commentator. In *Hardaker v Hill* (1978)[37] an action was brought by the secretary of the Football League for defamation concerning allegations by Jimmy Hill that the Football League had used threats against football clubs concerning freedom of contracts. The case was settled by an apology from Hill and his payment of the plaintiff's costs. Hill was again threatened with a libel action brought by members of the Football League management committee for defaming the league on television and in the press when he talked of 'overexposure' of football on television.

NOTES

1. [1935] 1 KB 110
2. *The Times*, 7 April 1977
3. *The Times*, 22 May 1980
4. (1912) *England and Empire Digest Repl Vol (Green Band)* 1(1) 36
5. [1964] Ch 413
6. [1991] 3 All ER 487
7. [1978] 1 WLR 302
8. [1978] 1 WLR 1520
9. [1966] 2 QB 633
10. *The Times*, 21 June 1978
11. [1938] 2 All ER 626
12. *The Times*, 4 December 1914
13. [1972] 3 All ER 158
14. [1897] AC 59
15. [1954] 1 WLR 1005
16. (1990) 3 WLR 55
17. (1973) 477 F2d 1292 23 ALR Fed 649
18. (1975) Pa Cmwlth 234 A2d 839
19. (1974) 411 F Supp 1396 (ND Ohio)
20. *The Times*, 29 July 1978
21. [1971] 2 All ER 36
22. (1932) 96 JP 371
23. [1938] 4 All ER 331
24. *The Times*, 21 May 1990
25. [1982] RTR 8
26. Mentioned in *Wooldridge v Sumner* [1963] 2 QB 43
27. (1972) 43 TLR 465
28. [1969] 2 All ER 923
29. (1939) 55 TLR 519
30. (1968) 120 NLJ 413
31. *Sunday Telegraph*, 31 July 1977

32. [1978] SLT 122
33. [1989] 3 All ER 389
34. [1937] 1 KB 818
35. [1931] AC 333
36. [1932] KB 431
37. *The Times*, 21 July 1978

The criminal law of England and Wales demands certain standards of conduct from everyone and sportspersons on the field of play have no special privileges compared with persons in the street. Participants in sport may, if their behaviour warrants it, be prosecuted and convicted in the normal criminal courts, and there have been several good examples of this process in recent years.

CRIMINAL BEHAVIOUR ON THE FIELD OF PLAY

In *R v Gingell*[1] in 1980, for example, Gingell pleaded guilty to assault after he punched an opposing player during a game of rugby football. The victim suffered a fractured nose, cheekbone and jaw. Gingell struck at least two blows, including one when the victim was on the ground; he was sentenced to six months' imprisonment. On appeal against the sentence, it was submitted that the sentence should have been suspended, on the basis that punching was 'accepted' in rugby football. The court decided that it was concerned only with enforcing a proper sentence for the assaults. Even given that the original blow may have been the result of some sort of provocation following the tearing of Gingell's shirt, there was no excuse for the subsequent blows. It was an assault that merited a term of immediate imprisonment, but the Court of Appeal decided that six months was too harsh and reduced the sentence to two months.

During the 1980s a new precedent was established when participants found guilty of committing an offence were actually made to serve jail sentences for the offence. PC Richard Johnson was jailed for six months for biting off part of another player's ear during a rugby match, when he was found guilty of wounding with intent to cause grievous bodily harm. He was jailed because an ordinary person committing the same offence would have been jailed. PC Johnson's appeal against his sentence was rejected by the Court of Appeal, yet the previous month the Welsh international rugby player Patrick Bishop, who punched an opponent in a club game, had had his one-month jail sentence for common assault suspended by the same court. The judge in the Johnson case did, however, comment on the leniency of Bishop's treatment.

In 1988 Steven Lloyd, another rugby player, was convicted of causing grievous bodily harm when he kicked an opponent in the head when the opponent was on the ground following a tackle by another player and he was sentenced to 18 months' imprisonment. His appeal against sentence was unsuccessful and the Court of Appeal said that the sentence was appropriate in the circumstances, even though it was the toughest penalty ever imposed in Britain for a 'sporting offence'.

Crimes may also constitute civil wrongs and in such a case the 'victim' may bring an action in the civil courts for compensation for the loss or injury suffered. For example, an 'assault' is both a crime and a tort (a civil wrong). Compensation is also available for injuries suffered as the result of a crime. Applications for such compensation must be made to the Criminal Injuries Compensation Board and the injuries sustained must be directly attributable to a crime of violence. It was because the board felt this requirement was not fulfilled that it initially refused compensation to Mark Johnson, a 29-year-old, fully qualified physical education teacher, who lost an eye during a rugby match. As a result of this injury he had to abandon his career. Johnson did not see who actually delivered the blow which precluded a civil case for compensation. On appeal to the board Johnson was awarded an interim payment of £15 000 with directions to file further medical evidence and loss of earnings as special damages for a final award.

Although a crime may have been committed, the police have a discretion whether or not to prosecute. Private persons may also decide whether or not to initiate criminal proceedings in addition to suing for civil damages, where this is appropriate.

To secure a conviction for a criminal offence the prosecution must prove two things. First, that the outward conduct of the accused was within the definition of a specific crime; this is known as the *actus reus*. Secondly, that the state of mind of the accused was that required for the crime concerned; this is referred to as the *mens rea*. *Mens rea* is a difficult concept, which does not mean simply a 'guilty mind', but rather an intention to commit an illegal act or to do a particular act regardless of its consequences. In other words, there must be an awareness in the mind of the accused that their actions may result in an illegal act or 'criminal conduct'.

Where criminal prosecutions follow incidents on the sports field, it is sufficient that the accused knew what they were doing at the time, and an intention to commit a crime does not have to be proved. In the case of *R v Moore* (1898),[2] for example, Moore, in trying to prevent a player from scoring a goal, had jumped with his knees against the player's back, which threw him violently forward against the knee of the goalkeeper. This caused internal injuries, from which he died and for which Moore was charged with manslaughter. The judge, in his summing up, said that although football was a lawful game and a rough one, no one had the right to use force likely to injure another, and anyone doing so had committed a crime. It did not matter whether the blow was deliberate or reckless; if it amounted to an unlawful act Moore was guilty. The jury returned a verdict of guilty, but sentence was postponed in view of Moore's previous good character.

Criminal offences take many forms and an act on the sports field could come within the 'definition' of more than one crime; we now consider some of the more likely of these.

The most serious is, of course, 'homicide' - the unlawful killing of another human being - and it may take several forms, of which the most well known are 'murder' and 'manslaughter'.

Murder is an unlawful homicide with malice aforethought, where death occurs within a year and a day of the act alleged to have caused it. 'Malice aforethought' means that there was an intention to kill or cause really serious harm to another person, whether by an act or an omission to do something. Special defences on a charge of murder include diminished responsibility, and provocation sufficient to cause a reasonable person to lose control and act as the accused did. Where the above defences are successfully pleaded, the charge will be reduced to manslaughter. Murder is triable only by jury, with a fixed penalty of life imprisonment.

Manslaughter is any unlawful homicide not classified as murder. It is also triable only by jury and the punishment ranges from life imprisonment to an absolute discharge. The law recognizes two types of manslaughter, namely 'voluntary' and 'involuntary'. Voluntary manslaughter occurs where a person has killed with malice aforethought, but the circumstances in which they have done so are regarded by the law as mitigating the gravity of the offence and the charge is reduced from murder to manslaughter.

Involuntary manslaughter, the more relevant offence in relation to recreational activities, is an unlawful killing, where the accused is regarded by the law as blameworthy, but did not have an intention to kill or cause grievous bodily harm.

Manslaughter is an ill-defined crime and has many forms, as reference to any criminal law textbook will illustrate. This lack of definition arises mainly because the state of mind of a person accused of this crime can vary from something short of malice aforethought to mere negligence.

To simplify matters, three definitions of manslaughter will be considered here. First, manslaughter which occurs when death follows an unlawful act, but there was no intention to kill or cause serious harm. In both *R v Moore* (above) and *R v Southby* (below), the accused were found guilty of manslaughter where death occurred following an unlawful act during a football match. In each case the sentence imposed was very light; Moore was bound over and Southby was conditionally discharged. They could have expected a harsher 'sentence' for a lesser offence from their local football associations. However, following the decisions in *Billinghurst* (below) and *Gingell* (above), it would seem that, in future, participants in recreation guilty of criminal conduct may anticipate punishments to fit the crime.

Secondly, manslaughter by neglect of duty occurs where a person, who has a legally recognized duty to others, causes the death of another; an example of this would be the neglect or ill-treatment of children by their parent or guardian. Finally, manslaughter may also be committed where a person does an act which is itself quite lawful, but the manner in which the act is done is so grossly negligent that it amounts to recklessness. In 1989 a water-skier and the driver of the speedboat towing him were found guilty of manslaughter when the tow rope knocked a 12-year-old girl over the side of her parents' boat, causing her death.

If the criminal conduct complained of does not result in the death of the victim, then it is likely to be charged as an 'assault', and English law recognizes various forms of this offence.

Assault and battery are 'common law misdemeanours', but their punishment is provided for by the *Offences Against the Person Act 1861*. They are separate offences. Assault occurs where a person intentionally or recklessly causes another person to fear immediate and unlawful force being used against them. Battery occurs where one person intentionally or recklessly uses unlawful force on another person. Assault and battery usually occur simultaneously, and for this reason the two offences are often referred to as 'an assault', although this is not strictly correct, as a battery only may occur if, for example, a person is attacked from behind and does not see their assailant.

Participants in recreational activities are answerable for any such criminal conduct occurring on the field of play. In 1981 an amateur football player was fined after being convicted of assault when he head-butted a member of the opposing team during a match. Where an incident occurs either before or after a match or other event, or it involves persons other than participants in that event, the participants concerned will naturally be liable for their conduct. Thus two players, Price and White, involved in an incident after a professional football match, were found guilty of assaulting both the trainer and the player of an opposing club. In 1972, Moran, a part-time professional footballer, was found guilty of an assault when he attacked a referee during a football match.

A threat, or use, of force cannot be an assault or a battery if either the victim validly consents to it or the accused has used reasonable force in self-defence. These are two defences that can be raised where a person is accused of 'assault'. The defence of 'consent' was discussed in *R v Billinghurst* (1978),[3] which decided that participants in recreation consented only to force 'of a kind which could reasonably be expected to happen during a game'. Self-defence, it was said in *Palmer v R* (1971),[4] 'is a straightforward conception. It involves no abstruse legal thought. It requires no set words by way of explanation. No formula need be employed in reference to it. Only common sense ...'

Self-defence occurs when a person is put in a position in which they have to defend themselves using reasonable force and it may even be a defence against a murder charge. Generally, the rules of recreational activities do not distinguish between an assailant and a victim who retaliates, whatever the provocation.

Both offend the playing laws, and there is also a tendency for officials to see only the response and not the initial provocation or blow. The law does recognize and excuse the act of self-defence if it is sufficiently reasonable and consistent with the degree of attack, but not when it is disproportionate to it, as in the case of *Gingell* (above).

Section 20 of the *Offences Against the Person Act 1861* provides another offence, that of unlawfully and maliciously wounding or inflicting any grievous bodily harm upon any other person, either with or without a weapon or instrument. This section creates two offences, one being an act resulting in the wounding of another and the other being an act resulting in the infliction of grievous bodily harm. A 'wound' occurs where the outer and inner skin are broken, and does not include bruises. Grievous bodily harm means really serious harm, as in the case of *R v Billinghurst* (1978) (above) where the victim was punched in the face, fracturing his jaw in two places. Billinghurst was found guilty of an offence under section 20 of the *Offences Against the Person Act 1861*.

Both these offences include the word 'maliciously' in their definition. This does not mean there must be proof of spite, it means that the accused must have known that the consequence of their act might be the infliction of some physical harm, however slight, on another person. These offences may overlap with the offences of common assault occasioning actual bodily harm but a person may be guilty of the latter offences where no 'grievous' bodily harm has been caused.

A further offence in this category is provided in section 18 of the *Offences Against the Person Act 1861*. This states that it is an offence unlawfully and maliciously to wound or cause grievous bodily harm with intent. The difference between the section 20 offence and this offence is that in this case it is sufficient to establish that the accused 'caused' as opposed to 'inflicted' grievous bodily harm. The prosecution must also prove, in this case, an intention to cause grievous bodily harm and not mere foresight. Considering these definitions, it is unlikely that many prosecutions resulting from incidents during recreational activities would arise under section 18, as it would be difficult to prove intent in the circumstances, whereas it may be possible to establish 'foresight'.

In *R v Doble* (1980)[5] a rugby captain was charged with causing an opponent grievous bodily harm with intent, when he allegedly punched the opponent hard in the left eye, causing the eyeball to collapse. Doble was acquitted by the jury as there was doubt as to whether or not he was the player who threw the punch. The judge accepted the verdict, but on the facts he said he would have found that the victim was unlawfully attacked by someone. Thus the ingredients of the offence were established, but there was no evidence to prove that the accused had been responsible for committing the offence.

Conversely, in 1992, an attempt to prosecute a professional football player Gary Blisset for this offence failed because the prosecution were unable to prove that the assault was deliberate. This prosecution, only the second involving a professional footballer, resulted from an incident when two players went for a high ball and Blisset had used his arms to gain height, and in so doing had hit John Uzzell in the face, causing serious facial injuries. While giving evidence, a chief executive of the Football Association described the challenge as 'entirely reasonable'. Uzzell is unlikely to play football again and was released by his club at the end of the season. Uzzell is now living on state benefit and considering whether or not to start civil proceedings.

Whatever the nature of the assault, it is for the prosecution to prove that the accused committed the act with the necessary *mens rea* (page 40), and for the accused to raise any defence such as self-defence which the accused feels is relevant. One alleged 'defence' in assaults arising from sporting events has been to suggest that the act complained of was within the 'rules of the game'. But no such rules can validate what has been regarded for centuries as a crime and the courts have been careful not to allow 'manly sports' to degenerate into criminal activities.

In *R v Bradshaw* (1878),[6] for example, Bradshaw was indicted for the manslaughter of a player killed during a football match. Bradshaw had 'charged' the deceased and struck him with his knee in the stomach, causing fatal injuries. Evidence varied according to whether Bradshaw tackled while the deceased had the ball or after he had kicked it away. The judge, in his summing up, said the jury must decide whether death was caused by an unlawful act. He continued thus: 'No rules or practice of any game whatever can make that lawful which is unlawful by the law of the land'. If Bradshaw had been acting according to the rules of the game and not acting in a way he knew was likely to cause death or injury, he was not guilty, but had he intended to injure the deceased he was guilty. The jury decided that in this case there was not sufficient proof that an offence had been committed and they returned a verdict of not guilty.

As can be seen from this case, participants have had a tendency in the past to consider themselves 'above the law', and many do not regard violence on the field of play as criminal conduct. However, the courts do not accept that unlawful acts committed by persons engaged in recreation should be considered as 'part of the game', nor do they accept that the victims, by partaking in these activities, have 'consented' to any harm they may suffer.

'Consent' was the defence put forward in *R v Billinghurst* (above). Here, during a rugby football match, Billinghurst had punched the opposing scrum-half in the face, fracturing his jaw, and had been charged with inflicting grievous bodily harm under section 20 of the *Offences Against the Person Act 1861* (page 43). The defence argued that in the modern game of rugby, players consented to the risk of some injury and that punching during a rugby match was the rule rather than the exception. The prosecution argued that public policy imposes limits on the violence to which a rugby player can consent and, whereas the player is deemed to consent to vigorous or over-vigorous physical contact 'on the ball', the player is not deemed to consent to any physical contact 'off the ball'.

The judge directed the jury that players were deemed to consent only to the force 'of a kind which could reasonably be expected to happen during a game', and that 'there must be cases which cross the line of that to which a player is deemed to consent'. He suggested that a distinction which the jury might regard as decisive was that between force used in the course of play and force used outside the course of play. He also suggested to the jury that their verdict in this case might set a standard for the future, as this was the first criminal charge concerning rugby football. Billinghurst was convicted by a verdict of 11 to 1, and given a 9-month prison sentence suspended for 2 years, as he was of previous good character.

When imposing sentence the judge said: 'Hereinafter, no one will be able to plead ignorance of the fact that violence of this sort on the rugby field is as much a criminal offence as it is off the field and that players, as well as spectators, are expected to behave like sportsmen'.

So ended the resistance of rugby players to intervention by the courts and their contention that incidents on the rugby field did not amount to criminal conduct. In the *Billinghurst* case, it was the employer of the victim who initiated the prosecution and not the victim himself. In many cases of violence on the field of play that would be adjudged criminal conduct, the matter is only dealt with by disciplinary proceedings of the sport's governing body or simply ignored.

In some cases, however, participants in sport who 'go over the top' are liable to punishment by the governing body of that activity as well as by the law. A footballer who was banned for life by the Football Association was also fined and ordered to pay compensation by a magistrates' court following his conviction for causing actual bodily harm to a referee when he punched him during a football match.

The reluctance of the players themselves to initiate prosecutions was illustrated in an incident concerning the Welsh rugby international J.P.R. Williams. In December 1978 Williams suffered facial injuries in an off-the-ball incident, but refused to initiate criminal proceedings. The players accept violence as a risk of the game, but the law in England and other countries does not accommodate this view.

Many offences against the person cannot in fact be committed if the victim has previously 'consented' to the particular act complained of. Whether or not a person can be said to have consented to the harm inflicted will depend on the circumstances. In 'lawful' sports, such as wrestling, consent could be given and justified on the basis that they are 'manly diversions, they intend to give strength, skill and activity, and may fit people for defence, public as well as personal, in time of need'. A 'manly diversion' includes boxing, which may cause serious injury, but has been distinguished from illegal fist fights known as 'prize-fights'.

In *R v Coney* (1882),[7] the accused, with others, was charged with aiding and abetting an assault by watching an illegal prize-fight, as the presence of a crowd was encouragement to the combatants to fight. The consent of the persons actually engaged in the fighting was no defence to the charge of assault. The definition of a prize-fight was discussed in *R v Orton* (1878),[8] which concerned a similar charge and the jury were directed that if it was a mere exhibition of skill in sparring it was not illegal, but if the parties met intending to fight until one gave in from exhaustion or injury received, it was a breach of the law and a prize-fight, whether the combatants fought in gloves or not.

The distinction between boxing and illegal prize-fights was further discussed in *R v Roberts* (1901).[9] Here 10 defendants, involved in the promotion of a boxing match, were charged with the manslaughter of a boxer in that contest. The aim of the prosecution was not only to punish the defendants, but to stop boxing contests which allowed a knock-out blow. The prosecution said that if the jury found the defendants guilty, they were saying that such boxing contests were unlawful. The knock-out rule concerned the ability of one of the parties to knock out an opponent so that the opponent could not rise within 10 seconds. If the jury decided that the whole purpose of the contest was to knock an opponent out, the prosecution contended that the fight was illegal. However, if the purpose was to demonstrate the skill of the contestants, the fight was legal. There was evidence that the fight was well organized and kept under control. The jury took the view that the injury causing death occurred during 'legal' boxing and the defendants were not guilty.

Attempts to ban boxing on the basis that it is a crime have failed, but there have recently been attempts to ban boxing on medical grounds as it may result in serious brain damage. If these attempts are successful it may simply result in the sport going underground and leading to more prize-fighting.

Although prize-fighting may have been thought to be an activity of the past, there is evidence to suggest that bare-knuckle fighting has been revived. In February 1981 police broke up a battle between two gypsies and dispersed a crowd of 600. At this fight wagers of up to £1000 had been made. No prosecution followed this incident, as the aim of the police was to prevent trouble occurring so they merely dispersed the gathering. The police claimed there was evidence to suggest that this was not an isolated incident.

The need to distinguish between legal and illegal fighting was explained by the judge in *R v Coney* (above) as follows:

When one person is indicted for inflicting personal injury upon another, the consent of the person who sustains the injury is no defence to the person who inflicted the injury, if the injury is of such a nature, or was inflicted under such circumstances, that its infliction is injurious to the public as well as to the person injured. The injuries given and received in prize-fights are injurious to the public, both because it is against the public interest that the lives and health of the combatants should be endangered by blows, and because prize-fights are disorderly exhibitions, mischievous on many grounds. Therefore the consent of the parties to the blows which they mutually receive does not prevent those blows from being assaults. In all cases the question whether consent does or does not take from the application of force to another its illegal character is a question of degree, depending on the circumstances.

This test is one of public policy and is based on whether or not it is in the public interest to allow the infliction of bodily harm in certain circumstances to be 'legal'. Consent in these cases does not cover any physical injury that may occur; it is subject to the qualification that, while a participant in a sport such as boxing or football validly consents to any physical harm normally incidental to that activity, the participant does not, and in law cannot, consent to a deliberate act intended to cause physical harm. Such an act would be deemed injurious to the public interest, as well as to the person concerned. It would be an impossible situation if footballers could legally resort to fist fights during a football match, just as it would be ridiculous if every injury on the field, however caused, became the subject of legal proceedings.

The courts have, therefore, drawn a distinction between incidents regarded as being part of the hazards of the particular recreational activity (such as 'on the ball' incidents in football) and incidents not expected to occur during a particular recreational activity ('off the ball' incidents). This distinction was illustrated in *R v Southby* (1969).[10] Southby was found guilty of manslaughter where death resulted from a punch thrown at an opponent following a certain amount of niggling between the two, when neither had, nor was about to have, possession of the ball.

Quite apart from actual assaults on the field of play, a participant's behaviour may be such that it constitutes a 'public order' offence such as breach of the peace or obstruction of a police officer. Breach of the peace offences are defined by statute as consisting of the use of 'threatening, abusive or insulting words or behaviour', either orally or by means of writing or gesture, whereby the public peace is likely to be disturbed. It can only be committed in a 'public place', at a public meeting or in such a way that it is visible or audible to the public. Such offences are now mainly contained in the *Public Order Act 1986*.

The magistrates, before whom a person charged with this offence appears, must decide in each case whether the behaviour complained of was threatening, abusive or insulting, in the ordinary meaning of these words. Should the magistrates decide that the conduct of the accused was within the definition of this offence, they must find also that there was an intention either to provoke a breach of the peace, or that the use of such words or behaviour was in a manner likely to cause a breach of the peace, for example, addressing an audience on a matter that is expected will cause a violent reaction. These offences have been widened by the *Public Order Act 1986* which provides that it is sufficient if the words or behaviour used are likely to cause harassment, alarm or distress.

'Public place' is defined as including 'any highway or other premises or place to which at the material time the public have, or are permitted to have, access, whether on payment or otherwise'. Where there is a place to which the public have or are permitted to have access, such as a football stadium, the whole area is a public place, even though the public are not allowed in certain parts of it, for example, the football pitch itself.

In *Cawley v Frost* (1976),[11] the definition of public place was discussed. Here the place concerned was a football stadium which consisted of a football pitch, surrounded by a speedway track and encircled by spectator stands. The speedway track was fenced off to prevent members of the public having access to either the track or the pitch. The defendant was a spectator at a football match, and was arrested when rival spectators started shouting abuse at each other and running on to the football pitch. He was charged with a breach of the peace under the *Public Order Act 1936* (now replaced and extended by the *Public Order Act 1986*), but his conviction by the magistrates was quashed by the Crown Court on the grounds that the speedway track was not a public place. On appeal by the prosecutor, it was held that the football ground included all the different areas, and as a whole was to be identified as a place to which the public had access, and was therefore a public place for the purposes of a breach of the peace.

Although the courts have stated that this offence should not be used where the behaviour complained of is not very serious, because such conduct was not the sort of incident Parliament had in mind when they framed the offence, it has nevertheless been extended to cover a variety of incidents concerning behaviour at sporting events. In 1972 James Dunne, a Fulham and Republic of Ireland half-back, was fined £35 and ordered to pay costs for an obscene gesture, during a football match, that was held to be insulting behaviour, likely to cause a breach of the peace when he appeared to push the ball into the face of a press photographer and then aim several blows at him during a Southampton v Norwich match.

On two occasions a police constable has actually walked on to a football pitch and cautioned a player for using language likely to cause a breach of the peace. The first occasion was in 1968 when a player responded to a kick on the ankle with foul language. Swearing by a footballer at his fellow players prompted a policeman to caution a player on the second occasion in September 1980. Although prosecution did not follow either incident, the second incident resulted in a caution for the player concerned. In both incidents the referee asserted himself as the 'man in charge' and doubted the right of the police to intervene. However, as both incidents occurred in a public place, the police, as enforcers of law and order, are ultimately responsible and therefore entitled to intervene if a breach of the peace is likely or any other offence is, or is about to be, committed.

Obstructing a police constable in the execution of that constable's duty is a crime defined in the *Police Act 1964*; it could happen that any referee or organizer of a recreational activity who tried to stop a police constable from intervening in a recreational activity because a criminal offence was being committed, would be guilty of this offence. Thus, in the two incidents described above, a referee, in ordering a police constable off a football pitch, might have been guilty of obstructing a police constable in the course of their duty.

This is by no means an exhaustive list of crimes of which participants in recreational activities may find themselves accused. As recreation develops more people become involved, and new activities are introduced, so the possibility of criminal liability increases. The advent of commercialism into sport, and the possibility of earning easy money, may result in crimes of fraud. This is illustrated by the case of 10 past and present footballers found guilty of conspiring to defraud by 'fixing' matches.

Organizers of developing sports may also find themselves involved in skirmishes with the criminal law, as a hang-glider pilot discovered when his exploits landed him in court. The accused was summonsed for flying an aircraft at below 1500 feet in a built-up area, endangering persons or property, contrary to the *Civil Aviation Act 1949* (now the *Civil Aviation Act 1982*). He had been soaring 50 feet above Bisham Cliffs; the cliffs and the beach below were frequented by holidaymakers. The accused pleaded guilty to flying an aircraft at less than 1500 feet, conceding that for this purpose a hang-glider was an aircraft within the meaning of the *Civil Aviation Act*. He was given a conditional discharge for 12 months. He denied a second charge of unlawfully causing his hang-glider to endanger persons or property and this summons was dismissed.

Participants in recreational activities, therefore, are not immune from criminal prosecution, even though participants themselves may be reluctant to initiate proceedings on the grounds that a person should not be branded a 'criminal' on the basis of incidents occurring on the field of play.

DRUG ABUSE

Before leaving the general topic of the criminal liability of participants, we may note the continuing problem of drug abuse, notably in the use of steroids to build up strength to improve performances and the use of stimulants for the same purpose. The use of drugs is universally condemned by governing bodies in sport, but the detection of offenders has been the main stumbling block to its elimination.

There is no specific law concerning the use of drugs in sport in England, but the *Misuse of Drugs Act 1971* makes it a criminal offence to use, possess or sell certain listed drugs. The drugs listed, however, do not include those used by participants in recreational activities to improve their performance. At present it is only an offence to sell prescription-only drugs which brings steroids under the *Medicines Act 1968*. In February 1991 the Home Secretary announced that it would be made an offence to supply steroids to anyone under 18, even when no payment was involved. The Department of Health was also to set up a survey of the use and misuse of hormone drugs, and to put more money into research on detection methods. This legislation has not yet been introduced, but renewed promises were made following the clenbuterol controversy in 1992 (below).

Belgium, France, Germany, Greece, Ireland, Italy, Luxembourg, Norway, Switzerland and Turkey have all introduced some form of laws or regulations prohibiting the use of drugs by participants in recreational activities. In 1992, nearly four years after the Canadian sprinter Ben Johnson was stripped of his gold medal at the Seoul Olympics when he tested positive for drugs, the Canadian government introduced tough penalties for anyone convicted of involvement in the illegal trade of anabolic steroids. Anyone caught and convicted of producing, importing or trafficking the muscle-building drugs may now be imprisoned for up to 10 years and coaches or doctors who give steroids for non-medical purposes will also be committing a criminal offence.

Although efforts to control the use of drugs by individual countries are commendable, it seems that the use of drugs should be a matter for the international governing bodies concerned, as the athletes from one country which has made it illegal to use drugs may find themselves at a disadvantage when competing against athletes from a country that has no such legislation. International governing bodies could then ensure uniformity in the control of the use of drugs and imposition of punishments for offenders.

One of the problems of leaving these matters to governing bodies is the diversity of punishments and the strictness with which they are enforced. One governing body of sport which has very strict rules concerning the use of drugs is the British Cycling Federation which provides for the disqualification and suspension of cyclists found to be using drugs. A fine of £1100 was imposed on and 10 minutes added to the time of Robert Millar, one of Britain's most experienced professional cyclists, who failed a drugs test during the tour of Spain in 1992. Millar was also warned that if he tested positive again within the next two years he would face a six-month suspension. Despite the strict application of these rules they have still been criticized by other governing bodies as being too lenient.

Governing bodies in British athletics have also taken strong measures to deal with the problem in Britain. In 1988 they introduced random testing throughout their structure and a register of nationally ranked British athletes willing to undergo such tests at any time. Only the names on that register will be considered for international competitions. Any athletes who register, but then fail to give a sample when required, will have their case heard by a special tribunal who will decide whether or not they should be removed from that register. The governing bodies treat a life ban as just that and in 1990 called on the International Amateur Athletics Federation (IAAF) to do the same instead of reinstating athletes after only 18 months when it is unlikely they will miss any major championships, thus making the risk worth taking.

International governing bodies, for example the IAAF and the International Olympic Committee (IOC) may also have very strict rules relating to the use of drugs by competitors in events organized by them, with resulting disqualification or suspension for offenders. In the 1972 Munich Olympics a competitor was disqualified for using medication for asthma which was found to contain a forbidden stimulant. During the World Cup in 1978, Scottish footballer Willie Johnson was suspended for life by the Scottish Football Association for using drugs. His action could have endangered the whole Scottish team, as it was within the power of the International Football Federation to ban Scotland from the World Cup.

Olympic athletes, through their chief spokesperson Sebastian Coe, won a pledge from the Olympic Congress in September 1981 that the control of drugs would be tightened up and penalties for the misuse of drugs would be increased. However, the IOC itself is powerless to punish offenders except at the Olympic Games and assumes that national governing bodies will act where necessary. Since then Britain has taken some of the boldest measures yet to deal with the problem. The British Sports Council has stated that sports governing bodies who do not adopt effective anti-doping measures will be liable to sanctions. Initially this would be the loss of use of the council's national centres and, as a last resort, cash grant aid could be withdrawn. They have also established a flying squad of drug testers in a specially equipped laboratory van to descend on sports events to carry out surprise tests on athletes. Eighty sporting associations agreed initially to co-operate and the flying squad will arrive unannounced at events at all levels.

When Ben Johnson, the Canadian sprinter, stripped of his gold medal in Seoul, only served a two-year ban and was then not only able to compete in the Barcelona Olympics, but also make a lot of money out of his comeback, the leniency of his punishment was severely criticized. Since his reinstatement Johnson has tested positive again and has now been banned for life. The IAAF have now introduced a policy of automatically banning athletes found to be using drugs or involved in irregularities during testing for four years. It seems, however, that the severity of this punishment may produce new problems in the fight to prevent drug abuse. Challenges from athletes affected both in the law courts and to the governing bodies themselves have resulted in the exposure of serious loopholes. In 1992 Katerina Krabbe, the world 100 and 200-metre champion, and two other German athletes were suspended for four years as a result of irregularities arising from drug tests during training in South Africa, because it was suspected that the same person had provided all three samples. However, Krabbe and her fellow athletes successfully challenged their suspensions on the grounds that at the time South Africa was not a member of the IAAF and that there had been delays in getting the urine samples to an accredited laboratory. Although Krabbe avoided suspension on this occasion, when she was tested later in the year, this time by the governing body for athletics in Germany (DLV), she was found to have been using clenbuterol and was automatically suspended for four years, but on appeal this was reduced to 12 months.

During the Olympic Games in 1992 two British weightlifters were expelled from the Games and suspended, as they were found to have taken clenbuterol in tests conducted just before the Games. The weightlifters, Andrew Davies and Andrew Saxton, immediately challenged their expulsion and suspension on the grounds that clenbuterol was not on any list of banned substances and that in any case it had been used for medicinal purposes since it was used for the relief of asthma as well as having muscle-building properties. The Sports Council advised the British Olympic Association to uphold the suspension, which they did. However, the British Amateur Weightlifting Association subsequently lifted the suspension on the grounds that it was not clear that clenbuterol was a banned substance and, it would appear, their doubt that they could justify the suspension if challenged in a court of law. This decision resulted in a threat from the Sports Council to withdraw funding from the sport.

Three of the German athletes, including Katerina Krabbe, suspended by their own governing body for the use of clenbuterol, having lost their appeals now considered an appeal to the British courts. This highlights another problem for international governing bodies, that is, the possibility their rulings will be challenged in legal systems where the most favourable result may be obtained.

To date, challenges in the English courts have met with little success. In *Gasser v Stinson*[12] in 1988 a Swiss athlete, Sandra Gasser, failed to prove that the procedure adopted in carrying out a positive dope test was not in accordance with the rules of the IAAF and therefore the IAAF had no power to suspend her. Gasser also failed in her claim that the IAAF rules purporting to ban or suspend athletes who fail drugs tests from competition were in unreasonable restraint of trade and therefore void. A similar decision was reached in *R v British Athletic Federation ex parte Hamilton-Jones*[13] in 1992 which upheld a four-year suspension imposed on Hamilton-Jones for failing to give a urine sample as this was properly done within the rules of the federation.

The clenbuterol incident has also exposed another real problem in the fight against drug abuse, namely that in an attempt to keep up with the development of new drugs, the rules refer not only to specific drugs, but also include general categories such as 'anabolic agents'. These general definitions may result in challenges in the courts to establish exactly which drugs are banned.

Challenges may result anyway due to the fact that long-term suspensions can prematurely end the career of a successful athlete. The desire to win that results in the use of drugs could also motivate an athlete to fight a suspension through the law courts. This is illustrated by the case of the American athlete, Butch Reynolds. Reynolds, the 1988 Olympic silver medallist and world record holder at 400 metres was banned by the IAAF for two years following a positive test for steroids after a meeting in Monte Carlo in August 1990. This ban also applied to Reynolds's status with his own governing body, The Athletics Congress (TAC). Reynolds took advantage of Article 9 of the United

States Olympic Committee's constitution, which allows suspended athletes on the verge of a national competition to take their case to the American Arbitration Association (AAA). The AAA lifted his suspension for the American national championships on the grounds that the two urine samples may have come from different people.

The IAAF protested because the national championships was a qualifying event for the World Championships in Tokyo and Reynolds's participation would 'contaminate' the other athletes. The president of TAC stated that national laws sometimes took precedence over international sports rules, and that this was one of those occasions, and therefore TAC was bound by the arbitrator. The IAAF did not accept this view on the grounds that every IAAF member undertakes to respect and follow the rules, and any departure from this principle could endanger continuing membership of the IAAF. Immediately before Reynolds ran in the national championships the IAAF confirmed his suspension and warned the Americans that they could be suspended from the IAAF, and that competitors at the meeting could also incur suspension for running against an ineligible athlete. The IAAF appeared to be relying on expert evidence that it was impossible to attribute different urine samples to any particular person.

Reynolds did compete in the championships and the IAAF warned that 'despite the special arbitration law which prevails in the United States any repetition of such a case would not be accepted in the future and the IAAF would not be able to justify in any way unlawful participation of this sort'. The IAAF added that Reynolds may have to face an increased suspension and any repetition would inevitably endanger the participation of the United States in major competition. Reynolds was subsequently eliminated in the American trials for the World Championships, thus avoiding any confrontations concerning his and the United States' eligibility to compete.

Reynolds also appealed to the arbitration panel of the IAAF to have his suspension overturned to enable him to compete in the Olympics in 1992. The arbitration panel decided to uphold the original decision and, as the suspension did not end until August 1992, he was unable to compete either domestically or internationally until then. In the mean time Reynolds had achieved the Olympic qualifying time by running in a special 400-metre event specially formed by organizers to protect other runners from being banned for running against him. The IAAF had made it quite clear that Reynolds could not compete in the Olympics and if he participated in the US trials any athlete who raced against him could also be banned from the Olympics. Reynolds challenged this ban successfully in the Supreme Court in America and obtained an injunction allowing him to compete in the Olympic trials. It was perhaps fortunate for all concerned that Reynolds failed to gain a place in the Olympic team.

This saga looks as if it may continue for some time following an award of the equivalent of £18.2 million damages to Reynolds by a district court in Columbus, Ohio. The response of the IAAF was that the award of damages was only effective in Ohio and that the court had no jurisdiction in the matter, and further that in continuing to maintain his innocence when there were no reasonable grounds for his doing so Reynolds was in danger of having a libel action brought against him by the IAAF. The IAAF firmly believes that had the issue been raised in the British courts Reynolds would not have been successful. The IAAF now face the problem of how to protect their drug control procedures, particularly in powerful countries like America where TAC found that Reynolds had no case to answer. With the IAAF set to see this case through to the bitter end it may require the International Court of Justice in The Hague to make the final judgment.

It is clear from such challenges that testing procedures and the results obtained must be watertight, because if the findings of any of the accredited laboratories were ever undermined by one result being found to be unreliable the implication would be that all the tests carried out by that particular laboratory were unreliable.

Action should also be taken against those who assist drug abuse by sportspersons because of the benefit they may derive personally from enhanced performances. Suggestions have been made that such assistance is not confined only to coaches but also to officials who are prepared to assist athletes to get round the testing procedures. Charlie Francis, Ben Johnson's coach, was banned for life in 1991 by the ruling body of Canadian athletics. That same year the doctor who prescribed anabolic steroids for Johnson was found guilty of professional misconduct and he was suspended and fined, although the suspension was only effective in the province of Ontario. Dr Astaphan claimed that he had prescribed the steroids for Johnson and other althletes because he feared they would kill themselves by administering their own treatment. The doctor admitted obtaining unlabelled steroids from an East German athlete on the black market. This latter point raises another problem that needs to be tackled, that is the supply of steroids and in 1992, following the break-up of the Soviet Union several top Russsian athletes were implicated in the smuggling of illegal substances worth large amounts of money.

To eliminate the problem altogether there must be international co-operation. This may soon be forthcoming because the IAAF have recently warned Germany that if they do not deal adequately with recent allegations of drug abuse by their athletes they will not be considered as hosts for the World Championships in 1995. In December 1990 Britain signed a pact with Australia and Canada allowing their sporting authorities to test each other's athletes while competing or training in these three countries; another step in the right direction. Other proposals to help the fight against drug abuse include the introduction of blood tests instead of urine tests which will yield more accurate results. Blood tests are to be used at the next Winter Olympics to detect substances which increase oxygen-carrying red blood cells.

In April 1993 the IOC and the Association of Summer Olympic International Federations announced their intention to spearhead a new initiative to standardize punishments and methods of testing for drug abuse. The two bodies met in Lausanne in June 1993 to work out a policy to be adopted by all sports. Main stumbling blocks to co-ordinating action against drug abuse will be getting the agreement of the 26 federations and overcoming legal problems. Present plans are to introduce a minimum period of suspension of two years for steroid offences. The IOC has the 'stick' of withdrawing television rights incomes from the Olympic Games to 'persuade' those federations that do not willingly co-operate. Although the IOC is not prepared to get involved with random testing it has promised funding to assist this practice. In an effort to keep sport out of the courts it is also expected the IOC will try and instigate a code of conduct to be signed by athletes wishing to participate in the Olympic Games which will include acceptance of rulings made by the court of Arbitration (set up by the IOC) instead of using the civil courts.

NOTES

1. (1980) 2 Cr. App R (S) 198
2. (1898) 14 TLR 229
3. [1978] Crim LR 553
4. [1971] 2 WLR 831
5. *The Times*, 11 September 1980
6. (1878) 14 Cox CC 83
7. (1878) 8 QBD 534
8. (1878) 39 LT 293
9. *Sporting Life*, 20 June 1901
10. 77 *Police Review*, 7 February 1969
11. (1976) 64 Crim App Reports 20
12. *The Times*, 16 June 1988
13. *The Times*, 28 December 1992

Spectators and neighbours | 4

Spectators have their own vital role to play in recreation, particularly in its sporting aspect, and it is hardly surprising that, over the years, the courts have had to take them into consideration when assessing the legal liabilities of promoters of recreation. The safety of spectators is obviously a vital priority and Parliament was forced to recognize this, in the wake of several sports stadium tragedies, by passing the *Safety of Sports Grounds Act 1975*.

At the same time, no one concerned with the provision of leisure facilities can afford to overlook the legal rights of those who live nearby; they are just as entitled to protection from injury, whether it be from errant golf balls or incessant noise and disruption to their nervous systems. This chapter looks at both these aspects of the law in relation to leisure.

SPECTATORS AND THEIR CONTRACTS

The law of contract governs not only the more obvious 'commercial' contracts which exist in sport (such as the contracts which professional footballers have with their clubs, which were examined in Chapter 2), but also the many and various arrangements under which people participate as spectators of sporting and other leisure activities.

In some cases, it is obvious that there must be some sort of 'contract', as for example where a football fan pays money and passes through the turnstile of the local football ground. In fact, whenever someone pays money to spectate, an increasingly common phenomenon in places such as swimming pools and squash courts, it is not difficult to anticipate that the law would regard the situation as a contractual one. What comes as a surprise to many is to learn that there is very often some sort of legal relationship created, even when the spectator is allowed in free of charge; one can say either that such a spectator enters under an implied contract with the organizer, or is allowed in as a 'licensee' (a word used here in a special, technical, legal sense). Either way, as a result, the organizer of the activity owes that spectator certain legal duties and the spectator must at least be taken to have agreed to behave.

The difficulty which lawyers face in situations such as these is that very little of the agreement between spectator and organizer has been put in writing, and one must search for the terms of the agreement by implication. It is not difficult to imply an undertaking by the organizer that the premises are safe and the event well organized (which is a duty imposed by the law anyway, regardless of whether or not there is a contract), and an agreement by the spectator that the spectator will be of good behaviour, a requirement of the criminal law, but what about the management's right to dictate what seat or place in the stand the spectator will occupy or their right to change the programme without warning?

There are no standard rules in areas such as this and the courts will either examine such written evidence as there is, for example, advanced publicity which reserved the organizer's right to change the programme or the seat number printed on the ticket which the spectator purchased, or 'imply' a reasonable understanding into the relationship, for example, the obvious need of the organizers to separate rival groups of football supporters and therefore to have the final 'say' on where the fans may sit or stand.

Some organizers seek to resolve this type of uncertainty by either printing conditions of entry on the tickets or simply referring on the face of the ticket to conditions under which it is bought which can be examined during normal business hours at the secretary's office or some similar place. At the same time, many of them take the opportunity of setting out 'exemption clauses' which absolve them from liability in the event of loss or injury, and again are either printed on the ticket itself, or contained in the conditions to which the purchaser is referred.

This type of ticket situation which arises in other contexts, such as the purchase of rail tickets or the use of a multi-storey car park, has been examined by the courts on many occasions in the past. The rule which has emerged is that conditions printed on tickets will not be effective unless, first of all, the purchaser was aware that they were being given something which referred to conditions and not simply a receipt for payment of the entrance fee and, secondly, that the nature of the conditions in question was 'reasonably' communicated to the purchaser.

Even then, as is explained elsewhere in this book, it is no longer possible, thanks to the *Unfair Contract Terms Act 1977*, for any sports organizers to exempt themselves from liability, either to a participant or a spectator, for physical injury or death, and any other kind of purported exemption, for example, relating to loss of property in a locker room, will be judged according to whether or not it is 'reasonable' (page 33).

This does not mean that the organizer is always liable for injury or loss to a player or spectator; simply that if they are found liable, under the general principles of law explained in this chapter and in Chapter 2, liability cannot be evaded simply by pointing to an exemption clause referred to in the wording on a ticket, or indeed in a notice displayed in the entrance foyer or around the ground.

When tickets have been sold in advance bad weather resulting in no play being possible at events such as cricket test matches and tennis at Wimbledon can cause real problems for the organizers. Generally, to protect themselves organizers will not allow refunds where there has been some play and will attempt to appease disgruntled fans, where possible, by making tickets sold for one day valid on another day. Where a condition relating to the sale of the ticket provides that no refunds are available if there is no play the organizers can, of course, rely on that condition, but to do so may in some circumstances lose the support of the public. During a test match in June 1992 the first day was completely washed out and money was refunded to all ticket holders. On the second day only two balls were bowled but the Test and County Cricket Board (TCCB) stood by the reimbursement clause on the back of the tickets which stated that refunds would only be made if, due to adverse weather conditions, no play whatsoever took place. Tickets for the second day were made valid for the last day of play, but this did not satisfy many of those affected. The TCCB itself was insured against losses incurred through bad weather, a fact that simply added fuel to the fire.

Following complaints and threats of legal action the TCCB negotiated a new deal whereby spectators buying tickets in advance for test matches for the 1993 season would be protected by a much improved insurance scheme against bad weather. A 'raincheck' scheme will give advance ticket buyers a full return on their money if, because of rain, only 10 overs or fewer are bowled in a day. There will be a 50% return if there are more than 10 but fewer than 25 overs.

Legal action did follow this incident and a judge at Birmingham County Court ordered the cricket authorities to refund the five spectators who brought the action their ticket money and costs. The judge did not allow the cricket authorities to rely on the exclusion clause for two reasons. The first was that as the clause had subsequently been amended this indicated their own feeling that the condition was unacceptable. Secondly, the judge pointed out that spectators who purchased tickets by telephone using credit cards had not seen the terms for refunds as they were printed on the back of the tickets. The Warwickshire County Cricket Club, against whom the action was brought, has yet to decide how to respond to this decision, particularly as all the gate receipts went to the TCCB.

Wimbledon introduced a similar policy in 1992, whereby spectators get back half their money if there is no tennis before 6 p.m. and the offer of a full refund for no play at all. The sale of Wimbledon tickets themselves resulted in legal action against the All England Club, which organizes the event, by a corporate hospitality company. The company was complaining that the practice of buying back tickets from debenture holders at an inflated price and then selling these tickets at a further inflated price to providers of corporate hospitality was unlawful due to the fact that debenture holders could only sell their tickets to the All England Club. A complaint was also made to the European Community Commissioner that this practice was an anti-competitive trading practice and therefore against European Community law. The Commissioner accepted the complaint and the Office of Fair Trading agreed to investigate the matter. The complaint was rejected because although the Club had a monopoly on tickets it was not in a monopoly position in the market for corporate hospitality.

Purchase of a ticket for a football match may include an implied, if not an express, term between the visitor and the occupier that there will be a reasonable view. Three Leicester City Football Club supporters successfully sued Millwall Football Club in the Woolwich County Court for the 'extremely poor view' during a third round FA Cup tie. They were refunded one-third of their admission money, and also travelling expenses and costs. Their view was obscured by a floodlight pylon, a high safety fence and one of the stands.

Organizers must also be careful to ensure that advance publicity is accurate as the non-occurrence of advertised events may result in prosecution under the *Trade Descriptions Act 1968*. Chipperfield's Circus were successfully prosecuted under this Act in April 1992 when the rare Siberian tigers that had been advertised failed to appear. The circus was fined £100 with £250 costs after admitting a false trade description.

OCCUPIERS' LIABILITY IN RELATION TO THE SPECTATOR

As was explained in Chapter 2, the 'occupier' of sports or leisure premises, who will be either the owner or the person who operates them, owes a legal duty to all persons who use them, including spectators, to ensure that they are 'reasonably' safe for the purpose or purposes for which those persons enter. In the case of a spectator, this means that the premises must be reasonably safe for spectating, which includes consideration of factors such as the safety of the seating in the stand, the structure of the stand itself and the proximity of the first row of permitted spectating to the event which is taking place. In activities which are not in the formal 'arena' setting, for example, perimeter spectating in motor-cycle scrambling, then the duty of the organizer is probably limited to marking out the course with ropes and putting up warning notices for spectators against the dangers of proceeding beyond the ropes.

Not only does an occupier owe a duty of care regarding activities on his premises, the occupier is also responsible for the static condition of the premises. This duty is a duty to take such care, which in all the circumstances of the case is reasonable, to ensure that a visitor will be reasonably safe while using the premises for the purpose for which the visitor was invited, or allowed by the occupier to be there. In *Francis v Cockrell* (1870),[1] the defendant who had had a grandstand erected on his land, was held to be liable when the grandstand collapsed and injured the plaintiff who had paid to enter the grandstand in order to watch horse-races. Similarly, in *Dougan v Glasgow Rangers Football Club* (1974),[2] Rangers were ordered to pay damages to the widow and family of a man crushed to death when a stand at their football ground collapsed. Accidents had occurred previously in this stand, but no action had been taken to remedy the situation.

Occupiers owe a duty of care to any visitors on their premises and this includes any police officers present on duty. In *Cunningham and Others v Reading Football Club Ltd* (1991)[3] several police officers claimed damages from the Reading Football Club for injuries resulting from rioting between fans. Two of the constables had been severely injured by pieces of concrete thrown at them by the fans. The police contended that as riots between opposing fans were foreseeable the football club was liable as an occupier of the football ground. The court decided the club was liable for injuries caused to the police officers because the injuries resulted from the club's neglect to take precautions against clearly foreseeable acts of violent supporters. In this case, given the dilapidated state of the ground, the conduct of the spectators was easily foreseeable in relation to loose concrete being a supply of missiles, particularly as similar incidents had occurred before and the club had not taken steps to remedy the situation.

Although the police have a 'duty' to attend situations where there may be trouble it has long been established that football clubs can be charged for 'extra' policing. At the beginning of 1991 proposals from the Home Office to make clubs pay the full economic costs of policing football matches were rejected by the all-party Parliamentary football committee on the grounds that a 'town cannot be deprived of its soccer club because the bill for policing bankrupts it'. Clubs can, however, be required to make a regular contribution to policing costs.

This duty of care also extends to the selection of persons to construct structures on land. The committee of a football club were found liable in *Brown v Lewis* (1896)[4] when a stand collapsed because an incompetent person had been employed to repair it.

It was, in fact, the publicity which attended the collapse of the Ibrox Park stand in 1971 (the origin of the *Dougan* case, above), which led to the passing of the *Safety of Sports Grounds Act 1975*. The Act will be dealt with in a later section of this chapter.

Although it will generally be the occupier who will be liable to spectators injured through their negligence, this liability may be shared by anyone else who was also responsible. In May 1985 a fire swept through a stand at Bradford City Football Ground killing 56 people and highlighting inadequacies in the *Safety of Sports Grounds Act 1975*. The main reason for the fire was a large amount of rubbish under the stand which had not been cleared for a long time. The club claimed it could not clear the rubbish because it would have meant dismantling the stand and they could not afford the expense. The judge, in an action for negligence, *Fletcher and Others v Bradford City Association Football Club*[5] in 1987, said this was irrelevant in relation to the duty owed to spectators which was to restrict entry to the stand or close it down. Both the club and the local fire authority were found liable. The fire authority was liable because they had set up a safety team under the *Safety of Sports Grounds Act 1975* to ensure safety at sports grounds and stadia. An engineer in the team had inspected the stadium and concluded there was a potential fire hazard. A letter was sent to the fire authority, but they did not follow it up and they were found liable for their inaction.

Generally damages will be paid to spectators who are injured in such incidents and dependants of those killed, but there was an attempt to extend this principle following the disaster at the Hillsborough stadium, the ground of Sheffield Wednesday Football Club. Ninety-five people were crushed to death at an FA Cup semi-final when crowds surged into the stadium. The incident was shown live on television, and relatives and friends of those killed or injured, who were present in the stadium or who watched it as it happened on television, claimed damages for nervous shock resulting from the negligence of those responsible. Nervous shock in this case was a psychiatric condition called traumatic stress disorder. Those responsible were the South Yorkshire police who were dealing with the crowds at the match, Sheffield Wednesday Football Club and engineers who had advised the club on the safety of the ground. All parties accepted responsibility and paid compensation, and the only contentious issue that was dealt with by the courts was who should actually be compensated and for what.

Most of the claims for nervous shock were rejected by the House of Lords and *Alcock and Others v Chief Constable of South Yorkshire* (1991)[6] decided exactly who could claim damages for nervous shock. Most of the claims failed on the grounds either that their relationship with those who died or their proximity with the disaster, through watching it on television, was not close enough. Generally claims for nervous shock caused by watching live or recorded coverage of a disaster will fail because the code of ethics followed by television authorities meant no pictures of recognizable suffering by individuals were shown, although simultaneous broadcasts of an event where there was a sudden disaster could in some circumstances give rise to a claim.

The House of Lords also rejected a claim in *Hicks and Another v Chief Constable of South Yorkshire* (1992)[7] from the parents of two sisters crushed to death for pre-death pain and suffering, as the parents had failed to prove that either girl suffered before death any injury for which damages could be awarded. The medical evidence was that they would have lost consciousness within seconds and died within minutes.

Following the tragedy the South Yorkshire police invited the West Midlands force to investigate its handling of the crowd and recommend whether charges should be laid against any of its officers. This investigation took 16 months and a report was submitted to the Director of Public Prosecutions, who decided that no individual officers should face prosecution. However the Police Complaints Authority (PCA) did decide that the officer who was ground controller at the game and the officer in charge of the control room should appear before a tribunal which could recommend several courses, including demotion or dismissal. But due to the retirement of the ground controller the PCA withdrew the charge against the officer in charge of the control room on the grounds that it would be unjust to proceed with this charge in the absence of his superior officer.

Many people felt that criminal proceedings should have been brought against those responsible for the Hillsborough disaster, but the Director of Public Prosecutions, having considered the matter, decided that there was not sufficient evidence. A subsequent attempt to initiate a private prosecution failed for the same reason, but in April 1993 families of victims were granted the right to challenge the way the inquest had been conducted through a judicial review.

There are ways in which an occupier may escape liability for damages relating to injuries or loss suffered on the occupier's premises. Warnings relating to a dangerous activity may enable an occupier to escape liability, provided the warning was given in time to enable a visitor to ensure their own safety; where children are involved, further steps, beyond a mere warning, may be necessary to discharge this duty.

In *White v Blackmore* (1972),[8] White, a member of a jalopy club, was competing in a race meeting and, as a competitor, had entered the grounds free of charge. A notice near the entrance exempted the organizers from liability for death or injuries to spectators, however caused. White was watching a race when he was killed by a car competing in the race. The court decided, in an action for damages by his widow, that the organizers of the race meeting, although negligent, were not liable as they had successfully limited their liability through the display of warning notices. There was no contractual relationship between White and the race organizers as he had entered the ground free of charge.

This defence has now been severely restricted by the *Unfair Contract Terms Act 1977* (referred to above), which provides that it is no longer possible to exclude or restrict, by contract or by notice, liability for negligence arising in a business context and resulting in death or personal injury. Whether or not liability for other forms of loss can be excluded will depend on the reasonableness of the exclusion, which will be a matter for the judge to decide. The Act covers not only the supply of goods and services, but also contracts of employment and the liability of occupiers of premises or land used for business purposes to persons entering on or using those premises or land.

There are two possible consequences of this legislation. One is that landowners may be reluctant to allow recreationalists on their land to pursue activities such as caving or pot-holing, as landowners cannot exclude their liability in relation to accidents occurring as a result of their negligence. Landowners in these circumstances may be exercising too much caution, as the Act relates to premises used for 'business' which may exclude such activities. However the *Occupiers' Liability Act 1984* has modified the 1977 Act to allow landowners to exclude liability for natural features on their land.

A second consequence is that a possible defence in relation to participants and spectators of recreational activities, that of *volenti non fit injuria* (page 27), may be expected to become more popular following the introduction of the *Unfair Contract Terms Act 1977*. This defence is a claim that the plaintiff consented to run the risk of injury, but this consent only applies to the known and normal dangers associated with that activity, and not to someone else's negligence. *Volenti* has been claimed successfully in several cases concerning injuries sustained by spectators of or participants in recreational activities. In *Murray v Harringey Arena Ltd* (1951),[9] a six-year-old boy was a spectator at an ice-hockey match, sitting in the front row, when he was hit in the eye by the puck. There was no evidence of such an incident occurring before. The court decided that the owners of the rink were not liable for the injury to the boy, as they had not been negligent. Such a danger was incidental to the game and could have been reasonably foreseen by any spectator, thus he had accepted the risk, whatever his age. This may now be subject to the *Occupiers' Liability Act 1957*, which varied the duty owed in relation to the character of visitors expected, including their age.

Similarly, in *Hall v Brooklands Auto Racing Club* (1933),[10] where a spectator at a motor race was injured when two cars collided in a race, it was held that the owners of the race track were not liable in respect of the spectator's injuries. In such cases there is no liability for dangers inherent in a particular sport which could have been foreseen by a spectator who therefore accepted the risk of them occurring.

The general nature of the defence of *volenti* was discussed, in the context of liability to participants, in Chapter 2.

It is also possible for the occupier of premises faced with a claim for damages from an injured spectator to claim that the spectator was partly to blame for those injuries in that the spectator was contributorily negligent. This potential defence was also dealt with in detail in Chapter Two in the context of liability for injury to a participant, but might equally well apply, for example, in a situation in which a spectator at a football match chooses to sit on the wrong side of a crowd barrier or where a speedway fan rushes on to the track to congratulate a winner.

OCCUPIERS' LIABILITY IN RELATION TO NEIGHBOURS

Occupiers owe a duty not to be negligent not only to persons actually on the premises they occupy, but also to persons outside their premises. The extent of this duty will depend on the foreseeability of the accident that occurred and the cost of taking precautions. In *Hilder v Associated Portland Cement Manufacturers Ltd* (1961)[11] the defendants allowed children to play football on their land, knowing that the football often went on to the adjoining highway. In an action resulting from an accident caused by a straying football, the defendants were held liable as the accident was foreseeable and was not a risk that could be disregarded. Similarly, in *Lamond v Glasgow Corporation* (1968)[12] the defendants, as owners of a golf course, were held to be liable when a golf ball struck a pedestrian on a public lane, as such an accident was reasonably foreseeable and should be guarded against.

However, in *Bolton v Stone* (1951)[13] a batsman, during a cricket match, drove a ball out of the ground whereafter it travelled 100 yards, clearing a 17 foot fence before striking and injuring the plaintiff who was outside the cricket ground. As a ball had only been hit out of the ground six times in the past 30 years the court decided that such an accident was not reasonably foreseeable and could not form the basis of a claim founded on the tort of negligence or nuisance; nuisance is another tort an occupier may be liable for, and is dealt with in a later section of this chapter.

LEGISLATION TO CONTROL AND PROTECT SPECTATORS

The *Safety of Sports Grounds Act 1975* has imposed extra duties on certain occupiers of premises used for recreational activities. This was the first statute specifically aimed at safety in sports grounds. As early as 1924 recommendations were made that a licensing system for grounds of a certain capacity should be introduced, but this was not put into effect until two fatal disasters had occurred, at Bolton in 1946 and the Ibrox Park disaster in Glasgow in 1971.

The purpose of this statute is to ensure the safety of spectators in relation to what is reasonable and practical for the club concerned. As it is based on 'reasonableness', it is not an absolute guarantee of safety. Any sports ground to be used by the public can now be required by the Secretary of State to hold a current safety certificate issued by the local authority.

A 'sports ground' is defined in the Act as any place where sports or competitive activities take place in the open air, and where accommodation, whether artificial or modified natural structures, is provided. Although the Act is aimed primarily at football clubs, it encompasses a large range of activities. Sports stadia, however, are the main target of this legislation which defines them as sports grounds where accommodation for spectators wholly or substantially surrounds the playing area.

Safety certificates issued under the Act are of two types. A 'general' certificate is the more usual and covers specific activities at a particular ground for an indefinite period. A 'special' certificate covers a single event or a short series of events. This certificate is relevant where a sports stadium stages events with which it is not normally associated and for which it does not hold a general safety certificate, and would apply, for example, to a 'pop' concert in a sports stadium.

By this statute, wide powers are conferred on the Secretary of State who may designate as requiring a safety certificate any sports stadium with a capacity of more than 10 000. In 1976, a statutory instrument designated all the first division football clubs, Wembley Stadium, Twickenham Rugby Union

Ground and Cardiff Arms Park. To estimate the capacity of a stadium, the Secretary of State may request any information needed from the sports stadium concerned, and failure to provide such information may result in a fine, and possible automatic designation. These powers also enable the Secretary of State to extend the provisions of the Act with any necessary modifications to sports grounds other than sports stadia with a capacity of 10 000 or more.

The Secretary of State has exclusive jurisdiction to hear appeals arising from the application of the Act in a manner detailed in the Act. Such appeals may relate to the refusal to grant a certificate at all, or not to a particular person, or the 'unreasonableness' of the contents of a certificate that has been granted. There is no right to an inquiry if an appeal is made, but an inquiry may be set up at the discretion of the Secretary of State.

The local authority is the central body around which the Act revolves, but powers are granted to county rather than district councils. This may lead to conflicts of standards relating to modifications done or required to be done to sports grounds and stadia by local planning authorities, which are the district councils. Detailed administration and implementation of this legislation is left to local authorities working within the framework of the Act with, hopefully, the co-operation of the clubs or occupiers concerned.

When a local authority receives an application for a safety certificate from a designated ground, they will first determine whether or not the applicant is 'qualified' to hold a safety certificate within the Act. Secondly, they can request details and enter the premises for necessary information on which to base decisions concerning any changes necessary to bring the stadium up to the standards required by the Act. Failure to co-operate with the local authority may result in the imposition of penalties provided in the Act or the issue of a certificate containing very restrictive terms. Cardiff City Football Club, on their failure to produce the information requested, had their ground capacity reduced so drastically that they were unable to stage a World Cup qualifying fixture between Wales and Scotland.

A local authority may require a club or occupier to take any measures it considers necessary to secure 'reasonable' safety. The factors to be considered concerning 'reasonable' safety include the maximum number of spectators to be admitted, the grouping of spectators within the ground, the number of exits and entrances, records of attendance and maintenance, and the existing provision of crash barriers. The cost of any alterations is not a factor to be considered, on the basis that persons involved in a commercial enterprise putting the public at risk should bear the cost of any statutory measures. A green guide relating to the factors that should be considered has been issued by the Home Office. Finally, local authorities have the power to amend and alter the terms and conditions of an existing certificate as time and circumstances dictate.

An inquiry was held into the fire at Bradford Football Club and following publication of the findings in the Popplewell Report the green guide to safety at sports grounds was updated and extended to 'all types of sports grounds where spectators are likely to be present'. Alleged breaches of the old guide formed a substantial part of the claim for negligence and the guide could be a useful weapon for plaintiffs in the future. An immediate consequence of the disaster was also the designation of all third and fourth division clubs in the Football League.

New legislation also followed this report, the *Fire Safety and Safety of Places of Sport Act 1987*, which amended the *Fire Precautions Act 1971*. The most important provision of this Act was the requirement of a safety certificate for a permanent stand which provides covered accommodation for 500 or more spectators at any type of sports ground: a requirement which could change the 'character' of events such as Wimbledon where spectators were allowed in during the late afternoon and could wander around freely, and stand and watch tennis matches.

Unfortunately this legislation was unable to prevent the disaster which occurred at the Hillsborough stadium which resulted in the Taylor Report. This report recommended the more stringent application of the provisions in the *Safety of Sports Grounds Act 1975* and particularly that all Football League clubs should have all-seat stadia. A deadline for first and second division clubs has been set for 1994, and all other clubs must be all-seat by 1999. These requirements in the Taylor Report were subsequently amended by the government because they could lead to the bankruptcy of smaller clubs. Outside the English Premier League and the Scottish Premier League it is likely that only clubs with average crowds above 10 000 will have to abolish standing terraces.

A Football Licensing Authority was established and charged, under section 13 of the *Football Spectators Act 1990*, with keeping under review the safety certificates issued by local authorities. The Football Licensing Authority employs nine inspectors to police the League clubs and check that certificates are up to date. It was subsequently discovered that some certificates issued in the late 1970s had never been reviewed and some had travelled unchanged from one ground to another when clubs moved to new grounds. The Football Licensing Authority has the power to force a local authority to amend a safety certificate issued to a club and can also sanction the suspension of a club.

Finance will be the main problem arising from the enforcement of this legislation and the Taylor Report. However, the government initially introduced a tax relief on expenditure to meet the requirements of the *Safety of Sports Grounds Act 1975* in the *Finance Act (No. 2) 1975*. Section 119 of the *Finance Act 1989* was introduced to offset a perverse ruling by a High Court judge in 1980. The judge refused to allow Burnley Football Club to offset against tax a £250 000 bill to replace an unsafe grandstand. Although this had been allowed by the Inland Revenue Commissioners, according to the judge 'no part, except the football pitch itself was necessary to the central activity of arranging professional football matches as a spectator sport. The club could have continued its activities without affording covered seats for those of its supporters prepared to pay for that amenity.' Section 119 now provides that tax relief can be claimed when expenditure is incurred in connection with issuing a safety certificate under the *Fire Safety and Places of Sport Act 1987*.

Some local authorities have been willing to grant loans to clubs to help them, but government assistance was only forthcoming following the recommendations of the Taylor Report. In September 1990 the Chancellor cut the pools betting duty in the budget, leaving football clubs £100 million better off over a five-year period. Any further aid from the Government will depend on evidence that football is making a significant contribution, in particular, that the Football League has introduced a money-raising scheme such as a transfer fee levy or diverting a percentage of television revenue to ground improvements. However, finance will always remain a problem, particularly when sports less affluent than football are involved.

Another solution sought by some clubs has been to attempt to build completely new stadia rather than trying to convert old grounds to meet the new requirements. However, two clubs attempting to do this, Southampton and Oxford United, have been experiencing difficulties in obtaining planning permission for the proposed new stadia.

SPECTATORS AND THE CRIMINAL LAW

As we have already seen in Chapter 3, the criminal law may be invoked in a variety of ways in connection with unlawful activities on the field of play. Equally, it is possible that the behaviour of a spectator falls foul of the criminal law and if, for example, the spectator assaults a player or another spectator, or indeed is simply guilty of aggressive behaviour which could constitute an 'assault' in the technical sense, for example, waving a fist under the nose of a referee as the referee leaves the field, then that spectator will be dealt with in the manner outlined in Chapter 3.

Regretfully, crowd behaviour has become a serious issue in recent years, and it is not unusual for fans arrested both inside and outside sports stadia such as football grounds, to be charged with offences like the possession of offensive weapons. More commonly, there comes a point at which the behaviour of some spectators, while not necessarily becoming overtly violent, constitutes a breach of the peace (as defined in Chapter 3) because of its provocative nature. 'Streaking' was an activity in point and not even turfs as hallowed as Lord's and Twickenham were immune from this activity during the years in which it was popular.

In *Brutus v Cozens* (1973)[14] the appellant stepped on to a tennis court, where the public are not allowed, during the annual open tennis tournament at Wimbledon. He blew a whistle, threw around leaflets concerning apartheid, attempted to give a leaflet to a player and then sat down on the court. Other people, on hearing the whistle, arrived carrying banners with slogans and distributed more leaflets. Play was stopped. The appellant was charged with using insulting behaviour whereby a breach of the peace was likely to be occasioned. The magistrates decided that this behaviour, although it angered the crowd, was not 'insulting'. On appeal to the House of Lords it was held that the magistrates must decide as a question of fact whether the accused's conduct was threatening, abusive or insulting in the ordinary meaning of these terms.

Although the existing criminal law can be applied to recreational activities, new criminal offences can be introduced by legislation to deal with problems relating specifically to recreational activities. This can be illustrated by consideration of attempts to control 'hooliganism' among football, rugby or other sporting fans. To date, hooliganism has been controlled by application of the existing criminal law, as indicated above, and in a large variety of cases fans have been punished, sometimes severely, for offences ranging from conduct likely to cause a breach of the peace, to behaviour resulting in grievous bodily harm.

Punishments have ranged from fines and imprisonment to being sent to a detention centre. Even before trial, restrictions may be placed on a person, for example, a ban from visiting any football stadium in the country as a condition of bail. In one case involving soccer hooliganism, an 18-year-old youth, Bruce, appealed against a 3-year prison sentence imposed for causing grievous bodily harm with a hammer, in an incident following a football match. The appeal was dismissed on the grounds that young persons who commit offences of violence on the occasion of football matches are liable to custodial sentences, however good their previous characters may be.

Violence among spectators is not confined to football supporters. Violent scenes erupted after a boxing contest, a world middleweight title fight, and one spectator involved was later imprisoned for throwing beer cans, one of which struck a television commentator.

Although crowd control is not the direct concern of the organizers of recreation, there have been suggestions that clubs concerned, and the governing bodies of the sports involved, should take measures to improve the situation. Where clubs have imposed sanctions on violent fans by banning them from their premises the courts have supported them, as happened when Bristol City Football Club and Swindon Town Football Club banned fans for persistent misbehaviour. In both cases, the court granted an injunction restraining the fans from entering the respective football grounds.

Following the publication of a report on football hooliganism in 1969 governing bodies of sport and individual clubs have been exhorted to take steps to curb violence, including the provision of all-seat accommodation at matches. Only relatively recently have any definite steps been taken towards controlling hooliganism among football and rugby fans. In Scotland the *Criminal Justice (Scotland) Act 1980* bans alcohol at major football and rugby matches by making it an offence to have alcohol at certain grounds and also in a coach travelling to or from a match. Being drunk on a coach, or while in or attempting to enter the ground is also an offence. These offences are punishable by a fine or imprisonment. This Act also gives the police wide powers to search people for offensive weapons. Early reports, following the implementation of this law, have been favourable. The first Scottish rugby union fan to be charged under this new law was ordered to lodge £60 as security for good behaviour over the following 12 months.

Similar legislation was subsequently passed in England and the *Sporting Events (Control of Alcohol etc.) Act 1985* bans alcohol on public service vehicles carrying passengers to or from designated sporting events. This Act also imposed a general ban on the sale of alcohol in football grounds, which caused consternation among football clubs because they derive a considerable income from such sales and because they expected people would give up their private boxes. However the Act does allow for exemptions to be granted under strict conditions, for example, where bars are not in sight of the pitch. Many clubs have taken advantage of this and have applied successfully to have the ban lifted in all or some of their bars or for particular matches.

British Rail meanwhile have taken matters into their own hands by introducing a by-law banning alcohol on football trains. In March 1981 a man, believed to be the first football fan to be charged under this by-law, was fined £40 for possessing vodka and being drunk on a football train to Portsmouth.

The Football Association has suggested that the government should intervene to control football hooliganism through special legislation or increased police powers. They also urged the provision of better facilities by football clubs. These suggestions were made because the Football Association felt it had done as much as it possibly could to control crowd behaviour during football matches, but it does not have the power to control hooliganism both before and after matches.

Some of these suggestions were implemented in the *Public Order Act 1986* which conferred discretionary powers on the courts to ban spectators committing public order offences from attending sporting fixtures by making them subject to an exclusion order following conviction for an offence under this Act or the *Sporting Events (Control of Alcohol etc.) Act 1985*. The Act has built-in powers of extension by the Home Office if the need arises. Exclusion orders were extended by the *Football Spectators Act 1989* to matches outside England and Wales. Such matches may be designated and fans convicted of football-related offences may be subject to a restriction order, and have to report to a designated reporting agency at a specified time and place (subject to offences for failing to do so). The order must last for at least 12 months.

The *Public Order Act 1986* also extended the provisions of the *Sporting Events (Control of Alcohol etc.) 1985* to any vehicle adapted to carry more than eight passengers and created offences of possessing alcohol, containers capable of causing injury and fireworks while at or trying to enter a designated sports ground. It also conferred powers to stop people and search them for any of the above articles.

In August 1991 the *Football Offences Act* came into force and this introduces three new offences which it is hoped will help rid the sport of the 'unsavoury minority' of spectators. It is now a criminal offence to do any of the following: throw any object on to the pitch or into any spectator area; run on to the pitch without good reason; chant indecent or racialist slogans. These offences can only be committed at designated football matches, that is, a designated association football match or a football match of a description designated for the purposes of the Act by order of the Secretary of State. Currently these are all Football League matches, European football competitions and all internationals.

Attempts by the government to introduce an identity card membership scheme for designated football clubs and a licensing scheme allowing clubs to admit spectators were thwarted by opposition from the clubs and governing bodies in football because of the difficulty of actually enforcing it. When the Taylor Report on the disaster at Hillsborough also opposed the scheme the government agreed to 'freeze' it indefinitely, although provision for such a scheme forms part of the *Football Spectators Act 1989*.

NUISANCE

However much the operator of sports and leisure premises may feel that the premises add to the amenity of the area, there may be neighbours who think otherwise. We have already noted how such neighbours may take legal action if they are physically injured as the result of a failure on the part of the occupier of leisure premises to take 'reasonable' care for their safety; another way in which the law protects them is by providing legal restraints against the commission of a nuisance either public or private.

A 'public nuisance' is a criminal offence of 'strict liability', which means that the offender may be convicted even though the offender may not have been at fault personally, but simply created a situation in which others were able to create the nuisance, which in law can be anything that interferes with the public's right to make use of a public place. This may occur where large crowds have gathered on a highway, making it impossible for other people to use that highway. Public nuisance may also occur where an activity makes the use of a public highway dangerous because, for example, golf balls are frequently hit over the road. In *Castle v St Augustine's Links Ltd* (1922)[15] it was held that there was a public nuisance where golf balls were often hit on to or over a public highway from a nearby golf course, thus endangering users of that highway. The 'public' is usually deemed to mean a substantial number of persons are affected, not just one or two.

For this offence, it is not necessary to prove that the accused knew that their action would create a public nuisance. In *Moore* (1832)[16] the accused was found to be guilty of a public nuisance when he organized pigeon shooting on his land and in consequence a large crowd of people collected on the highway to shoot at pigeons as they escaped. This caused an obstruction of the public highway, preventing other people from using the highway. Such an offence is now covered by statute, for example the *Highways Act 1980*. Many instances that have in the past been judged to amount to a public nuisance, including polluting rivers (which could occur through the use of motor boats), and causing excessive noise and dust, are now the subject of special legislation, and proceedings are unlikely to be brought at common law where a statute covers the situation, but it nevertheless remains available.

Although public nuisance is primarily a crime, it can also give rise to an action for civil damages by anyone who has suffered more loss or damage than simply the general inconvenience to the public. However, if a neighbour is the victim of loss or damage in relation to that neighbour's own private property (as opposed simply to their interests as a general member of the public), then it is more appropriate for them to sue for 'private' nuisance.

A successful action in private nuisance relies on the existence of five elements in the action complained of:

1. there must be an interference with the plaintiff's enjoyment of their land;
2. the interference must be continuing and not one isolated incident;
3. the interference must be unreasonable;
4. the interference must have been either created by the defendant, caused by the defendant's neglect of duty or continued by the defendant;
5. generally the plaintiff must suffer actual damage.

These elements will be considered individually, beginning with the requirement that the interference must affect the plaintiff's enjoyment of their land. The plaintiff must have an interest in the land affected by the action complained of in order to sue.

In every case of nuisance there must be an element of continuity, for example, a series of explosions or continuous noisy activities. The interference may take the form of a threat of danger or discomfort to the plaintiff, as well as actual discomfort or damage. Actions in nuisance may be brought against participants in and organizers of recreation, concerning, for example, a nuisance caused by balls frequently landing on private property. In *Miller v Jackson* (1977)[17] the action brought concerned the playing of cricket on a village green. Cricket had been played there since 1905. In 1970 houses were built near the green. These houses were liable to have cricket balls hit into their gardens. The plaintiff bought one of these houses in 1972 and sued members of the cricket club for damages for negligence and nuisance, due to incidents that had caused physical damage to the house and the apprehension of personal injury. The court decided, first, that there was negligence on the part of the cricket club, as the risk of injury was foreseeable. Secondly, it was decided that the playing of cricket did constitute an unreasonable interference with the plaintiff's enjoyment of land and was a nuisance. Finally, however, the court decided that there were special circumstances, namely, that the plaintiff knew when he bought the house that cricket was played on the green and, also, as the village as a whole had an interest in the existence of a cricket ground, the plaintiff would only be awarded damages and would not be granted an injunction, which is the usual remedy when nuisance is established, to stop cricket being played on the green.

In *Kennaway v Thompson* (1980)[18] the Court of Appeal allowed an appeal against a decision to award damages in lieu of an injunction because of public interest in the club concerned. In this case the plaintiff had built a house on land next to a man-made lake on which a motor-boat racing club was already organizing motor-boat racing and water skiing. During the five years after the plaintiff went into occupation of her house, there was a considerable increase in the activities of the club and race meetings were held most weekends between April and October with large, noisy boats taking part. The plaintiff brought an action in nuisance claiming damages and an injunction, but was refused an injunction by the High Court. However, the Court of Appeal allowed her appeal and granted an injunction on the grounds that, in cases of continuing actionable nuisance, the jurisdiction to award damages ought only to be exercised under very exceptional circumstances and in this case the public interest in continuing the activity constituting the nuisance did not prevail over the private interest in obtaining an injunction which would therefore be granted to reduce the noise and number of race meetings.

There is no exact definition of what amounts to an 'unreasonable' interference, but the test used is what would be reasonable according to the ordinary habits of people living in a particular area. In deciding what is reasonable, the courts balance the interests of the various occupiers against each other and, in weighing up competing interests, the courts will take into account the extent and duration of the interference, and the encroachment on the ordinary use of the plaintiff's property. If the interference is due to the fact that the plaintiff is using their property for a special purpose which makes it unusually sensitive to interference, then there is no nuisance.

If the interference only affects the plaintiff's enjoyment and convenience, and there is no actual damage to property, that interference must be substantial and one of which a person of ordinary feelings would complain.

A further consideration is the nature of the locality, for example, a plaintiff suffering discomfort from the trade carried on at a shop opened next door to the plaintiff cannot complain if there are a lot of shops in the area in which the plaintiff lives, but such a plaintiff could probably establish nuisance if the area concerned is a select residential area.

Finally, where a defendant is found to be acting maliciously, what might normally constitute a reasonable interference may be held to be unreasonable.

Only the person responsible for causing, or continuing, the nuisance can be sued. Where a nuisance occurs on a person's land, that person will be responsible if the person is aware of it, even though they did not create it.

Generally an action in nuisance will not succeed unless actual damage can be proved. However, there are two exceptions to this rule. First, where the interference is with an 'easement', such as a right of way or a fishing right, it is not necessary to prove actual damage, so the nuisance is said to be actionable *per se*, that is actionable without proof of loss, injury or damage; secondly, where a plaintiff brings an action for an injunction to prevent a nuisance occurring in the future.

To escape liability in an action for nuisance, the defendant may be able to prove one of the following defences: *volenti non fit injuria*, contributory negligence, statutory authority as a reason for creating the nuisance and, finally, that a right to continue the nuisance has been acquired as a prescriptive right because it has existed openly and continuously for 20 years.

Remedies available for nuisance are damages, an injunction, which is an order to stop the activity creating the nuisance or 'abatement' of the nuisance. Abatement is the removal of a nuisance by the person affected by it, such as lopping branches off an overhanging tree and is subject to three conditions. These are as follows: that in the circumstances an injunction would have been granted anyway; that no unnecessary damage was done; and that where it involved entry on to another person's land prior consent was obtained, unless it was an emergency. The courts, however, do not favour abatement because of the possible consequences of such action.

Private nuisance actions have been brought in several cases concerning recreational activities. Four cases, *Walker v Brewster* (1867),[19] *Winter v Baker* (1887),[20] *Inchbald v Robinson* (1869)[21] and *Becker v Earls Court Ltd* (1911),[22] concerned, respectively, the holding of fêtes with firework displays, a fair and rifle gallery, a circus and an exhibition with sideshows, all these activities being held on a regular basis. In each case local residents complained of noise caused by the activity itself and the crowds they caused, and in each case the court decided there was an actionable nuisance and granted an injunction to stop these nuisances.

Stretch v Romford Football Club Ltd (1971)[23] concerned speedway racing, recently introduced at the defendant's football stadium. A nearby resident, in what was essentially a quiet, residential area, complained that this was a nuisance because of the substantial increase of noise above that caused by football matches and this disturbed his family. Witnesses claimed they too found the noise disturbing and the defendants were unable to establish as a defence that the family was unusually sensitive to noise. Actionable nuisance was established and a perpetual injunction was granted.

Remedies do exist, therefore, for people troubled by balls hit on to their property or noise caused by persons taking part in recreational activities. They may, however, be deterred by the expense involved in bringing an action and problems of proving a nuisance have been created, particularly where the organization concerned has the money and expertise to resist such a case successfully. Enforcement of a judgment may also be difficult and expensive. Individuals adversely affected by such activities may be more likely to complain to the local authority, who have many statutory powers available under environmental health legislation, which could make life difficult for the organization concerned.

SUNDAY OBSERVANCE

Many spectator events are now organized on a Sunday and this creates a potential difficulty under the Sunday observance laws. The *Sunday Observance Act 1780* provides that it is an offence where 'any house, room or other place ... shall be opened or used for public entertainment, or for publicly debating on any subject whatsoever, upon any part of the Lord's Day, called Sunday, and to which persons shall be admitted by the payment of money, or by tickets sold for money ...'.

This offence is not confined to entertainments in buildings, a point discussed in *Culley v Harrison* (1956).[24] In this case, a motor-cycle scramble had been held in a fenced-off area within a large park, to which members of the public who purchased a ticket were admitted. The organizers were charged with an offence under the *Sunday Observance Act 1780* for using, on a Sunday, a place for public entertainment to which people were admitted on payment of money. They contended that 'other place' should be construed in relation to the preceding words 'in any house, room', and that a park was not a 'place' within the meaning of the section. The court decided that 'other place' in the Act was not restricted by the words 'house' and 'room', preceding it, and that the part of the park used for the motor-cycle scramble came within the Act, so an offence had been committed.

Williams v Wright (1897)[25] concerned payment for admission to an entertainment on Sunday. In this case, tickets for a concert held on a Sunday evening stated 'admission free, reserved seat 1 shilling' and the court decided that charging for a reserved seat was not incompatible with admission being free, so no offence had been committed.

This law is relevant to organizers of recreation wishing to arrange activities on a Sunday, although the offence is only committed where admission is by payment. The decision of the Football League to allow league matches to be played on Sundays caused a lot of controversy and the Lord's Day Observance Society threatened to test the legality of the games if they looked like becoming a part of the sporting scene. Limits have been placed on the number of games that can be played on a Sunday and instead of tickets spectators have, in some cases, been sold 'official programmes' which entitle them to enter the ground to overcome the *Sunday Observance Act 1780*. It is questionable whether this device does actually overcome the Act as the programmes could be described as 'tickets', especially if entry is refused to anyone who has not purchased a programme. However, the solution derived by Colchester United of making spectators 'temporary members' of a supporters' club would appear to comply with the Act. In fact, with most football matches being attended by ticket holders (bought in advance) and season ticket holders very little cash is paid on the day.

Perhaps the most bizarre scheme to circumvent the Act was that devised by the Jockey Club for its first Sunday meeting at Doncaster in July 1992. This first Sunday programme was, ostensibly, not a race meeting at all, but a series of musical concerts with 'concert goers' paying £5 or £10, depending on their preference for the acoustics of the grandstand or the silver ring. No on-course betting was allowed, but bets could be placed in advance or through the use of bookmakers' credit or Switch cards, the latter being considered currently not to be cash, with off-course bookmakers. Bands played with intervals for refreshments which coincided with the races. The racing industry felt they were unlikely to be prosecuted as the most likely prosecutor, the local authority, owned the racecourse.

By the 1990s schemes to get round this archaic legislation had been abandoned with apparent impunity by sports such as football, tennis and golf and there is now so much sport on Sunday that television has a *Sunday Grandstand*. Yet attempts to pass an Act to legalize spectator sports on Sunday have been unsuccessful.

NOTES

1. (1870) LR 5 QB 501
2. *Daily Telegraph*, 24 October 1974
3. *Times Law Report*, 22 March 1991
4. (1896) 12 TLR 455
5. *The Times*, 24 February 1987
6. [1991] 4 All ER 907
7. [1992] 2 All ER 65
8. [1972] 3 All ER 158
9. [1951] 2 All ER 320
10. [1933] 1 KB 205
11. [1961] 3 All ER 709
12. [1968] SLT 291
13. [1951] 1 All ER 1078
14. [1973] AC 854
15. (1922) 38 TLR 615
16. (1932) 3 Band Ad 184
17. [1977] 3 All ER 338
18. [1980] 3 All ER 361
19. (1867) 5 Eq 25
20. (1887) 3 TLR 569
21. (1869) 4 Ch App 388
22. (1911) 56 SJ 73
23. (1971) 115 SJ 741
24. [1956] 2 All ER 254
25. (1897) 13 TLR 551

Recreational clubs and governing bodies

5

Many recreational activities are enjoyed and organized through clubs or similar organizations, that is, groups of people joining together to pursue a particular pastime according to their own rules. Where members of these clubs desire it, they may become affiliated to the governing body of their particular sport or pastime, thereby agreeing to become subject to the rules of that governing body. An example of this system is the organization of gymnastics and rambling through clubs which are affiliated to the British Amateur Gymnastics Association, and to the Ramblers' Association, respectively.

The law does not define a 'club' at all and a club may take many forms; but all of them have one thing in common, they are a group of people drawn together to pursue a particular pastime. A club may be registered as a corporation and attain legal status, being recognized by the law as having an identity separate from its members. It is not essential that a club should be registered, but it may be advantageous should it wish to engage in a particular activity such as running a bar.

We may therefore conveniently begin our examination of the way in which the law controls recreational clubs by considering the various forms which such clubs may take.

UNINCORPORATED ASSOCIATIONS

Many clubs are not registered as corporations and are termed unincorporated associations. Such clubs have no independent legal 'personality', but are regarded by the law as a group of separate individuals. There are many types of unincorporated associations, ranging from informal groups of people enjoying a sport or pastime such as bird-watching societies, to more formal cricket and golf clubs, and up to vast and highly influential groups including trade unions and unincorporated employers' associations. The latter have become so important that the law has had to accord them a legal 'personality', and make special rules relating to them.

Generally the law does not regard these associations as independent groups, but treats their property as the joint property of all the members. Contracts made on their behalf are treated as the contracts of the particular person who made them or authorized their making. This means that the individual concerned, and not the club, is bound by the contract. The law also holds members of such clubs individually responsible for torts they have committed themselves or have authorized through the combined activities of the group. For example, in *Brown v Lewis* (1896)[1] the committee of a football club employed a person to repair a public stand, but the work was done so badly that the stand collapsed and a member of the public was injured. The committee who had authorized the work were held responsible and not the members of the club generally.

There are, however, some important exceptions to this general rule. One is that, where several people have the same interest in any proceedings, the proceedings may be brought against one or more of them as representing them all. In *Pidington v Hastings* (1932)[2] the defendant, Hastings, was named as a representative of the committee of the polo club, the Ranelagh club, against whom this action for negligence was brought.

A further exception occurs in some cases where an unincorporated association has an interest in property and that property is held by trustees on their behalf. The trustees are recognized as the legal owners, although responsible to members of the association for their actions concerning the property. Any legal actions in respect of the property will therefore be brought against the trustees.

Finally, the law does recognize that unincorporated associations may make rules that are binding on their members, and they may confer authority on certain members to 'govern' other members. An example of this is the powers of expulsion often conferred on committees, such as the stewards of the Jockey Club. In *Banks v De Walden and Others*[3] in 1978, John Banks contested in the High Court a three-year ban by the Jockey Club from their courses. The racing ban was imposed on Banks with a £2500 fine, following a Jockey Club Disciplinary Committee ruling that he and John Francome, former champion hurdles jockey, had broken Jockey Club rules. Francome was suspended for five weeks and fined £750. In view of the threat to the employees of Banks, due to the ban, the Jockey Club issued a statement that they could represent Banks's company 'on the rails'. Banks did not appeal, as he had threatened, against this decision and the committee refused his request that they review the decision.

An unincorporated association may cease to exist in a number of ways. The rules of the association may provide for dissolution following the occurrence of specified events. All members of an association may agree to the termination of that association or the courts may make an order that an association should cease to exist. For whatever reason an unincorporated association ceases to exist, when it does so all joint property it holds should be distributed among those who are members at the time of dissolution.

REGISTRATION OF CLUBS AS COMPANIES

A club may acquire special status at law through certain Acts of Parliament by becoming a 'body corporate' or an incorporated association. The *Companies Acts 1948, 1967, 1980, 1981* and *1985* provide for the incorporation of an association as a limited liability company. Registration as a company gives a club a legal status separate from individual members of the club. Proprietary clubs, which are those owned by a proprietor, may also be registered as companies to protect the owner against personal loss, should the club run into financial difficulties.

Clubs incorporated as limited liability companies under the *Companies Acts* have memoranda and articles of association instead of rules. These must conform with the rules of the governing body of the club which, for example, for football clubs would be the Football Association. Through its articles of association a company club creates a contract with each member, each member becoming a shareholder of the company. The memorandum and articles of association respectively define the objects of the company club and the way in which these objects will be achieved. A company club is administered by appointed and elected directors. The articles of association, or the statutory Table A under the *Companies Acts*, will usually regulate the procedure for amendment and alteration of a company club. An example of this occurred in *Berry and Stewart v Tottenham Hotspur Football and Athletic Company Ltd* (1935),[4] when a takeover bid of the defendant company club was planned and the club was able to rely on its articles of association to block its company share transfers in the High Court.

In 1951 a minority shareholding in the Bristol Rovers Football Club Ltd, being dissatisfied with the affairs of the company, instituted an inquisition into the affairs of the company, under the provisions of the *Companies Act 1948*. A more recent case concerning a company club was *Hobbs and Leadbetter v Castle, Bristol City Football Club Ltd and Others* (1978),[5] where the court refused to interfere with a resolution, properly taken, of the company club.

Registration as a company and acquisition of a separate legal status means that a club can sue or be sued in its own right, without directly involving individual members or the proprietor. Registration also involves many duties and obligations on the part of the club, including the filing of annual returns and the holding of statutory meetings. Such a step merits serious consideration by a club before it is taken and a wise step would be to consult a solicitor first.

REGISTRATION OF CLUBS AS INDUSTRIAL AND PROVIDENT SOCIETIES

Clubs which are not suitable for registration as companies do have alternatives available to them. Registration with the Registrar of Industrial and Provident

Societies, under the *Industrial and Provident Societies Acts 1965, 1968* and *1975*, is available to members' clubs which exist with the object of benefiting the community by provision of, for example, certain recreational facilities. A club fulfilling the requirements of the Acts, and being registered with the Registrar of Industrial and Provident Societies, acquires certain advantages which include becoming a 'corporation' at law, with limited liability for members in relation to club debts. Once registered, a club comes under the supervision of the registrar and must comply with many requirements, including the submission of accounts and annual returns, and the issuing of shares. This type of club is often termed a members' club because it exists for the benefit of the members who themselves control the club.

REGISTRATION OF CLUBS AS FRIENDLY SOCIETIES

A further alternative exists for clubs with the purpose of 'social intercourse, mutual helpfulness, mental and moral improvement, and rational recreation', which may register under the *Friendly Societies Act 1974* and *1992*, as a friendly society, with the Friendly Societies Commission. The Commission was introduced by the 1992 Act and replaced the Registrar of Friendly Societies. Members' clubs that come within the definition of a friendly society may choose to be incorporated or unincorporated and existing unincorporated friendly societies may change their status to incorporated in order to extend the kinds of services it may undertake. Incorporation will be more relevant to friendly societies offering mutual insurance. Many members' clubs who will come within the definition of a friendly society. Registration as an incorporated association does not give the club a legal personality of its own. It does, however, have a definite advantage because it vests the club assets in trustees who are given a certain degree of protection concerning club debts by virtue of this registration. Registration does involve the acquisition of administrative duties, including the submission of annual returns, the appointment of certain officers and selection of investments for club funds.

REGISTRATION OF CLUBS AS RECREATIONAL CHARITIES

Finally, some clubs, though obviously not proprietary clubs, may obtain registration as charities. A club that is so registered gains certain benefits for itself, which includes extra tax relief over and above that normally available to members' clubs on profit from internal trading. A club registered as a charity is also entitled to a reduction on rates paid to the local authority and may qualify for further reliefs.

However, unless a club registered as a charity is classed as an 'exempt' charity (as are charitable clubs which are also registered under the *Industrial and Provident Societies Acts* or the *Friendly Societies Acts*), it comes under the control of the Charity Commissioners and must register with them. Such a club must also comply with the rules and regulations detailed in the *Charities Act 1960* and *1992*. In relation to recreational activities this legislation is supplemented by the *Recreational Charities Act 1958*.

The establishment of recreational activities as 'charities' has given rise to many problems and much litigation over the years, mainly due to the complexity of the law relating to charities. A 'charity' is established by a particular form of trust, known as an 'express trust'. A trust is a legal device which enables one person to settle an amount of money or property in the hands of another person or persons, to hold it for the benefit of a third party. The law governs the actions of the persons holding the trust, the 'trustees', to protect the interests of the person or persons benefiting from the trust, the 'beneficiaries'.

Charity, as generally understood, differs in meaning from the way in which that word is used by lawyers. Over the years a definition of the term charity has evolved, using guiding principles rather than definite rules in deciding whether or not a given body should be granted charitable status. These guidelines reach back as far as the preamble of the *Statute of Charitable Uses 1601* which formed the basis of a test established by Lord MacNaughten in *Commissioners for Special Purposes of Income Tax v Pemsel* (1891)[6] which was that, provided a trust was set up for the public benefit, then trusts which would qualify for charitable status would be those for:

1. the relief of poverty;
2. the advancement of education;
3. the advancement of religion;
4. other purposes beneficial to the community.

Case law since 1891 has enlarged on this test, but only recently have proposals been suggested to modify this definition, notably in the Goodman Report on Charity Law.

Neither the *Charities Acts 1960* and *1992,* nor the *Recreational Charities Act 1958* actually define a charity, although section 1(1) of the 1958 Act provides:

It shall be and be deemed always to have been charitable to provide, or assist in the promotion of facilities for recreation or other leisure-time occupation, if the facilities are provided in the interests of social welfare. ...

As long as nothing in this section shall be taken to denigrate from the principle that a trust or institution to be charitable must be for the public benefit.

This Act was passed following the decision in *Inland Revenue Commissioners v Baddeley* (1955)[7] which decided not to accord charitable status to a trust for the promotion of 'religious, social and physical well-being' on the basis that this was too wide a definition. The Act validates trusts for recreational and leisure-time activities provided they are for the public benefit and they satisfy the requirement of being in the interests of social welfare.

In *Guild v Inland Revenue Commissioners (1992)*[8] a testator's bequest of residue 'for the use in connection with the Sports Centre in North Berwick or some similar purpose in connection with sport' was held to be charitable and exempt from capital transfer tax. This case concerned an appeal from the Scottish courts' refusal to allow the bequest to be registered as charitable. Their Lordships decided the bequest came within section 1 of the Recreational Charities Act 1958 whereby it was sufficient if the facilities were provided with the object of improving the conditions of life for members of the community generally and that the wording of the bequest, although very wide, was construed as meaning that a 'similar purpose' should display the leading characteristics of a sports centre.

Institutions or trusts for the promotion of sport or recreation can qualify for charitable status in two ways, either under the second or fourth head of MacNaughten's classification, for the advancement of education or 'other purposes beneficial to the community', or under the provisions of the *Recreational Charities Act 1958*.

'Advancement of education' was the purpose of the trusts discussed and accepted in *Re Mariette* (1915)[9] which concerned the provision of a fives or squash court and an annual prize for athletic sports. In *London Hospital Medical College v Inland Revenue Commissioners* (1976)[10] the athletic, social and cultural activities of a students' union were held to be charitable as furthering the educational purposes of the college. To satisfy this test it had to be shown that the promotion of sport was subservient to the main object, the advancement of education, which was charitable. Also in *Re Dupree's Deed Trusts* (1945)[11] the promotion of an annual chess tournament for boys and young men resident in the city of Portsmouth was a valid charity as it was of educational value.

Trusts solely for the promotion of sport, as in *Re Nottage* (1895)[12] which concerned yacht racing, *Re Clifford* (1911)[13] concerning angling and *Re Patten* (1929)[14] which involved funding a cricket club, are not considered to be charitable. The grounds for such a decision were that the immediate object of the trust was to benefit only the members of a particular society, which did not satisfy the criteria of being beneficial to the community. This criteria was satisfied in *Re Gray* (1925)[15] concerning the provision of recreation for an army regiment, as the promotion of the physical fitness of the army was beneficial to the community.

To achieve charitable status under the *Recreational Charities Act 1958*, two criteria must be satisfied. The trust must be provided for the public good and must be in the interests of social welfare. Section 1(2) of the Act states that the interests of social welfare imply that:

(a) the facilities are provided with the object of improving the conditions of

life for the persons for whom the facilities are primarily intended; and
(b) either (i) these persons have need of such facilities as aforesaid, by
    reason of their youth, age, infirmity or disablement, poverty or social
    and economic circumstances; or (ii) the facilities are to be available to
    the members or female members of the public at large.

The Act has not solved all the problems concerning the definition of a recreational
'charity', as was illustrated in *Inland Revenue Commissioners v McMullen*
(1978).[16] Here a trust had been established in 1972:

> to organize or provide or assist in the organization and provision of
> facilities which will enable and encourage pupils of schools and universities
> in any part of the United Kingdom to play Association Football, or other
> games or sports, thereby to assist in ensuring that due attention is given to
> the physical education and development of such pupils, as well as the
> development and occupation of their minds ... and to organize or provide
> or assist in the organization or provision of facilities for physical recreation
> in the interests of social welfare in any part of the United Kingdom ... for
> boys and girls who are under the age of 21 years, and who by reason of
> their youth, or social and economic circumstances have need of such
> facilities.

The Charity Commissioners decided to register the trust as a charity under
section 4 of the *Charities Act 1960*. The Inland Revenue Commissioners
objected to this registration and appealed to the High Court, which upheld the
objection on the grounds that the trust was merely for the promotion of sport
and did not come within the *Recreational Charities Act 1958*, because the true
construction of the words 'social welfare' indicated there must be some
deprivation to be alleviated. This decision put a very narrow construction on
the Act.

An appeal to the Court of Appeal[17] was dismissed on the same grounds that
it merely concerned the promotion of sport, and not the advancement of
education and did not satisfy the requirements of the 1958 Act, concerning
social welfare. However, when the case came before the House of Lords,[18]
their Lordships reversed the decision and allowed the registration of the trust
as a charity, because they felt first of all that it was not only to organize the
playing of association football in schools or universities, but also to promote
the physical education and development of students as an addition to their
formal education. A second ground for their conclusion was that the provision
of sporting facilities contributed to providing a balanced education, also it was
for the advancement of education being limited to schools and universities.

This decision has therefore widened the definition concerning the 'advancement of education', but it remains to be seen whether the narrow construction
of 'social welfare' in relation to the 1958 Act will be applied to future cases.

The question of what is a charity, in relation to recreation, remains complex and confused.

The *Charities Acts 1960* and *1992* provide that most charities must be registered in registers kept by the Charity Commissioners and, where appropriate, by the Secretary of State for Education and Science. Both the commissioners and the Secretary of State have general supervisory powers over trusteeships of charities and, in particular, they share with the courts the power of sanctioning 'schemes' for the administration of charitable trusts. Legal proceedings in respect of charitable trusts can be brought by the trustees and certain other parties with the authority of the Charity Commissioners. Where the commissioners refuse to register a trust there is a right of appeal to the High Court. Conversely, where the commissioners do register a trust as a charity, there is also a right of appeal against registration. Such an appeal is usually brought by the Inland Revenue Commissioners on the grounds that they do not accept the exemption from taxation inherent on registration as a charity. This occurred in *Inland Revenue Commissioners v McMullen*, discussed above.

The *Charities Act 1992* has extended the powers of the Charity Commissioners, allowing them to intervene in the running of all registered charities. Every charity has to submit annual accounts and the submission of false information is a criminal offence. The commissioners have the power to appoint a receiver to take over a charity whose affairs are being mismanaged. They can also disqualify anyone from acting as a trustee who has been convicted of a criminal offence involving dishonesty. This Act also gives charities the power to take out an injunction to prevent professional fundraisers acting on their behalf without permission. These additional powers are aimed at enabling the commissioners to intervene quickly when abuse is suspected.

Where, in certain instances defined in the *Charities Acts*, the original purposes of the trust cannot be carried out or cannot be carried out in the manner originally intended, or the objects of the charity have become impossible, the doctrine of *cy pres* may apply. This means the court may sanction a scheme to which the funds may be devoted which is as near as possible to the original charitable object. This occurred in *Re Geere's Will Trusts (No. 2)* (1954),[19] where a school which already had a swimming pool was given a valid charitable bequest to build one, and in *Re Morgan* (1955),[20] where a valid charitable bequest for the provision of a recreation ground had been made to a village which already had a recreation ground.

In *Oldham Borough Council v Attorney-General*[21] in 1992 the Court of Appeal reversed a High Court decision in a judgment that could have far-reaching consequences. Oldham Borough Council had applied for the court to authorize the sale or exchange of playing fields on land conveyed to the council by deed of gift. The council proposed to sell the original land to developers and with the substantial proceeds replace the playing fields with newer and better ones and still have money left in the charity for maintenance and other purposes. The Attorney-General defended the action as a representative of the interests of charities generally. The Court of Appeal decided they could supply the *cy pres* doctrine in this situation and such land could be sold with the consent of the court or of the Charity Commissioners and the appeal was allowed. On the basis of this judgment it would seem that charities can now consider relocation if their present accommodation is worth disproportionately more than a suitable alternative.

The present law relating to charities, particularly concerning recreational activities, has been the object of much criticism on the basis that, although the concept has been expanded to meet changing needs such as the preservation of our national heritage, as in *Re Verrall* (1916),[22] it should continue to develop and that the payment of a subscription to join a club which provides recreational facilities should not, as it does now, disqualify that club from registration as a charity. In fact the Rugby Football Union announced its intention in April 1993 to challenge legal precedents that prevent clubs from gaining the benefits of charitable status.

Finally, it should be mentioned that charities and voluntary organizations in England and Wales could be adversely affected by a Directive proposed by the European Community Commission in 1992 which will be to the effect that companies and firms should have the same rights and freedoms to provide services throughout the Community, and the only exemptions will be 'non-profit making' organizations. As these proposals could jeopardize tax concessions for charities the Home Office has appealed to the Community to make exceptions.

The discussion so far has concentrated on the types of club which may exist, other than purely proprietary ones. The next section will deal with more specific matters concerning the constitution of such clubs.

THE CLUB CONSTITUTION

Clubs generally are regulated by a 'constitution' which is a collection of rules and agreements controlling the day-to-day running of the club. Where a club has acquired a particular legal status, a detailed and comprehensive constitution may be required, with rules governing such matters as membership, meetings and voting rights. A proprietary club, on the other hand, may only have rules relating to rights of admission and membership subscription. Whatever the constitution of a club, it must be complied with by the members. This is a condition on which a member is permitted to join a club. The constitution is also the basis on which a registration certificate or licence (page 103) for the sale of alcoholic drinks is granted and for this reason it also must be adhered to.

Licensed or registered clubs run the risk of losing their 'licence' or certificate if they fail to observe their own rules, either because the club is no longer being conducted in good faith as a bona fide club or because of a direct offence under the *Licensing Act 1964*, such as sale of alcohol to members of the public unconnected with the club.

A club may change its constitution by altering the rules within it by agreement of the members. In some cases certain rules **must** be contained in a constitution; for example, clubs registered as companies may have to observe rules imposed by the *Companies Acts* themselves and failure to observe such rules may amount to a criminal offence.

The constitution of a club regulates the relationship between one member of the club and the other members of the club, and in some cases also between the member and the club itself. The relationship varies according to the legal status of the club.

The rules of a members' club are the basis of a contract between the members (see Chapter 2). This contract is formed when a new member joins a club, and is between that member and other members of the club. Such a contract may be legally enforced, as illustrated in *Clarke v Dunraven* (1897)[23] also dealt with in Chapter 2. In this case the club rules stated that each yacht owner undertook to compensate the owner of any other yacht damaged by that owner's yacht during a regatta. The case concerned the owners of two yachts who had entered a regatta organized by the club, the Mudhook Yacht Club. One of the yachts, the *Satanita* caused another, the *Valkyrie* to sink. The House of Lords decided that the owner of the *Satanita* should pay damages to the owner of the *Valkyrie,* because of the contract which had been made by the acceptance of the club rules on becoming a member.

Precise, comprehensive rules are therefore essential so that each member is aware of their relationship with other members and the club. Members do not have to sign any agreement relating to their willingness to be bound by the rules of a club; agreement is implied when membership is applied for and granted. There is no general duty to provide members with a copy of the rules, although they must be readily available to members wishing to consult them. Clubs registered as a friendly society or an industrial and provident society, however, must supply a copy of the rules to any member requesting them, at a minimal charge.

The rules of a proprietary club form a contract between the members, and also between the proprietor and each member. Every person accepting membership of a proprietary club agrees to be bound by the rules of the club, as does the proprietor.

Clubs registered as industrial and provident societies, friendly societies or Companies must comply with certain statutory regulations concerning their rules and their constitutions must be approved by the relevant body.

CLUB OFFICIALS

Whether or not a club is governed by a committee, it generally has certain officials bearing certain well-known titles and to whom certain special responsibilities are given. Usually such officers are elected by club members and the club itself will define the duties of various officials. Below is a general indication of the officials one might expect to find in a club and a suggestion of their possible duties. Some club officials, particularly secretaries, may be salaried appointments and employment law, which is discussed in Chapter 7, will also be relevant.

The **president** is generally the 'figurehead' of a club and has little active power. A president may be elected for a long term of office and do little more than officiate at important club functions.

A more important official is the **chairperson**, who is usually the chairperson of the governing committee whose meetings it is one of their functions to control. The chairperson will also usually chair general meetings of the club. Although all-powerful when chairing a meeting, the chairperson must act impartially and according to the rules of natural justice. The chairperson or secretary is expected to represent the club before the licensing justices on matters relating to registration certificates and to sign forms, for example, for bar extensions and registration certificates, as well as dealing with official club correspondence.

In addition to the above duties the secretary has the responsibility of dealing with all the paperwork relating to the club and for this reason is perhaps its most important official. Usually the secretary is the one who deals with third parties on behalf of the club, and who is regarded by the court as sufficiently responsible to be named in relation to the registration certificate, and to be responsible for matters concerning it. The secretary is generally regarded as having the authority to make contracts on behalf of the club by which the club will be bound.

Finally, the **treasurer** is the person responsible for the financial affairs of the club, from the collection of subscriptions to the preparation of the club accounts for auditing and presenting at the annual general meeting. Usually a treasurer cannot make payments without the authority of at least one other official. Special conditions attach to this office where clubs are registered as either friendly societies, industrial and provident societies or charities.

A club normally has a committee to control its activities, which will include the above officials (except the president) and other members elected by the club, usually at the annual general meeting. This committee deals with the day-to-day running of the club and meets regularly to do so. All the power in a members' club lies in the general body of the members, except where they have delegated certain powers and functions to the committee.

MEMBERSHIP OF CLUBS

Issues may arise concerning admission to the membership of a club or activities of individual members which are not covered in the club rules and in such cases the courts may be called upon to impose guidelines to resolve issues arising from conflicting claims of the club and the member.

Admission to membership of a club is one possible area of conflict. Membership is governed not only by the rules of the club itself, but also by the licensing laws and the status of the club. Here it is possible only to discuss the 'usual' situation.

Where election to membership is through the committee, usually the names and addresses of proposed members are 'posted' on the club notice-board to allow existing members to make objections if this is felt necessary. The committee then decides whether or not a person should be elected to membership and need not give any reason for rejecting anyone from membership. It would seem that a disappointed applicant has no redress against a club for refusal, except for two reasons: first, where false or damaging information has led to the applicant's rejection, which may give the applicant grounds for an action in defamation; second, where that rejection is based on racial grounds. Clubs are governed by the strict race relations law contained in the *Race Relations Act 1976* and certain 'associations of persons' are not allowed to discriminate against applicants for membership on racial grounds. 'Discrimination' includes outright refusal of membership or an offer of only a reduced form of membership. In 1984 a Sikh was awarded £150 damages against the Wrekin Golf Club for refusing him membership on the grounds of race.

The 'associations of persons' includes all clubs with 25 members or more, whose admission rules are in the constitution. These conditions must also be complied with to gain a registration certificate. This Act applies to virtually all clubs, including proprietary clubs, but its aim is only to prevent discrimination and, where there is another genuine ground for refusal, such as the applicant's character, the club will not be liable under the Act. However, it is legal, albeit illogical, for persons of the same racial or ethnic origins to form exclusive clubs for themselves.

Clubs are also covered by the *Sex Discrimination Acts 1975* and *1986* which seek to ensure sexual equality by providing that women should not be discriminated against, although there is one important exception. Such discrimination in membership shall not be unlawful in the case of any organization 'carried on otherwise than for profit', and which was not 'set up by any enactment'. In other words, it would seem that members' clubs may discriminate against persons of a particular sex, whereas proprietary clubs may not.

Proprietary clubs must have clear rules laying down the conditions on which the proprietor will allow a person to become a member of the club. Although the licensing laws are less rigid in these matters than they are concerning members' clubs, they will almost certainly insist on some form of rule ensuring there are no 'instant membership' agreements, which would make the club the same as a public house. These clubs are also subject to the *Race Relations Act 1976*.

Another cause for conflict between a club and its members may be the payment of subscriptions. A member's first subscription becomes due after election to membership. A subscription is paid in exchange for the privileges of membership. Once a person is a member their subscription becomes payable according to the rules. Provisions for a 'fine' may be made in the rules if subscriptions are not paid by the date due. In theory, a club may sue a member for a subscription, although a club that does not have a separate legal personality may find difficulty in actually doing so.

Subscriptions are, in simple language, payment for the use of club facilities. In the absence of any rule to the contrary, a person lawfully expelled from a club may not bring an action for a refund of any unexpired portion of their subscription, although they may be sued for any arrears of subscriptions due, unless the club concerned is registered as a friendly society.

Fixing of subscriptions should be the responsibility of the committee or members in general meeting and the exact amount should not be stated in the rules in order to facilitate changes. The rules should also allow for a method of altering the subscription.

Subscriptions to join a proprietary club are based on a commercial agreement concerning payment of a fee for use of facilities made available by the proprietor.

Finally, mention should be made of guests of members. Guests of members may only be admitted to a club if the rules allow it and such guests may buy alcoholic drinks only if the rules permit it. Club rules may include conditions relating to the number of guests allowed. As far as proprietary clubs are concerned, the licence granted by the justices will dictate whether or not members' guests are allowed on the premises.

LIABILITIES AND DUTIES OF A CLUB

Liability varies according to the type of club concerned. The proprietor of a club is classed by law as the 'occupier' of the club premises and, under the *Occupiers' Liability Act 1957*, must therefore take reasonable care for the safety of all those who are 'invited' on to the premises by the proprietor (see Chapter 4). This includes members, their guests, entertainers and delivery men. A proprietor who employs staff will also be vicariously liable for injuries caused by those employees to people on the premises (page 124).

The situation is not so clear where members' clubs are concerned, because although in theory a member injured on club premises should be able to sue the club, this is not always possible. Where a members' club has a legal status separate from its members, it is possible to sue the club as the company/club is the occupier of the premises. Where this is not so, the injured party would be trying to bring an action against 'the club' which is represented by all the members of that club. Thus any member attempting to sue the member's own club would, in effect, be trying to sue the member themself, a legal impossibility. The 'occupiers' of such a club are the total membership, who therefore owe a duty of care to each other and themselves. An injured member has thus failed in the duty of care that member owes to themself!

Indeed, in *Robertson v Ridley and Another* (1988)[24] a member of a members' club was riding his motorcycle out of the club grounds when he failed to see a pot-hole in the driveway, fell off and was injured. The member claimed damages in an action for negligence in respect of injuries sustained, but the Court of Appeal decided that a members' club was not liable either in contract or in tort to its members in respect of such injuries, unless the rules of the club expressly so provided. The court also stated that a provision in the rules that the chairperson and secretary were responsible in law for the conduct of the club did not render them liable to the club's members in respect of such injuries. However, in *Jones v Northampton Borough Council* (1990)[25] the court stated that a duty of care may exist where a club officer or member of a committee has taken it upon themselves to perform a task on behalf of the other members and, if in the course of performing that task acquires knowledge of circumstances that give rise to risk of injury to club members, then there is a duty to warn the other members of such a risk. In this case a club official while organizing a game of five-a-side football was told that the floor of the hall was wet due to a leaking roof and was under a duty to warn other club members of the danger arising therefrom.

An injured member who has no action against the club, because the club has no legal status, may be able to sue a member of staff if that person could be shown to be responsible for the member's injury. Where a member is injured as the result of another member's negligence then an action will lie against that member directly and personally, without involving the club at all.

A club can no longer escape liability for injury to members or other persons on its premises, by putting up a notice to the effect that 'the management regrets that it is unable to accept liability ... ', the effect of which used to be to include an exclusion clause (page 25) as a term of the contract of admission. The *Unfair Contract Terms Act 1977* stopped this practice by providing that no one could, by means of a contractual term or a notice displayed on the premises, try and restrict or exclude their liability for death or personal injury arising from negligence. Therefore, a club that would normally be liable cannot escape this liability by introducing an exemption clause through a notice on the door or a term in the club rules. However, this does not make any difference to the position of members of a members' club which has no separate legal status. Also, a club that can show that the injured party 'volunteered' for the risk or was adequately warned of it, may not be liable (page 27).

As far as a club's liability for loss of, or damage to, property on club premises is concerned, the area of law concerned is again negligence (page 23). Thus, a club will be liable in damages, for example, where a member's clothing is damaged because a chair has a nail protruding, unless the club concerned is without a separate legal status.

In practice, the most common type of loss experienced on club premises is the theft of the belongings of members or other persons. The club, or the proprietor, can only be held liable if it can be shown that there was negligence and that reasonable care had not been taken. It must be shown that negligence caused, or at least contributed to, the theft, for example by failing to lock a cloakroom or employing dishonest staff. Some such actions have been known to succeed, and there have also been cases in which damages have been recovered from a proprietor following theft of property by a member of staff of the club. Any attempt to exclude liability through an exclusion clause will be prevented by the *Unfair Contract Terms Act 1977*, unless it is 'reasonable' to impose such an exception. These points were also made in Chapter 2 in connection with the belongings of a sports participant.

A club may also be sued by a third party, that is a non-member who was injured or suffered loss while on club premises. The position is the same for all clubs; either the club or the proprietor will be sued and, where a club has no separate legal status, then the action will be brought against a member or members of that club. A club is liable, as the occupier of premises, to anyone lawfully on those premises, to take reasonable care to ensure their safety. A third party has more right to sue for loss or injury sustained on club premises than a member has. Normally a third party would sue the committee which is responsible for the running of the club and its activities.

Where a club has trustees (discussed below), it is usual to sue them in their official capacity as trustees, because they have been elected specifically to represent the members of the club. An individual member or trustee who has been successfully sued as a club's representative may not be able to claim recompense from the club, unless this is provided for in the club rules. Such a member or trustee may therefore have to bear the loss personally.

In view of their liability to members and third parties concerning loss or personal injury, clubs would be well advised to take out an insurance policy to cover such liability, as well as insurance to cover property belonging to the club or left on club premises. An insurance policy is a contract between the insurance company and the party insured, and the terms of such a policy are agreed by the parties concerned. Clubs taking out insurance policies should therefore ensure that the policy is adequate for their needs. A club which employs people is obliged by law (under the *Employers' Liability (Compulsory Insurance) Act 1969*), to insure against their liability for personal injury to their employees.

Debts are another form of liability that may arise in a club. Most clubs will be involved in trading, as they will be purchasing equipment and supplies for the bar, and also may be involved with other matters, including building altera-tions. Such liability in a proprietary club is solely the concern of the proprietor. Where a club is registered as a limited company, the financial liability of each member for the trading debts of the company is limited to any unpaid portion of that member's shareholding. The situation is not so clear where other types of club are concerned.

In 1975 the club treasurer of the Holme Hale Social Club in Norfolk was held to be personally liable for a debt of £3500 owed by the club to a local builder. The club itself had no funds to pay the debt, and the bailiffs were ready to take the treasurer's house and furniture in settlement of the debt. Only intervention from outside bodies saved the treasurer here, because all that was done was in compliance with the law. This situation occurs where a club has no separate legal status and the only way an action can be brought against such a club is to sue individual members. Where a club has no trustees then a creditor will usually sue the person with whom the contract was agreed. Thus a club member who makes a contract on behalf of their club may become personally liable, unless it is made clear at the time that only the funds of the club are being pledged in satisfaction.

The committee of a club will be held liable for contracts entered into on their behalf by their employees, for example, where a club steward orders stocks for the club's bar. However, the committee has no authority to incur liability on behalf of ordinary members of the club, unless those members ratified the transaction in question at a general meeting of the club.

Thus, for individual members of a club, there is little risk of incurring liability on behalf of the club; all the risk is borne by the committee, all or any of whom may be personally sued for the debt. In the Holme Hale Social Club case discussed above, actions were actually started against the treasurer, secretary and chairperson, but only the treasurer owned his own house, so the creditor sought settlement from him.

A club can avoid the above situation in three ways. The first way is by ensuring that in every contract made with a third party there is a clause clearly stating that in the event of legal proceedings or debts being incurred, the creditor may obtain satisfaction from club funds only. This must be stated clearly in each contract and it is not sufficient to give the contractor a set of club rules stating this to be the case, as the rules are a contract between the club and each individual member only.

A second method of avoiding the imposition of personal liability on committee members is for the club to become a limited company, which makes the club a separate legal entity and the club funds independent from those of its members and the committee. Legal liability of individual members, including those on the committee, is limited to any unpaid portion of their shareholding. Once the club funds are exhausted a creditor cannot bring an action against individuals belonging to the club for settlement of the creditor's account.

The third method is by appointment of trustees.

TRUSTEES OF CLUBS AND ASSOCIATIONS

Where a club does not have a separate legal status, trustees may represent the club in all legal matters. Trustees can also be used to protect individual members from claims for debts arising out of contractual obligations (above), or from claims arising from loss or injury sustained by third persons lawfully on club premises (again, discussed above).

The systems to be used for appointing trustees should be dealt with fully in the club rules. Basically, the trustees should be compelled to act at all times on the instructions of the committee, and on no other authority, even their own. Where a club has trustees there is no lessening in the powers and authority of the committee, as the trustees themselves should have no power and no discretion other than that conferred on them by the committee, who will guide and instruct them at all times. Trustees are in essence 'figureheads', representing the club as a whole.

Usually there are two trustees who hold office for as long as possible or as long as is convenient to ensure continuity. They should be appointed by the club as a whole at a general meeting and be over the age of 21. Although it is desirable that they should be club members, it is better if they are not committee members and have no direct links with the committee, in order to avoid possible conflicts of interest. There is no reason legally why a trustee should not be a committee member, unless the club is registered under the *Friendly Society Acts* which state that a trustee cannot be either a secretary or treasurer of a club.

Trustees making a contract on behalf of the club may, by the inclusion of a suitably worded clause, make it clear that it is the club making the contract and not the trustees themselves. They may also limit their personal liability with a further clause that only club funds are to be used in pursuance of the contract.

DISCIPLINARY ACTION AND ENFORCEMENT OF RULES

Clubs may sometimes have to discipline members who are in breach of club rules or guilty of behaviour repugnant to other members. This situation can occur equally in a proprietary club or a members' club. To avoid complications and hostility, the rules should state clearly the procedure to be followed in these circumstances.

Any member who has paid the current subscription is entitled to use the club's facilities unless that member is guilty of behaviour punishable by the withdrawal of this privilege and the situation is dealt with in the club rules. Any club seeking to deprive a club member in this way, with no authority in the rules or in a manner not in accordance with the club rules, may find themselves subject to a legal action.

Even though a club may have its own rules concerning the disciplining of members it will still be subject to the law in two ways. First, the rules must be in accordance with the law. Second, the courts can be asked to intervene in a dispute on behalf of an individual involved, where the dispute has been resolved contrary to club rules or contrary to the rules of natural justice. In *Young v Ladies' Imperial Club* (1920)[26] the court refused to interfere with a decision properly taken according to the club rules to expel the plaintiff from the defendant club, on the grounds that the court was not a court of appeal from the decisions of club committees 'provided the committees are properly constituted and properly summoned, and deal with the matter in a way not contrary to the principle of natural justice'.

Dawkins v Antrobus (1881)[27] was also an action concerning expulsion of a member from a club. The rule concerned, correctly passed at a general meeting, was that a member guilty of conduct injurious to the club could be expelled by a two-to-three majority of a general meeting. The plaintiff was so expelled, for conduct injurious to the interests and character of the club. The court refused to interfere on the grounds that there was no proof the club had acted maliciously and, even though the decision may be unreasonable it was in accordance with club rules which had been properly exercised.

More recently, in *Hobbs and Leadbetter v Castle, Bristol City Football Club* (1978),[28] the court refused to interfere with a resolution passed at an emergency general meeting by the defendant club to increase the club's issued capital by 80 000 £1 shares, as there was no evidence to warrant interference. However, the court did award damages against the defendant member who, in voting for the resolution on behalf of Leadbetter, a shareholder, had not voted in accordance with his instructions.

The court did intervene in *Hartington v Sendall* (1903)[29] to restrain a club from expelling a member for refusing to pay the annual subscription, recently increased by the club. An injunction was granted to restrain the club from expelling the member on the grounds that the rules of the club prescribed the amount of the annual subscription, but did not contain any provision for its amendment or alteration.

A club, wishing to avoid interference by the courts, may attempt to exclude their jurisdiction by including in the rules one which states that members should not have recourse to the courts following decisions made by the club or its governing body, which shall be final. The courts will not accept any such rule attempting to oust its jurisdiction on the basis that it is against public policy, and will, as in *Baker v Jones* (1954),[30] strike out that particular rule.

As explained above, all clubs, when dealing with matters of discipline involving a member, are bound by what are referred to as 'the rules of natural justice'. Since these also arise in the context of disciplinary hearings by the governing bodies in sport and recreation, and since most of the case law in this area concerns such governing bodies, detailed consideration of this topic is deferred to the final section of this chapter.

Problems may arise in the interpretation of club rules relating to the disciplining of members, particularly where they provide that a member may be disciplined for 'conduct injurious to the club', or some such other behaviour.

Difficulties arise in deciding just what sort of behaviour comes within the definition. Those eventually making the decision must use their own judgement; this is acceptable provided that they act impartially. Where this is felt to be the case, a court of law is not generally prepared to overrule that decision, whatever their feelings on the matter.

A person successfully appealing to a court of law concerning disciplinary proceedings may, by court order, be reinstated as a member, be granted an injunction to stop the club from refusing admission to and use of the premises, have any claim that member has against the club enforced or even, in some cases, be awarded damages. Sometimes the court may be sympathetic to the club, as in the case of Swindon Town Football Club who, in November 1980, were granted an injunction banning a 20-year-old fan from their ground for the rest of the season. The fan in question had already been ejected from the ground four times in the last two seasons for misbehaviour and, in May 1980, had been fined £100 for threatening behaviour.

Finally, all clubs should enforce their own rules, more particularly where the club has a bar, to ensure compliance with relevant licensing laws.

Attempts have been made to employ legal action as a means to force the management of a club to enforce its own rules, with mixed results. A member of a members' club has a legally recognized right due to an equal share in the joint assets of the club and the courts, recognizing this right, will allow such a member to apply for an order to force the committee to act in accordance with the rules. This occurs because such a member is entitled to take action to protect their share of the club's assets. It is usual for a club to have a rule giving the committee a discretionary right to act in the general interests of the club as a whole, which may circumvent the need to apply all the rules of the club strictly. In practice, therefore, it is extremely unlikely that a member will go to the bother and expense of court action to enforce the rules strictly. The usual procedure is to remedy the situation by taking appropriate action at the next annual general meeting of the club.

DISCIPLINARY COMMITTEES OF GOVERNING BODIES

These bodies form a 'domestic tribunal' which, in many cases in which they are contemplating disciplinary action, are in effect deciding on someone's future livelihood. None the less, the law recognizes their right to discipline their own members and will not normally interfere.

Any abuse by these tribunals will, however, be checked by the courts, as their decisions may be examined by the law courts on certain grounds, one ground being that the tribunal has exceeded its power. This is called acting *ultra vires*. In *Davis v Carew-Pole and Others* (1956),[31] Davis, an unlicensed race-horse trainer, was declared a disqualified person by the National Hunt

Committee, according to their rules. Davis brought an action claiming the decision was *ultra vires* and void, and asking for an injunction to stop the committee from treating him as a disqualified person. He was granted an injunction on the grounds that on the true construction of the rules the committee had no power to declare Davis a disqualified person.

Pett v Greyhound Racing Association Ltd (No. 2) (1970)[32] concerned an action against the National Greyhound Racing Club which virtually controlled greyhound racing. Pett was alleged to have drugged a greyhound he had trained and raced. At the ensuing hearing Pett was refused legal representation which he claimed was *ultra vires* and sought an injunction preventing the hearing until he had legal representation. An injunction had already been granted in the earlier case of *Pett v Greyhound Racing Association Ltd* (1969).[33] However, in this case the court decided the tribunal was not acting contrary to the rules of natural justice in refusing legal representation, as legal representation was not a prerequisite of a hearing of this kind, and the inquiry was in all other respects a fair one, even though the decision may affect his future livelihood and reputation.

The above case brings us back to an issue raised in the context of disciplinary action by a club, namely 'the rules of natural justice'. This applies whether the decision was a judicial decision, that is, settling a dispute between members, or an administrative decision concerning details of the club's organization. The rules of natural justice are rules imposed by the courts on bodies empowered to make decisions; they therefore apply both to clubs and governing bodies. They are referred to as the rules of natural justice because they are rules every ordinary, reasonable person would consider fair. There are two rules. The first is that no person should be judge in their own cause. This means that no one should act as judge where that person has an interest in the matter. The second rule is that each side to a dispute must be given a fair hearing. Generally this means that persons involved in proceedings of a tribunal should be informed of the case against them, given the date of the hearing, allowed time to prepare a defence and finally permitted a chance to give their defence or other representation to the tribunal. There is no right actually to appear before such a tribunal and no rule that a tribunal should hold an inquiry on the lines of a formal prosecution. A person can present a case to a tribunal orally or in writing. As long as a tribunal is thorough and impartial the courts will not interfere with its decision.

In *McInnes v Onslow Fane* (1978)[34] an action was brought by the plaintiff against the British Boxing Board of Control following their refusal to grant him a manager's licence on the grounds that no reasons had been given for the refusal and he had not been given a hearing before the Board. In such a case, the court decided, the law must be reluctant to allow an implied obligation to be fair to be used as a means of reviewing honest decisions of bodies exercising jurisdiction over sporting and other activities which those bodies were far better fitted to judge than the courts, even where such bodies were concerned with the means of livelihood of those taking part in such activities. The plaintiff was unsuccessful because the board's refusal to grant a licence did not cast a slur on his character, it did not deprive him of any statutory right and there was no apparent dishonesty relating to the decision. In this case the court referred to a duty to act 'fairly', which appears to be the same as obeying the rules of natural justice.

In *Birne v National Sporting League Ltd* (1957)[35] Birne brought an action following his expulsion from the league for alleged non-payment of wagering debts. He claimed that his expulsion was void and brought an action in defamation regarding letters relating to his expulsion. The court decided that his expulsion was void because the hearings of the committee were against the rules of natural justice, as both sides had not been heard, although a letter from the complainants had been read. The expulsion being void, the letters were found to be defamatory.

Finally, a tribunal or disciplinary committee should make its reasons for a decision known to the parties involved and the courts will insist on this as far as possible.

A reason for non-interference by the courts in the disciplinary affairs of governing bodies may be the expertise of the body concerned. This was the reason given in an unreported Court of Appeal case in 1973 when a footballer, Machin, appealed against a decision by the Football Association Disciplinary Committee that he had deliberately kicked another player. The committee had based their decision on television evidence, and the court declared itself satisfied and impressed by the care given by the committee to the case.

The courts will also not interfere where they are generally satisfied with the procedures for resolving disputes adopted by governing bodies. Indeed, the courts welcome the establishment of such procedures, as they are not happy at the possibility of their being used as the means of settling disputes concerning participants and organizers of recreational activities, although as explained above they will interfere to ensure that any such procedures are fair and reasonable, and that the correct procedures have been followed.

Reel v Holder (1979)[36] concerned an action brought by Taiwan against the International Amateur Athletics Federation (IAAF), an unincorporated association controlling international athletics, because they had voted to exclude Taiwan from membership, although Taiwan had been a member for the previous 22 years. The exclusion was based on the contention that Taiwan was not a 'country' within the rules of the IAAF, as mainland China governed both Taiwan and China. This contention was not accepted by the court, which decided that as China and Taiwan were separate geographically they could be defined as countries. Second, the court declared that the IAAF, having accepted Taiwan as a member for 22 years, could not now exclude them on the basis that their earlier decision had been contrary to their own rules. This was an application of 'equitable estoppel' whereby a person or body of persons is prevented from behaving 'unfairly', for example, going back on an earlier decision, although their behaviour may not be against the law.

CHALLENGING DECISIONS OF GOVERNING BODIES

In *Law v National Greyhound Racing Club* (1983)[37] the decision, not to interfere with a decision by the National Greyhound Racing Club, was based on the fact that there was a contractual relationship and therefore a remedy in private law, thus excluding the possibility of the public law remedy of judicial review. This decision was followed when the Jockey Club was challenged for refusing to allocate fixtures to a new racecourse at Telford in 1991 because most of the Jockey Club's decisions affected people who voluntarily and willingly subscribed to its rules and procedures. The wider public had insufficient interest to make such decisions reviewable. Occasionally, however, as in the exercise of the quasi-licensing power, the Jockey Club may be subject to review.

The issue of whether or not governing bodies could be subject to the public law remedy of judicial review was again raised in *R v Football Association of Wales ex parte Flint Town United Football Club* (1990).[38] Here Flint Town United Football Club had requested judicial review to challenge the decision of the Football Association of Wales not to agree to their club transferring to another league run by the English Football Association. The court decided that the public law remedy of judicial review was not, in this case, the correct procedure as the authority of the tribunal was derived solely from contract, in other words, there was no 'public' interest involved. In this particular case the court did, however, comment on the situation and stated that it felt the Football Association of Wales had dealt fairly with the matter, because it had considered the application properly and had turned it down on the basis it was about to establish a new league itself which would result in a better standard of football in Wales (the reason Flint Town had requested a transfer), and that their decision had been taken within the best interests for the progression of Welsh football.

In *R v Jockey Club ex parte the Aga Khan* (1991)[39] the judge declined to intervene in the Jockey Club's decision to disqualify the Aga Khan's winner of the Oaks after a banned substance, camphor, had been found in its urine. Although the judge expressed some disquiet that such issues were apparently excluded from the public law remedy of judicial review, he was nevertheless bound by earlier decisions to this effect. This decision was challenged on appeal to the Court of Appeal by the Aga Khan. The Court of Appeal decided unanimously in December 1992 that the decision of the Jockey Club could not be challenged through judicial review and would not recommend that the case be sent to the House of Lords. It would therefore appear to have been established that the relationship between the Jockey Club and racehorse owners was private and consensual, and participation in the sport required acceptance of the rules. It is established law that the High Court will not exercise its review powers over bodies whose jurisdiction is based on consent, and there were no grounds for distinguishing between the Jockey Club and any other governing body in sport. To have decided otherwise could have had very far reaching implications for all governing bodies in sport.

In *R v the Football Association Ltd ex parte the Football League Ltd* (1991)[40] the judge again ruled that the decision of the Football League to set up a Premier League which had been challenged by the Football League was not susceptible to challenge by the public law remedy of judicial review. The judge did, however, go on to express his view that the Football Association, in seeking to promote a Premier League, was acting within its powers.

These cases expressed reservations about the current law that public remedies were excluded where the issue concerned a domestic tribunal that derived its powers from a contractual relationship, where the remedy would be a declaration that the tribunal was exceeding its powers or an injunction to prevent it from doing so. It is clear from these judgments that the feeling is that where there is some element of 'public' interest the public law remedies should be available, but this situation can only be remedied by the judgment of a higher court or statutory intervention.

When the Commonwealth Games Federation refused to allow Annette Cowley, a swimmer, to represent England in the Commonwealth Games because she was not domiciled in England, she took the federation to court. However, the court decided that she had no right to question the decision of the federation who was acting within its own rules and 'reasonably' and that the contractual relationship was between the national association and the federation, not between the individual swimmer and the federation.

The court's refusal to intervene, unless gainful activity is involved, was confirmed in *Currie v Barton* (1987).[41] Here Currie was disputing a decision of the Essex Lawn Tennis Association to ban him for three years from eligibility for selection in county teams and the judge refused to interfere because selected team members received no reward but that of honour. However, the public nature of some sporting bodies has been acknowledged by the English courts in the past. In *Martell v Consett Iron Co. Ltd* (1955)[42] the Anglers' Association was allowed to maintain an action by an individual riparian owner, because the court recognized the association had a sufficient common interest in the subject matter of the plaintiff's claim and was defending the collective interests of members.

From the precedents already established it would appear that the courts will not interfere with decisions of governing bodies provided they are acting fairly, within their own rules and being reasonable. Perhaps the long-term solution would not be to include sporting bodies within the public law remedy of judicial review, but to seek an alternative dispute resolution. Generally speaking the courts are not a suitable forum for the settlement of disputes involving sportspersons and governing bodies or federations. In 1983 the International Olympic Committee recognized the need for an alternative means of resolving disputes and established the Court of Arbitration for Sport (CAS). CAS is based in Lausanne and has been reasonably successful in resolving disputes between sportspersons and their corresponding governing bodies in disciplinary matters. The Central Council for Physical Recreation has recently established a Sports Arbitration Panel to achieve the same purpose in the UK. The success of such bodies depends ultimately on their acceptance by the persons concerned and serious threats to such a system have been posed by the drug abuse disputes discussed in Chapter 3.

NOTES

1. (1896) 12 TLR 455
2. *The Times*, 12 March 1932
3. *The Times*, 4 May 1978
4. [1935] Ch 718
5. *The Times*, 7 July 1978
6. [1891] AC 531
7. [1955] 1 All ER 525
8. *Times Law Reports*, 2 March 1992
9. [1915] 2 Ch 284
10. [1976] 2 All ER 113
11. [1945] Ch 16
12. [1895] 2 Ch 649
13. (1911) 106 LT 14
14. [1929] 2 Ch 276
15. [1925] Ch 362
16. [1978] 1 All ER 230
17. [1979] 1 All ER 588
18. [1980] 1 All ER 884
19. [1954] CLY 388
20. [1955] 1 WLR 738
21. *The Times*, 5 August 1992
22. [1916] 1 Ch 100
23. [1897] AC 59
24. [1989] 2 All ER 474
25. *The Times*, 21 May 1990
26. [1920] 2 KB 523
27. (1881) 17 ChD 615
28. *The Times*, 7 July 1978
29. [1903] 1 Ch 921
30. [1954] 1 WLR 1005
31. [1956] 1 WLR 833
32. [1970] 1 QB 46
33. [1969] 1 QB 125
34. [1978] 1 WLR 1520
35. *The Times*, 12 April 1957
36. [1979] 1 All ER 1041
37. [1983] 1 WLR 1302

38. QBD transcript, 11 July 1990
39. *The Times*, 4 July 1991
40. *The Times*, 22 August 1991
41. *The Times*, 27 March 1987
42. [1955] Ch 363

Generating income

6

All clubs and associations, and groups of people concerned with a purpose or a particular activity, need money to finance themselves. Very few associations are self-supporting in the sense that an annual subscription paid by members covers all the running costs of these associations. Most associations have to have an income to cover costs and this may be derived from a variety of sources, from bar profits of licensed clubs to large sponsorship programmes of governing bodies. There are legal implications in activities associated with the raising of an income and these will be considered in relation to the activities concerned.

SALE OR SUPPLY OF ALCOHOL

One of the most usual means by which a club or association derives an income is by the sale or supply of alcohol to members through the establishment of a bar.

Before any club can install a bar to sell alcoholic drinks to members, it must either be registered under the *Licensing Act 1964* (amended by the *Licensing Acts* of *1988* and *1989*) and granted a registration certificate, or it must be a proprietary club and granted a licence. A proprietary club is owned by one 'individual' known as the proprietor, who usually runs the club as a commercial enterprise. 'Members' of such a club have no right to any of the club assets and can only become members because the proprietor has decided to allow them to have access to the club premises.

Proprietary clubs do not necessarily always make a profit. Some clubs such as church social clubs may be run as proprietary clubs for convenience, with the minister or a parish official as the 'proprietor' and licence holder.

The main distinction between proprietary clubs and other clubs lies in the ownership of the assets. Where club assets are held by some private individual, not club members themselves, the club is recognized as a proprietary club by the law. A 'proprietor' is not necessarily one individual but may be, for example, a company or a partnership. This distinction may be blurred in the case of sports and social clubs attached to large companies, but generally the involvement of the parent company indicates classification as a proprietary club.

A proprietary club does not qualify for a registration certificate under section 39 of the *Licensing Act 1964* as it lacks the essential element of joint ownership of its assets by its members. If it wishes to serve alcoholic drinks it must therefore apply for a justices' licence. There are various justices' licences available, for example the 'Full on licence' held by licensees of public houses and the 'Residential licence' held by hoteliers. A proprietor wishing to run a club to which admission is regulated by membership, such as a works' social club limited to employees of the parent company, may be granted a special form of club licence for the club, under section 55 of the *Licensing Act 1964*. Although a proprietor can apply for a full on licence if it is felt such a licence is necessary for the club, the justices will probably impose a condition limiting sales to members and their guests only, so effectively this becomes the same as a club licence.

In contrast, a registered club or members' club is a form of co-operative in which all the assets of the club, for example, the land, building and fittings, are owned in equal shares by the members of the club. Each person, by virtue of membership, has the right to be heard in the management of the club.

Important legal consequences result from this situation. One is that the serving of alcoholic drinks to members is regarded by the law as a 'supply' rather than a 'sale', which renders such a club exempt from tax on its bar takings in so far as they come from members. As with all unincorporated associations, on the dissolution of a registered club the remaining assets must be divided equally between the current members.

Most registered clubs are run by elected committees, although this is not a legal requirement, but committee members, including the president or chairperson, are nevertheless accorded the same rights, and no more, as ordinary members. A registered club is thus a financial democracy, governed by the consent of its members (hence the term 'members' club') and regulated by a constitution. This non-commercial status results in such clubs being given a privileged status in section 39 of the *Licensing Act 1964*. This allows them, subject to certain qualifications, to apply for a registration certificate authorizing supply of alcoholic drinks to members, and in some cases their guests, instead of having to apply, like a publican, for a justices' licence. Qualifications relating to an application for this certificate are detailed in the *Licensing Act 1964*, and include such things as minimum membership and the nature of the premises the club occupies.

Clubs granted registration certificates are subject to the laws governing registered clubs and are dealt with separately in the *Licensing Act 1964*.

Most recreational clubs existing in England and Wales which serve alcoholic drinks are believed to operate under registration certificates, as this is the method usually adopted. In practice justices considering whether or not a club qualifies for a registration certificate will take into account all the circumstances and the 'spirit' of the arrangement, rather than the letter of the law. This may result in works' sports and social clubs being allowed to register under section 39, even though the club premises may be owned by the parent company, who may also pay the salaries of club staff, including a full-time general secretary appointed as a full-time, salaried employee of the company. It should be noted that works' sports and social clubs tend to be non-profit making and frequently subsidize the activities of their members.

As stated earlier, to obtain a registration certificate the constitution of a club must comply with the requirements of the *Licensing Act 1964*. Friendly societies and industrial and provident societies comply through the requirements necessary for registration under the relevant Acts. A club registered as a company, although complying with the *Companies Acts*, may not have sufficient rules to qualify for a registration certificate, a deficiency which would have to be remedied before a certificate would be granted.

A members' club may therefore be both a company and also a registered club under the *Licensing Act 1964*. Each 'member' of the club is a 'shareholder' of the company and the 'committee' of the club is the 'board of directors' of the company. It is, however, a complicated procedure for a club to become a club/company.

The procedure for applying for either a registration certificate or a justices' licence is set out in the *Licensing Act 1964*. Applications are dealt with by the licensing justices in the magistrates' courts.

A club with the necessary qualifications for a registration certificate would probably find a registration certificate preferable to a justices' licence, one reason being that the justices have a wide discretion concerning the grant or refusal of a licence, but they cannot refuse to register a club with the relevant qualifications. Also, a licence must be renewed annually, whereas a certificate can, following the first renewal, be granted for any period not longer than 10 years. Finally, whereas a licensed club is subject to all the conditions and prohibitions contained in the *Licensing Act 1964*, a registered club enjoys certain privileges such as the right to serve alcohol to someone under 18.

An application for a new licence or registration certificate, or renewal of an existing one, may be opposed by the police, local authority or fire authority and any other person directly affected, for example immediate neighbours. A registration certificate or licence may have to be surrendered if the police, local authority or fire authority apply for a cancellation, usually on the grounds of a failure to comply with relevant conditions.

In April 1993 the Government announced its intention to completely revise the licensing laws which could affect the types of licence available to clubs and associations.

SALE OF FOOD

Where food is sold by a club, which is often done in conjunction with a licensed bar, the club concerned becomes subject to the *Food Safety Act 1990* and Food Hygiene Regulations introduced under this Act. These apply to any clubs serving food or drink and not exclusively to clubs running a catering service. The regulations lay great emphasis on cleanliness and sanitation, as well as the proper storage and preparation of food. They are concerned mainly that clean sanitation areas must be provided and that the handling of food or drink must be in places entirely separate from these areas. These regulations concern the bar and the kitchens of the club.

Clubs employing staff must comply with strict regulations concerning hygiene and the handling of food, as must the employees themselves.

The community physician must be informed if anyone working on premises serving food or drink develops certain infections such as food poisoning. Food offered for sale must be kept separate from food not fit for human consumption, and persons handling open food and drink must wear clean and washable over-clothing such as jackets and overalls.

Local authorities enforce the Food and Hygiene Regulations through inspectors appointed for the purpose and conferred with wide powers. These powers cover private clubs, as well as hotels and restaurants, and the greatest power is the right to enter and inspect premises at any reasonable hour of the day, to ensure that the regulations are being complied with. Where entry is refused or resisted an inspector may obtain a warrant authorizing entry by force if necessary.

Penalties for breach of these regulations are severe, including heavy fines for the original offence, and additional daily fines for every day the breach continues. Where a serious breach of the regulations occurs the court may, at the request of the local authority, prohibit premises from being used for catering purposes. A club could therefore be banned from serving drinks under a licence or registration certificate as the result of such a prohibition order.

GAMING AND GAMING MACHINES

Another source of income for recreational clubs or associations may be derived from the installation of gaming machines on their premises for the use of members. This would render the club subject to the gambling laws. 'Gambling' may be used to describe the whole of gaming, lotteries, fruit machines and betting. Each of these are subject to separate laws and will be dealt with in turn.

Gaming is defined in the *Gaming Act 1968*, the current legislation, as 'the playing of a game of chance for winnings in money or moneysworth, whether any person playing the game is at risk of losing any money or moneysworth or not'. Gaming machines, such as fruit machines, may also be included with gaming. These are defined under the Act as machines 'constructed or adapted for playing a game of chance by means of the machine', in which the machine 'has a slot or aperture for the insertion of money or moneysworth in the form of cash or tokens'.

All 'gaming' therefore requires the playing of a game of chance, whether a machine is involved or not. 'Games of chance' do not, however, include any 'athletic game or sport', nor do they include any game of pure skill. Games combining skill and chance are included, which can cause problems of definition of activities such as darts, snooker, whist and bridge. Snooker and darts are regarded as games involving pure skill, but any games involving cards must always be classified as gaming, because of the element of chance when the cards are dealt, regardless of the player's skill.

Something of value, usually money, must be staked on the outcome of an activity for it to be classed as 'gaming'. A club may therefore organize a 'gaming' evening using, for example, matchsticks as stakes, provided that the matchsticks are not later exchanged for money or goods. The law treats all forms of gaming, from roulette to bridge, in basically the same way; bingo, however, is dealt with separately.

Gaming may be operated by a club in five different ways.

1. *Gaming under a gaming licence.* This concerns what might be termed 'hard core' gambling in a casino run as a commercial enterprise, including such games as blackjack, roulette and *chemin de fer*. The means by which casinos become licensed are complicated and strict, and not relevant to our purpose, which is to consider gaming in the context of entertainment for club members and/or a source of funds for the club.

2. *Gaming under a gaming certificate.* The 1968 Act enables genuine members' clubs, offering a wide variety of facilities to their members, to include gaming without having to obtain a gaming licence. Such clubs cannot offer the same gaming facilities as a commercial casino, nor are they subject to such strict controls. A gaming certificate may be issued under Part 2 of the *Gaming Act 1968* which covers a club for limited varieties of gaming, other than bingo.

   An application for a gaming certificate is made to the local licensing authority. Applicants must comply with certain conditions, and are limited concerning the gaming allowed under the certificate. A certificate must be renewed annually when a fee is payable, but following one renewal, an applicant may, on request, be granted a certificate for up to 10 years. Members of a registered gaming club are limited to the more familiar, and probably less profitable games, such as bridge, whist, cribbage and backgammon. Strict rules apply to holders of such a certificate

3. *Gaming under Part 1 of the Gaming Act 1968.* A club that does not possess a gaming licence or a gaming certificate may conduct certain types of gaming, provided the rigid and demanding rules of Part 1 of the *Gaming Act 1968* are obeyed. So stringent are these rules that a club may not feel this method is worth considering, which was probably the intention of Parliament when the Act was passed.

4. *Gaming at entertainments not held for private gain.* A club holding neither a gaming licence nor a gaming certificate, operating outside the narrow

rules of Part 1 of the 1968 Act, may still comply with the gaming laws, provided certain conditions are observed, as detailed in section 41. These conditions govern the types of game, the stakes and prize money, but most important, the games must be played at 'an entertainment promoted otherwise than for purposes of private gain'. In other words, this section is intended to enable bona fide members' clubs to hold 'gaming sessions' as part of a social programme and as a means of raising funds. Games that can be played under these terms include whist, bridge, dominoes and bingo.

5. *Gaming as an amusement with prizes.* The provisions of the 1968 Act do not apply where gaming is organized as an 'amusement with prizes', as a part but not a main attraction of a social event, such as a fête or sporting event, the main event being conducted for purposes other than private gain, such as the raising of funds. Gaming machines are included in this context, where prizes (not money) are played for. This type of gaming is now covered by the *Lotteries and Amusements Act 1976*.

The *Betting and Gaming Duties Act 1981* levies duty on most types of games played on premises with a gaming licence, but not on games played on premises with a gaming certificate, unless the gaming concerned is bingo.

Bingo is dealt with by the law as either a commercial enterprise or an entertainment. Where it is being operated as a commercial enterprise it must be done under a gaming licence provided under Part 2 of the *Gaming Act 1968*. This is known as a 'Bingo only gaming licence' and subjects the operator to strict controls and conditions. Bingo can also be played under a gaming certificate and within the rules of Part 1 of the 1968 Act.

However, most clubs in the context being considered would be concerned with bingo being played as an entertainment and not for private gain. The same conditions apply here as to gaming as an entertainment and this is the most common use of section 41 of the *Gaming Act 1968*. A registered club, that is, one with a registration certificate, may organize bingo sessions as one of its normal activities, making a lump-sum charge, not exceeding a prescribed maximum for admission and stakes. The stakes may be of any size, but total prize distribution is subject to a maximum. Stakes must go towards one or more of the following; prizes, expenses, club funds, or some other purpose other than private gain, for example a charity. Bingo may also be organized as an 'amusement with prizes' as part of a larger social event, but not being the main attraction.

A 'gaming machine' is defined by the *Gaming Act 1968* as any machine by which a game of chance may be played. The Act distinguishes two types of machine, those found on club premises and known as 'jackpot' machines, and those found on any other premises which are termed 'nonjackpot' machines.

The 'jackpot' machine pays a cumulative prize which is variable and only paid when a particular combination appears on the machine. These machines may only be used in genuine clubs and the club must have a licence or certificate to cover them. Only premises either licensed or registered for gaming under the 1968 Act, or registered for the use of machines only under that Act, may provide these machines. A club already licensed or registered for gaming is automatically covered for two jackpot machines on its premises.

Clubs not wishing to become registered or licensed for gaming may apply for registration under Part 3 of the *Gaming Act 1968*, which allows a club the provision of two jackpot machines on its premises. A Part 3 registration certificate is available to all genuine clubs, although the magistrates concerned would seem to have an absolute discretion regarding its granting to a proprietary club. Application for this certificate is made to the local licensing justices and certain conditions concerning the club must be complied with before it will be granted. A fee is charged for this certificate which must be renewed every five years at a reduced charge. It may be cancelled, following a hearing, at the request of the local police and may be relinquished any time.

Any club authorized for the provision of jackpot machines must, whatever form the authorization takes, comply with stringent rules regarding their use. These rules include a provision that all prizes must actually be paid out of the machine, and in cash, not tokens. The Home Secretary can, at any time, fix a maximum for jackpot pay-outs. Currently there is no limit. Jackpot machines cannot be used on club premises at any time during which members of the public have access to those premises.

Use of a non-jackpot machine may be authorized by permit under Part 3 of the 1968 Act. This type of machine is primarily intended for use in premises such as public houses and restaurants. Clubs may apply for such a permit, although non-jackpot machines are less attractive because, as the name implies, there is no chance of winning a jackpot. A club must apply for a permit to the local licensing justices if it is licensed or registered to sell alcoholic drinks or, in other cases, to the local authority. A fee is charged for the permit, which may be granted for any period of not less than three years. This permit may be transferred or cancelled. Again a club must comply with stringent rules relating to the use of these machines.

Not only does the law regulate the type of machine that can be made available, but the 1968 Act also lays down strict regulations concerning those who supply and maintain these machines. However, these provisions do not directly concern the club. Complications may arise where a club acquires a machine through a hiring agreement rather than an outright purchase. Hiring agreements and some sale agreements are dealt with in the Act.

Money may only be collected from inside the machine by an 'authorized' person, which for club purposes will be an official member of the club or a designated employee of the club.

The *Betting and Gaming Duties Act 1981* provides that a gaming machine licence duty must be paid before any gaming machines can be provided for use on club premises. The amount of duty payable depends on whether or not the premises have local authority approval under the *Gaming Acts* and the rate at which duty is charged. The latter varies according to the denomination of coins which may be used to operate the machine. Gaming machine licence duty is not payable when the machine in question is used as part of a 'charitable entertainment', subject to certain conditions being satisfied.

LOTTERIES

Lotteries can also be a source of club funds. A lottery occurs where prizes are distributed to people selected by chance, for example, drawing numbers from a drum, as in a raffle or prize draw. The law relating to lotteries has been codified in the *Lotteries and Amusements Act 1976* which ensures that club lotteries are subject to the control of the local authority and in certain cases the Gaming Board (if the lottery is used to raise money from members of the public). Where a lottery is promoted only among members there are no such controls.

There are three types of lottery allowed by the Act: the 'small' lottery; the 'private' lottery; and the 'society's' lottery.

The small lottery is one organized as part of a social function, such as a dinner or sporting event in which non-members may take part and the object of which is entertainment. Certain conditions must be observed, which include paying all the proceeds to the club once expenses have been deducted, not paying any cash prizes, and only selling tickets at the time and place of the main entertainment.

A private lottery, as defined in the Act, includes a lottery conducted among members of the same club or a section within a club. Such a lottery must be organized by a person authorized to do so by the club committee; the whole proceeds, less expenses, must be devoted to club funds, and the lottery may be advertised and conducted only on club premises. Every ticket sold must have on it the name and address of the promoter, and a description of the people to whom sale of tickets is limited, that is, club members.

Finally, the society's lottery is one conducted by a club or society for charitable or other purposes, but not for private gain, for example, to raise funds for the club. Many conditions are imposed on this type of lottery by section 5 of the *Lotteries and Amusements Act 1976*. They include requirements that the lottery must be promoted in Great Britain, conducted in accordance with a scheme approved by the club and all proceedings, less expenses, must go to club funds. A club wishing to run such a lottery must be registered for the purpose with the local authority, that is, the district council, the procedure for this being contained in Schedule 1 of the Act. Within three months of the lottery the promoter must send a return to the local authority stating, among other things, the purposes and proceeds of the lottery. A club cannot promote more than 52 lotteries in any 1 year and these must be at least 7 days apart, unless they are being conducted simultaneously at a sporting event or social function. The promoter must be an 'authorized' member of the club, and the promoter's name and address, and the date of the lottery, must appear on all the tickets. Many other detailed requirements are also listed in the Act.

When a club wishes to organize a lottery to raise total stake money of more than £5000, the scheme must be registered beforehand with the Gaming Board. It appears that the board is obliged to register such a scheme, unless there is any irregularity in its organization. A fee for registration is payable to the board and accounts relating to any such lottery must be produced for the board at their request.

A lottery is not lawful until the club concerned is registered with the local authority for lottery purposes. This includes lotteries also registered with the Gaming Board. Subject to each individual local authority's requirements, the main regulations concerning registration are the payment of an initial fee and a subsequent annual renewal fee, and the genuineness of both the club concerned and the purpose of holding lotteries. Clubs already registered under the *Betting, Gaming and Lotteries Act 1963* automatically became registered under the 1976 Act, which replaced the 1963 Act.

New regulations were introduced in 1978 concerning the details of a scheme to be followed in the organization of a lottery, whether or not this scheme is submitted for registration with the Gaming Board. The requirements are very detailed on the promotion of the lottery, sale of tickets and proportion of proceeds allocated for prizes. Such a scheme, once approved by a club, must be followed in the organization of the lottery or that lottery becomes illegal.

Lotteries are advantageous to a club as they provide a source of income and, in the case of some amateur sports clubs are their 'life-blood'. The disadvantages of a lottery include the need to register the lottery and compliance with so many detailed conditions.

OTHER FUNDRAISING ACTIVITIES

Apart from statutory controls such as those outlined above, there is no limitation on the methods of fundraising adopted by a club, other than the ordinary criminal law. It is open to anyone to make an appeal to the public for funds in any manner for any object. Some activities, such as auctions, are of course governed by the ordinary law, in this case the law of contract, which covers any fundraising activity involving the sale of goods.

House-to-house collections may be organized, but must be registered with the local licensing authorities who will grant a licence for a period specified in the application, which must not exceed 12 months. Although local authorities should only restrict such collections to the extent necessary to ensure that they are bona fide and the collection is properly conducted, there may be a tendency to restrict the number of collections in their areas to recognized 'charities' only.

Regulations concerning street collections are made by police authorities and may differ from district to district. A permit has to be obtained from the Commissioner of Police and applications must be made in the name of a committee or other body consisting of not less than three people. The permit will state the day, time and areas where the collection can take place. Collectors must not obstruct or annoy anyone, as it is a criminal offence to obstruct the highway. They must occupy a stationary position, not more than two at one place, they must not be under 16 years of age, they cannot use a table which would cause an obstruction or any table exceeding a specified size. They must not use a box on the end of a pole to reach upper windows of houses or top decks of vehicles. The collecting boxes used must be numbered, securely closed and be marked permanently with the name of the fund. Collectors must not be paid for their services. Accounts relating to the collection must be registered with the Police Commissioners within a month of the collection.

ENTERTAINMENTS HELD BY CLUBS TO RAISE FUNDS

A further means of supplementing club funds is by holding dances, square dances and discothèques open to members and bona fide guests. Such activities may require a 'late' bar. This may involve an application to the licensing justices for an 'exemption order', an order exempting the club from closing the bar at the normal time and allowing them to continue serving drinks until a specified time. An unlicensed club may apply for an 'occasional permission' which would allow the sale of alcoholic drinks just at that one function.

A club planning to hold such functions may also require an entertainment licence. This licence is issued under the *Local Government (Miscellaneous Provisions) Act 1982* which replaces earlier legislation relating to the grant of music and dancing licences. The 1982 Act designates the district councils in England and Wales as the authority for licensing places outside Greater London for:

1. public dancing or music or other public entertainment of a like kind; and
2. any entertainment which consists of, or includes, any public contest, exhibition or display of boxing, wrestling, judo, karate or any similar sport.

Special procedures apply in Greater London by virtue of the *London Government Act 1985*, including a requirement to advertise the application both in the press and on the premises. Applications are dealt with by the council of the London borough concerned or the Common Council of the City of London.

A provisional grant of an entertainment licence may be made under the 1982 Act in respect of premises which are about to be or are actually being built, extended or altered.

Although places used for public entertainment are licensed the licence is issued to, and is personal to, the licence holder. The holder may apply to the district council at any time for variation of any terms, conditions or restrictions attached to the licence.

The Act confers on district councils the power to make regulations concerning the particulars and notices that an applicant must give and to charge a 'reasonable' fee for granting, transferring or renewing a licence. This fee may be waived if the council thinks the entertainment is educational or for a charitable purpose.

If the authority refuses to grant, renew, transfer or vary a licence, or attaches conditions or restrictions to the licence, an applicant for or holder of an entertainments licence may appeal to a magistrates' court.

An entertainments licence will generally remain in force for one year, but the issuing authority may issue one for a shorter period. Licences may also be granted for particular occasions only. Licences are renewable and transferable at the discretion of the issuing authority.

This is an important matter as a club may face criminal proceedings if public entertainments are organized without an entertainments licence where such a licence is required. The licence may be revoked if the holder is convicted for exceeding the terms of the licence. The Act also provides rights of entry and inspection to the licensing authority, and to the police and fire authorities. The latter two authorities also have a right to express a view regarding the issue of a licence and the issuing authority must have regard to those views.

An entertainments licence is only required for 'public' entertainments and is not necessary for private entertainments open to club members only. However, such entertainments must relate to genuine clubs and in *Lunn v Colston-Hayter* (1991)[1] the organizer of an entertainment open to 'club' members only was convicted as those attending the entertainment, an all-night dance in an aircraft hangar, had to join a 'club' by obtaining their tickets no later than 24 hours before the party.

COPYRIGHT IN RELATION TO PUBLIC PERFORMANCE OF MUSIC

A further aspect of the 'public' performance of music by a club concerns the requirements of the law relating to copyright. Copyright is the legal right a person possesses in respect of artistic works such as literature or music. A club's main concern with copyright would be expected to be where it concerns music. Such a copyright may be owned by the original composer or may have been sold to a publisher or a recording company. In any event a copyright expires 50 years after the death of the composer, at which time it ceases to apply.

Copyright owners are entitled to bring a legal action under the *Copyright, Designs and Patents Act 1988* (which replaced the *Copyright Act 1956*) against anyone infringing the copyright by performance of the music in public without permission. Permission generally requires payment of a fee. Separate copyrights may exist covering composition, recording and lyrics, and infringement of three separate copyrights is possible by the playing of one record. In *Performing Rights Society Ltd v Aristidou* (1978)[2] an action was successfully brought against a restaurant owner for playing musical works in public on a record player in his restaurant.

Members of a club are regarded as 'the public' for the purposes of the *Copyright, Designs and Patents Act 1988* as illustrated in *Performing Rights Society v Rangers Football Club* (1974).[3] In this case an action was brought by the holder of the copyright and licensing rights of three musical compositions that had been performed before members of the defendant club. The court decided this constituted a performance 'in public' and awarded damages for breach of copyright.

There are exceptions to this strict rule, one being that there is no infringement of copyright where a sound recording is heard on premises on which people live or sleep, for example, a residential club. Thus, a holiday camp playing recorded music through loudspeakers over the camp was found to be within this exception in *Phonographic Performances Ltd v Pontin's Ltd* (1967).[4] The second exception occurs where sound recordings are played as part of the activities of a club established mainly for charitable purposes. Although it is not clear exactly which clubs this covers, it would certainly apply to friendly societies, youth clubs, church clubs and clubs organized for educational purposes.

For practical reasons concerning the enforcement of copyright the majority of copyright holders have combined as the Performing Rights Society, which now controls copyright in most music and the Phonographic Performance Ltd, which controls records. These organizations make contact with establishments where copyright music is likely to be performed, assess the music to be performed and charge an annual fee which is passed on to the copyright owners. The clubs involved are issued with a licence protecting them from actions for infringement of copyright.

Clubs that are not licensed are assessed and charged under a tariff imposed by the society. The rate is fixed by reference to the type of music the club is providing, that is, whether it takes the form of live performances of music or records used for background music. For background music a fixed annual rate is charged. Clubs should be aware of the current tariff and where they feel the fee charged is too high they can approach the Performing Rights Society directly or appeal to the Copyright Tribunal for a ruling on the reasonableness of the tariff under which it is being charged.

The remedies given by the *Copyright, Designs and Patents Act 1988* for infringement of copyright are of two classes, civil and criminal. Civil remedies include damages or an injunction, or any other suitable remedy that may be available. It is also a criminal offence to infringe copyright, punishable on summary conviction.

Television and radio are also included in the law of copyright. Both these media may infringe copyright by broadcasting certain material. They are also protected by the law, as it is an infringement of copyright to show in public a recording of a television programme. With the increasing popularity of video equipment, clubs should therefore be aware that the showing of recorded television programmes to club members may be an infringement of copyright. In February 1981 an international construction company agreed to pay damages and costs for infringing the copyright of television programmes, in an out-of-court settlement, when video-recorded programmes were shown to their employees overseas. Video Performance Ltd licenses the public performance and broadcast of prerecorded videos.

SPONSORSHIP

Finally, another source of funds for clubs is sponsorship. This occurs when a business organization donates money to a club under a mutual agreement. This agreement usually relates to some form of publicity for the organization by the club, for example, the wearing of sports clothes bearing the name of the sponsor or use of the name of the organization for a particular event. The display of advertisements, however, may be regarded as the provision of a service and therefore subject to value added tax for the supply of services (page 118).

A sponsorship agreement is beneficial to both parties concerned. The club concerned obtains additional funds with relatively little effort; such funds are not taxable, provided they are used for the benefit of the club. Sponsors gain, as they obtain relatively inexpensive publicity and tax relief on moneys used for sponsorship.

Sponsorship is based on agreement between the parties concerned and is therefore essentially governed by contract. However, such deals may fall foul of the law in countries such as France and Australia where advertising tobacco products has been made illegal, thereby making it impossible to televise a grand prix in which cars sponsored by tobacco companies are racing. However, so important is sponsorship by tobacco companies to motor racing that following their ban on advertising of tobacco products in 1992 the French government offered substantial compensation to the sport. But, such bans may prevent the countries concerned from holding world class events.

INVESTMENT OF CLUB FUNDS

Generally clubs have a surplus of funds from year to year which must be held for the members, usually through investment. This section is designed to point out basic legal requirements concerning the investment of club funds. Any advice concerning actual investment should be sought from an accountant or broker.

The assets of a members' club belong in equal shares to the members, who should, in theory, have a say in any matter concerning those assets. Practically, there is usually a club rule authorizing a certain person or persons, usually committee members, to handle investments on behalf of the club, those investments to be held in the club's name or by its trustees acting on the committee's instructions. Such a rule may also specify the type of investments which may be made, otherwise, in theory, any investment is possible. Trustees acting on behalf of the committee may make a 'bad' investment, in which case the members, the beneficiaries, could bring an action against them for damages to cover the loss. Consequences of this nature should be avoided if at all possible. One method of overcoming this problem may be to choose investments within the guidelines contained in the *Trustee Investments Act 1961*. Following these guidelines will not mean that the trustees are not liable if anything should go wrong, but the scheme laid down in the Act should lessen the chances of anything going wrong.

A club, therefore, wishing to invest funds rather then leaving them in a bank account, should do so through trustees directly controlled by the committee. If a named official of the club organizes investments in the official's own name, that official will be regarded in law as acting as a trustee for the members and therefore liable for any loss resulting from bad investments.

TAXING OF INCOME

Unless they fall within any of the exempted categories, recreational clubs, associations and governing bodies are liable to pay taxes in the same way as any other organization. Exemptions from income tax occur where the club is registered as a charity with the charity commissioners (page 80) or registered under the *Friendly Societies Acts* (page 80), or where it is registered as an industrial and provident society and trading within the club is referred to as 'supply to members'.

A members' club with a registration certificate is not subject to taxation concerning gains arising from 'mutual trading', which is profit derived from members, for example, bar takings. However, where a club has an income through dealings with independent third parties such as banks and investments trusts, that income is taxable as corporation tax.

Investment income may be paid as 'taxed' or 'untaxed' investment. 'Taxed' investment income is taxed at source before the club receives it, for example, interest on building society investments. 'Untaxed' income is paid without deduction of tax. Corporation tax is paid at a higher rate than basic-rate tax, so further deductions may be necessary on 'taxed' income. A club's accountant must be very careful to distinguish these types of income when preparing club accounts for tax purposes.

Many clubs may be exempt from paying tax when certain types of transactions, known as 'charitable exemptions', are involved. The provisions governing these exemptions are complex and detailed, and expert advice should be sought on the matter. Where a club or organization is regarded in law as a charity (page 80), however, income used for the objects and purposes of the charity is not taxable.

Charities enjoy almost complete exemption from income tax and corporation tax, provided their funds are applied for charitable purposes only. The only exception is that profits from a trade are not exempt from tax, unless the trade is exercised in the course of actually carrying out the primary purpose of the charity or the work in connection with the trade is mainly carried on by the beneficiaries of the charity. Charities do not pay capital gains tax on disposals by them. There are also reliefs from taxation available to donors to a charity.

Several cases have arisen concerning club or society exemption from taxation, the majority being in relation to registered charities, when the issue has been whether or not the club is a 'charity'. These cases were discussed in Chapter 5, concerning the definition of 'charity'. It may be that some recreational organizations, though not charities, would qualify for other tax relief. In *Peterborough Royal Foxhound Show Society v Commissioners of Inland Revenue* (1936),[5] the society concerned was founded to promote the interests of foxhound breeding and for that purpose held an annual foxhound show. The court decided that the society did not satisfy the requirements of a charity, but that being an agricultural society, the profits of the show were exempt from income tax.

A recreational club not qualifying for exemption from income tax will be liable to pay this tax, as was decided in *Carlisle and Silloth Golf Club v Smith* (1913).[6] This case concerned green fees collected from visitors by an ordinary members' golf club. As the number of visitors concerned was larger than would normally be expected in a golf club, the court decided that the club was carrying on an enterprise beyond its ordinary functions and that any profit deriving from visitors' green fees, after deduction for maintenance, was taxable, and that separate accounts should be kept for this purpose.

RATING OF CLUBS AND SOCIETIES

In 1990 a new system of rating was introduced for club premises when business premises, including sports clubs, became subject to the uniform business rate. In many cases this involved a substantial increase in relation to the amount paid in rates which would force large increases in subscriptions that could ultimately result in decreasing membership and closure of the club. Because many amateur clubs have premises in prime locations and subsequently high rateable values they face massive increases following revaluation, the first since 1973. However, the blow is to be softened by a five-year phasing-in period.

Under the *Local Government Finance Act 1988* local authorities do have a discretion to grant non-profit-making organizations not registered as charities up to 100% exemption from this rate, but they are under no obligation to exempt such organizations from any part of the bill. Under the new arrangements the local authority would be able to offset 75% of any relief against the new uniform business rate pool leaving the council tax payers to meet only 25% of the bill. This is a recognition of the contribution that non-profit-making sports clubs make to the local community. It is up to the local authorities to demonstrate their willingness to play their part and grant relief from rates in appropriate cases. However, there is concern that councils may be loath to ask residents to pick up the bill for rate relief. Whether to grant relief will be decided locally according to the local authority's policy and the individual merits of each case. An authority's decision may be challenged in the courts should an organization feel that the authority has failed to exercise its discretion properly.

By the end of 1991 there had been several challenges by riding schools on the grounds that equestrian establishments were being rated under the industrial system. Nevertheless, the disproportionate increase in overheads has forced many riding schools out of business. The Central Council for Physical Recreation (page 158), having been alerted to the fact that many local authorities were failing to comply with the government's Practice Note issued in November 1989 exhorting local authorities to give rate relief to voluntary non-profit-making sports clubs, have also joined the battle against the new tax.

An organization does not become ineligible because the accounts show a profit at the year end; to avoid confusion in framing applications any excess of income should be shown as 'surplus' because no club can be expected to operate properly without budgeting for a surplus.

In Scotland councils can draw from a fund to offset the cost of allowing exemptions and rates are not paid in Scotland by any club which does not have a bar. It has been suggested that a similar scheme be introduced for England and Wales. However, it is expected the whole system will soon be subject to revision.

Charities are still granted mandatory relief of at least 80% so perhaps the answer for some clubs would be for clubs to establish charitable youth sections.

VAT ON RECREATIONAL FACILITIES

Value added tax (VAT) is an indirect tax charged on the supply of goods and services in the UK in the course or furtherance of a business. The provision by a club, association or organization of the facilities or advantages available to its members in return for a subscription or other consideration, falls within the definition of the 'carrying on of a business'.

VAT is charged on the supply of goods and services in the UK where the supply itself is taxable, and the supply was made by a taxable person who is, or should be, registered for VAT purposes. An association which is treated as carrying on a business and making taxable supplies is required to register for VAT purposes, if that income exceeds a certain limit. In 1992 the limit was £36 600.

'Supply' for VAT purposes covers all forms of supply and transactions such as sales, hirings and performance of services. An association providing facilities or advantages to members, in return for subscriptions or other consideration, is making a supply and, where the association should be registered, is subject to VAT at the standard rate, currently 17.5%, unless it is an association specifically exempted or zero-rated (for example, trade unions and youth clubs).

All clubs and associations have to pay VAT on purchases of goods and services, although VAT paid by a registered association on supplies purchased for the purpose of the business is recoverable. This includes tax on supplies purchased for the provision of advantages or facilities to members. It must first be established that the supplies were purchased for this purpose. In *British Olympic Association v Customs and Excise Commissioners*,[7] a VAT tribunal case in April 1979, it was decided that input tax incurred on the provision of uniforms for the British Olympic team in 1976 and on fees paid to the fund-raising agents were not recoverable, as these related to an activity not connected with the provision of facilities to members.

Most countries apply a tax similar to VAT, although its applicability to recreational associations varies. Denmark, Italy, Norway and Germany apply a similar system to that of the UK, although probably not as strict, but VAT is applied to organizations engaging in profit-making activities, although amateur recreational associations are exempt. Ireland applies a mixed system, where subscriptions and admission charges are exempt from this tax, although purchase of equipment and receipts from bars are not. Belgium applies VAT in principle to sports clubs, but a provision of the VAT code makes services supplied by managers of sports facilities exempt from the tax when these managers pursue non-profit-making goals and when receipts are used exclusively to cover running costs.

In French legislation sports clubs have a privileged position as they are assimilated to non-profit-making associations, a status not altered even if such an association engages in profit-making activities, provided that the profits are reconverted within the association itself and they are managed benevolently. Sporting associations in The Netherlands are also exempt from VAT, provided their receipts do not exceed a certain limit.

Recreational organizations in the UK feel very strongly that they should be exempted from payment of both direct and indirect taxation on the supply and purchase of goods and services, so that all their profits may be used in the promotion of their particular activity. In this particular area there is felt to be a case for specific legislation in relation to recreational activities, as illustrated by the following examples.

In 1980 the government in Britain announced that VAT would be levied on the full amount of fees for entry to competitions and events, and on drinks and refreshments served to visiting teams in the clubhouse. However, following a campaign of resistance to these measures, spearheaded by the Sports Council, the Central Council for Physical Recreation and many governing bodies in recreation, exemptions were granted where the competitions and events were staged by non-profit-making bodies.

A campaign to reduce VAT on British bloodstock, that is on all sales and transfers of horses inside or outside the country had also been successful. British horse owners and breeders had been at a disadvantage, as their main competitors, Ireland and France, were granted privileges in relation to VAT. In Ireland bloodstock was exempted altogether from payment of VAT and in France VAT was charged only on the 'carcass value' of bloodstock, resulting in a greatly reduced rate. Early in 1980 the British government relaxed the restrictions imposed on British bloodstock. However, in 1991 Britain's bloodstock breeders were again in dispute with the government when VAT at 17.5% was imposed on sales of bloodstock. Breeders were particularly worried as the removal of trade barriers in the European Community in 1993 meant VAT would be applied in the country of purchase. France was allowed to set a 5.5% rate for bloodstock and Ireland was allowed to keep its 2.7% level, thanks to bargaining with the Community. Britain could reduce its rate, but ministers initially refused to do so because, they argued, if it was done for one industry it would have to be done for others.

The problem had arisen because racing in the UK has been regarded as a hobby rather than a business which has prevented racehorse owners from registering for VAT and thus being unable to claim back the tax. Following representations from people involved in all areas of the sport and a threat that Tattersalls, Europe's leading auctioneers, would move their prestigious Houghton Yearling Sale from Newmarket to Fairy-house near Dublin in January 1993 the government announced their intention to modify aspects of VAT regulations in relation to horse breeding in the March Budget. The proposed plan included allowing bloodstock breeders to register for VAT and to inject more cash from betting turnover back into racing through a reduction in betting tax in the hope the resulting higher prize money would allow owners a better chance to recoup their expenses.

In relation to taxation generally, governing bodies in sport and recreation seem to take the view that they should be exempt from taxation, so that all profits could be used to promote their activity and for this reason they should be regarded as a special category by the law.

NOTES

1. (1991) 89 LGR 754
2. *The Times*, 6 July 1978
3. [1974] SLT 151

4. [1967] 3 All ER 736
5. [1936] 2 KB 497
6. [1913] 3 KB 75
7. *The Times*, 17 November 1979

The employment of staff | 7

Whenever professional sportspersons are recognized as employees they are subject to the employment law of that country. In most countries the law concerning the professional sportsperson as an employee is not specific, but rather tends to be drawn into the framework of the law relating to employment law generally. This has been the case in England and Wales where the law offers professional sportspersons protection in relation to their conditions of employment.

Employment legislation in Britain is generally enforced not through the law courts, but in tribunals specially created by this legislation. Such tribunals usually comprise a legally qualified chairperson and two other non-legal persons, one of whom 'represents' employers' interests and the other employees' interests. The aim of these tribunals is to dispense justice quickly, cheaply and informally. Industrial tribunals deal with matters such as claims for redundancy payment, unfair dismissal and discrimination at work. Appeals from the decision of an industrial tribunal are heard by the Employment Appeal Tribunal and, from there, if the issue concerns a point of law, there is a right of appeal to the law courts.

EMPLOYEE OR INDEPENDENT CONTRACTOR?

Professional sportspersons, however, are not the only employees in recreation in England and Wales. There are also others responsible for the running of recreational facilities, including people from managers to catering and cleaning staff.

Employers in recreation range from clubs which may employ both professional sportspersons and general staff, managers of recreational facilities to governing bodies in recreation who may employ clerical staff.

Both organizers of recreation who employ people and professional participants in sport who are employees are therefore affected by employment law. This area of the law is very complex and continually changing. The contractual position of the professional sportsperson has already been examined in Chapter

2, and included in the following pages will be those laws which govern the rights and duties of all sports employers and employees. A separate section will deal with taxation, although this is a branch of the law in itself.

To some extent employment law is an extension of the law of contract, as it is centred around the contract of employment. There are two types of contract of employment, one made between an employer and an employee (which is a contract **of** service) and the other between an employer and an independent contractor (which is a contract **for** services).

It is necessary to distinguish between these two types of contract, due to the differing rights and responsibilities that arise from them. For example, the rights relating to dismissal apply to employees, but not to independent contractors; an employer is 'vicariously' liable for the negligent actions of an employee, but not those of an independent contractor; an independent contractor owes no loyalty to an employer in the way an employee does.

The law has evolved tests to decide into which category such a contract falls. These centre on such considerations as the amount of control exercised over the person concerned, the importance of that person's work to the employer's business, who pays the wages and how, the payment of income tax and the form in which the contract is drawn up. However, there is no one simple test to decide the issue and where legal problems arise, the court will determine the issue according to the circumstances. Some situations are quite clear: for example, a full-time swimming pool attendant obviously has a contract of service, whereas a building contractor employed to undertake alterations to changing facilities at the pool would have a contract for services. Somewhere in the middle (and falling into one category or the other, depending on the circumstances), will be specialists such as golf professionals and tennis coaches 'associated' with a particular club.

This section is concerned with the contract of service, and the rights and responsibilities that arise from it in relation to employment.

THE CONTRACT OF EMPLOYMENT

A contract of employment is governed by the general law of contract and, with a few exceptions, may be written or oral. Only recently has legislation required that certain provisions should appear in a contract of employment. The law governing employment is rapidly changing and developing, and the present law governing the formation of contracts of employment is the *Employment Protection (Consolidation) Act 1978*, as amended by the *Employment Acts 1980* and *1990*.

This Act provides that every employee is entitled to a written statement from their employer containing basic information specified in the Act. Such a statement must be provided within 13 weeks of the start of employment and must give the following information.

1. the names of the employer and the employee;
2. the date the employment started;
3. the rate or scale of pay, or the method by which it is calculated;
4. the intervals when remuneration is paid, that is, weekly or monthly;
5. hours of work;
6. any terms and conditions relating to hours of work, whether or not any period of employment with another employer will count towards 'continuous employment' with the present employer for the purposes of future calculation of redundancy pay, or entitlement to protection from unfair dismissal;
7. any terms and conditions relating to holidays and holiday pay, sickness and sick pay, pensions and pension schemes, discipline and the right to complain to someone if not satisfied with conditions;
8. the title of the job the employee is employed to do;
9. the length of notice the employee is obliged to give, or entitled to receive if their employment is to be terminated, certain minimum periods being specified in the Act;
10. the date of the expiry of the term if the contract is for a fixed period.

This document should also inform the employee of certain statutory rights conferred on them by the various statutes relating to employment. These include the following:

11. The right to join any trade union of the employee's choice and to take part in its activities, including such matters as 'closed shop' agreements which may affect the employee.
12. The right to be disciplined under disciplinary rules where these exist. Such rules must be laid down in the written notice or be reasonably accessible to the employee in a document referred to in the written statement, however, it would not appear that the existence of such rules is compulsory.
13. Notice of an employee's right to complain if the employee is dissatisfied with any disciplinary action taken against them, or any other aspect of their employment. The written notice defines the person to whom such a complaint should be made, and the manner in which it should be made.

Where there are no details that can be entered under any of the above headings, it should be stated that no details are available; for example, because no pension scheme exists. An employee must be notified in writing of any changes relating to details contained within the document.

The contract of employment is not this statement. This statement is a record of the terms of the contract, binding on both parties and it applies from the first day of employment, whenever it may actually be received.

For practical purposes it would be impossible to include all the detailed provisions relating to employment in one document and an employer is entitled by this Act to refer employees to relevant documents for current provisions and future changes.

Generally an employee working less than 16 hours per week does not have to be provided with written terms of the employee's contract, unless that employee was originally employed to work more than 16 hours a week or had been working between 8 and 16 hours per week 'continuously' for 5 years. Where an employee is a husband or wife of an employer, there is no obligation to provide written terms.

There is a developing European dimension to employment law and many of the proposals in Community legislation will have direct relevance to the contract of employment. A proposed Directive has been introduced on the basis that uniform provisions relating to written statements will facilitate free movement of workers between Member States. This proposed Directive will introduce an entitlement to a written statement where the employee works eight or more hours a week.

Should a person be provided with a formal, written contract containing all the conditions which the employee should be made aware of, that employee does not also need a written statement of the terms of the contract as the requirements of the law will have been satisfied. The terms of the contract of employment may only be varied with the consent of both the employer and the employee.

PAYMENT OF WAGES AND SICKNESS ALLOWANCE

The common law imposes on employers certain duties which could also be termed the 'rights of the employee'. Remuneration, or payment for work done, is the first duty. The amount to be paid will be stated in the contract of employment, either by agreement between the employer and employee, by the incorporation of a local or national collective agreement relating to that particular work or by statute, for example, the *Wages Councils Act 1979*. Where wages have not been agreed as above, then it is implied that a reasonable sum will be paid for the work done.

There is no duty imposed on an employer to provide work for an employee, although there is sometimes a duty to pay an employee when no work is available. A contract of employment may imply an obligation to provide a reasonable amount of work to enable an employee to earn premium payments for night shift and overtime working, as the employee would if they were working under normal conditions.

Apart from remuneration for work done, there are other aspects relating to this duty, such as holiday pay and sick pay. Entitlement to holiday pay depends on the terms of the contract of employment, although in some cases, for example young people in factories, specific provision may be made by statute.

Provision is usually made in the contract for the payment of sick pay. Apart from any such provision an employer is now under a statutory duty to pay sick pay. The provisions of the *Social Security and Housing Benefits Act 1982*, amended by the *Social Security Acts 1985* and *1986*, make it the responsibility of employers to pay to their employees statutory sick pay for the first eight weeks of absence through illness. Any amounts paid may be recouped from the state through national insurance contributions or, if this not enough, from the monthly tax return.

An employee is not prevented from claiming full wages, even though the employee may be receiving social security payments for sickness. The usual benefit is full pay for a certain period, then half pay. This is designed to protect an employee from unanticipated incapacity. A sick-benefit scheme will often specify certain classes of injury that do not qualify for entitlement, which may include self-inflicted injuries, or injuries caused by the employee's own misconduct. Sporting injuries may also be excluded, but generally this occurs only where the employee engages in sport professionally and the injury is not incurred in the course of that employment. Where employees participate in a particularly hazardous sport, those employees may be unable to claim sick benefit on the grounds of misconduct, because employees are under a general duty to their employer not to engage in activities in their spare time which would prevent them from performing their duties.

As employees are under a general duty to their employer not to use their leisure time in a manner that would render them unfit to perform their duties, where a contract of employment does not specifically state that certain injuries are exempt from sick pay, it may be that engaging in recreational activities would be a breach of this duty.

Incapacity through sports injuries may also lead to the termination of the contract of employment. The contract may possibly be frustrated because it has become impossible for an employee to perform duties under the contract, although frustration is normally only relevant where the contract of employment is for a long term which cannot be determined by notice. It would not be relevant where the employment could be terminated by notice. Where the contract allows for a period of sick leave it is unlikely the contract can be terminated before that period has expired. In such circumstances it would be easier for an employer to give notice to terminate the contract, as the fact that an employee is no longer capable of doing the job is considered a fair reason for dismissal.

These problems may arise in relation to employees in recreation as many such employees, not only professional sportspersons, tend to be actively engaged in recreational activities. The question that arises here is whether an employer should have to bear the financial consequences of all sports injuries sustained by their employees or whether the employer should limit the liability. Employees must then decide whether to limit their own recreational activities or to protect themselves through an insurance policy (page 30).

As the involvement of employees in potentially dangerous sports is likely to increase, it seems unreasonable to expect employers to bear the financial consequences of all sports injuries sustained by their employees. The extent of liability for sick pay should therefore be clearly outlined in the contract of employment. Employees engaging in hazardous sports should perhaps insure themselves in relation to possible injury, and not expect their employers to bear the loss occasioned by such injury.

TIME OFF WITH PAY

There is also a duty to pay an employee who is not actually working in circumstances other than maternity leave. These include suspension of an employee with at least four weeks' service on medical grounds under orders set out in Schedule 1 of the *Employment Protection (Consolidation) Act 1978* and under a provision of a Code of Practice issued under section 16 of the *Health and Safety at Work etc. Act 1974*, because their place of work has become a health hazard. This entitlement lasts for a maximum of 26 weeks.

Where an employee has been put on short time or been 'laid off' temporarily, there is a duty to pay that employee during suspension from work for all or part of the normal working hours, provided the contract has not been terminated. This duty arises from the provisions of section 88 of the *Employment Protection (Consolidation) Act 1978*. There are two exceptions to this duty, first if such a term was deliberately excluded from the contract and secondly where the failure to provide work is due to circumstances beyond the employer's control, for example, a secondary strike.

If the contract of employment does not provide for pay on workless days, there is a right to a statutory guaranteed payment. This is provided for in the *Employment Protection (Consolidation) Act 1978*, as amended by the *Employment Act 1980*, which states that any employee not provided with work is entitled to a maximum daily payment for no more than five days during any three-month period, provided the employee is not involved in a trade dispute, has not refused suitable alternative employment and has not taken any action to prevent their services being available to their employer.

In some circumstances an employee may have time off with pay during working hours. This applies to independent trade union officials who are entitled to time off to carry out their duties or undergo training relating to their duties and also to employees who have had notice of redundancy, who may have time off to look for new employment or make retraining arrangements, provided that employee has been continuously employed for 2 years for at least 16 hours a week.

If an employee is a member of certain public bodies, an employer must also allow a reasonable amount of time off work to enable such an employee to pursue those duties consequent on such membership and this covers such duties as a magistrate, local councillor, member of a statutory tribunal, health authority, educational governing body or a water authority. There does not appear to be any duty to pay an employee for time taken off in this manner.

DEDUCTIONS FROM WAGES

The actual manner in which employees are paid is also controlled by legislation which has established two basic principles, that wages must be paid in the current coin of the realm (but not necessarily in cash) and that payment to workers 'in kind' is illegal and invalid. Valid deductions may be made from wages for such things as rent, accommodation and tools. Legislation has also authorized deductions in relation to disciplinary fines, bad workmanship, damage to an employer's property and the use of materials. Provision for such deductions must be included in the contract of employment, and the amounts involved must be fair and reasonable. These matters are dealt with by the *Wages Act 1986*.

It is lawful for an employer to make a deduction from a worker's payment at the request of that worker for payment to a third party, provided such an arrangement forms part of the contract of employment. An example would be deductions made relating to membership of a works' sports and social club, dealt with by means of a form signed by every new employee and processed by the personnel department of the parent firm.

An employer must now deduct certain sums decreed by law from wages, including income tax, national insurance and attachment orders. Income tax is deducted under a pay-as-you-earn system, which means that the tax is based on earnings during the current year and is collected in instalments. Both employers and employees pay national insurance on a sliding scale, except where the employee earns less than a set gross weekly amount. Under the *Attachment of Earnings Act 1971* the courts have the power to issue attachment of earnings orders. These relate mainly to maintenance awards to wives or children, judgment debts and fines. Where such an order applies, the person owing the money has it deducted from their salary by the employer before the employee actually receives the money. The employer then sends the money to the 'collecting officer' of the relevant court. An employer must also inform the employee every time such a deduction is made and for which a 'handling charge' can be levied.

TRADE UNION MEMBERSHIP

Duties relating to trade union membership of employees are imposed on employers by the *Employment Protection (Consolidation) Act 1978*, amended by the *Employment Acts 1980, 1982, 1988* and *1989*. The Acts state that every employee has the right not to have any action taken against them by an employer to stop or deter them from joining a trade union or taking part in trade union activities, nor can they be compelled to join a trade union which is not 'independent' of the employer. The employee must first seek the agreement of the employer before engaging in union activities during working hours. Although an employer still has the right to dismiss an employee for participation in union activities, if an employer exercised this right that employer would almost certainly face an action for unfair dismissal. Any employee genuinely objecting on religious or 'conscience' grounds to joining a trade union cannot have any action taken against them by the employer to compel the employee to join a trade union. Where an employee feels that rights relating to trade union membership are being infringed, that employee can complain to a industrial tribunal which could order the employer to pay compensation to the employee.

The *Employment Act 1990* has further amended the *Employment Protection (Consolidation) Act 1978* to the effect that it is unlawful to refuse employment, or any service of an employment agency, on grounds related to union membership or non-membership.

An employee who belongs to an 'appropriate' trade union, that is, one recognized by the employer, must be allowed to take time off to partake in all union activities, except actual industrial action, where it is an activity of an appropriate trade union to which the employee belongs or an activity where the employee is acting as a representative of such a trade union. Only a 'reasonable' amount of time off may be permitted. Codes of Practice have been issued as guidance on this matter. Whereas an official of such a union is entitled to pay in respect of time off for such activities, this does not appear to apply to ordinary members of unions.

Officials of 'independent' trade unions are entitled to time off during working hours to carry out union duties related to industrial relations with employers or associated employers and their employees. Time off is also allowed for undergoing training relating to industrial relations relevant to an official's duties, or approved by the Trades Union Congress (TUC) or the union of which the employee is an official. Again the time taken off must be 'reasonable', in accordance with any Code of Practice issued on the subject, and must be with pay. Where an employee entitled to time off work is unreasonably refused this right, that employee may bring a claim before an industrial tribunal.

DISCRIMINATION

Acts of Parliament which relate to discrimination must be observed in the recruitment of staff and the framing of terms of employment. The *Race Relations Act 1976* deals with, among other things such as club membership, discrimination in employment. It is unlawful for an employer to discriminate against a potential employee on the grounds of race, colour, nationality, or ethnic or national origins, which the Act calls collectively 'racial grounds'. Discrimination may be unfavourable treatment of an applicant for a job, offering less favourable terms of employment than other persons might expect or simply refusing a person's application. Discrimination may also occur once a person is actually in employment, through lack of opportunities for promotion, transfer and training, refusal of benefits or facilities normally available to an employee, or unreasonable dismissal.

Any action taken concerning an employee for a genuine reason unconnected with racial grounds is not discrimination; for example, it is reasonable to refuse employment to a person who does not have the necessary qualifications, regardless of their colour or race. Exceptions are allowed if certain jobs require members of a particular race, for example Chinese waiters in Chinese restaurants.

A person claiming that they have been discriminated against may bring a case before a specially constituted industrial tribunal. Sometimes settlement of a complaint may be attempted by a conciliation officer appointed by the Arbitration and Conciliation Advisory Service (ACAS) before referring it to the tribunal.

Once a tribunal is satisfied a complaint is genuine, it can make an order declaring the rights of the parties, which may result in the employer having to make financial compensation to the employee concerned or take a particular course of action, for example reinstatement or the offer of a job.

Discrimination based on sex is also unlawful, following the *Sex Discrimination Acts 1975* and *1986*, and the *Employment Act 1989*. For the purposes of these Acts, discrimination is treating a person less favourably than persons of the opposite sex would be treated or making a job unnecessarily difficult for a person of the opposite sex. Discriminating against a married person because they are married is also unlawful. The rules relating to sex discrimination do not apply where the number of people employed by the employer does not exceed five. This may exempt many recreational clubs with a small staff, but not professional clubs where the players themselves are employees.

Where being a male or a female is a genuine 'occupational qualification' for a particular job an employer may insist on employing only a male or female applicant. This includes matters of privacy and decency, but not strength or stamina.

These provisions, therefore, make it unlawful to advertise for a male or female specifically and an employer in breach of this provision may be summonsed by the Equal Opportunities Commission and heavily fined, as may the newspaper publishing such an advertisement. It is, however, lawful for clubs to advertise for a 'steward with a wife to assist', for example. All applicants for a job should receive application forms and all applications should be treated equally. It is unlawful for an employer to discriminate against a woman in the arrangements made in determining who should be offered employment and this includes the type of questions asked at an interview.

These were two of the issues discussed in *Saunders v Richmond Borough Council* (1977)[1] which also involved more complicated issues such as the suitability of a woman as a golf professional. Miss Saunders had applied for a job with Richmond Borough Council as a golf professional. Due to an oversight following a morning interview Saunders was not invited to attend a second interview the same afternoon. She complained to an industrial tribunal that she had been discriminated against in the procedure used and in questions asked at the interview. The industrial tribunal dismissed her complaint as there was no evidence of discrimination. She appealed to the Employment Appeal Tribunal claiming that the only grounds on which the council failed to offer her an appointment were based on discrimination. The appeal was dismissed on the basis that the questions asked did not amount to discrimination; there was genuine confusion concerning the second interview for which she should have been called and, finally, although her qualifications were excellent, they were not so superior to those of the successful candidate to suggest the council were guilty of discrimination.

An appeal to an industrial tribunal by a female judo referee on the basis she had been discriminated against because she had been banned from refereeing international matches did, however, meet with success.[2] The ban had been imposed on the grounds she did not have the strength to separate two hefty male fighters, but the tribunal said that Mrs Petty, a fully qualified national referee and club coach, should be considered 'on her merit' for national men's contests. In June 1981 an Employment Appeal Tribunal rejected a claim by the British Judo Association that its policy of not allowing women to referee men's national competitions was lawful.

As illustrated above, a complaint under the *Sex Discrimination Act 1975* can be brought before an industrial tribunal with an appeal from their findings to the Employment Appeal Tribunal. Conciliation may first be attempted to solve the problem before it reaches a tribunal. Where a complaint is found to be genuine a tribunal may make a declaration of the parties' rights, which may be an order to make financial compensation or take a certain course of action, such as offering an employee a job or reinstating an employee.

MATERNITY RIGHTS

A female employee who is expecting a baby is entitled to maternity pay, provided she has been continuously employed for not less than 2 years by the 11th week before the expected confinement. This entitlement is for a period of up to 6 weeks beginning 11 weeks before the expected week of confinement and is not affected by whether or not there is an intention to return to work later. An employer must be informed that she will be absent from work because of pregnancy at least three weeks before the absence begins unless this is impracticable, in which case it must be as soon as reasonably practicable. The amount due under this provision is nine-tenths of a week's pay, less the social security maternity allowance. Under the *Social Security Act 1986* statutory maternity pay is payable through the employer who recoups it from national insurance contributions.

An employee expecting a baby is also entitled to time off with pay for antenatal care, on production of a certificate stating she is pregnant and an appointment card showing that the appointment has been made.

There is a right to return to work following confinement, provided the employee has been continuously in the same employment for two years and has informed her employer of her intention to return to work. This entitlement to return to the same employment and same status lasts for a period of 29 weeks, beginning with the week of confinement. The employee must notify her employer of her intention to return at least three weeks before her intended return. An employer can request written confirmation of an intention to return to work 7 weeks after the confinement and the right to return will be lost if the request is not answered within 14 days of receiving it or as soon as reasonably practicable.

The right to return to work has been excluded by the *Employment Act 1980* in two situations. First, where immediately before the maternity leave was taken the employer had no more than five employees and it is not reasonably practicable to reinstate her in her original job or to offer her suitable alternative employment. Secondly, where, regardless of the size of the firm, it is not reasonably practicable to reinstate her in her original job, for reasons other than redundancy and suitable alternative employment is offered and she either accepts or unreasonably refuses that offer. Where a job is lost through redundancy she is entitled to a suitable vacancy or, if no such vacancy exists, she may claim redundancy pay.

EQUAL PAY

Another legal requirement concerning the payment of wages is that defined in the *Equal Pay Act 1970*, which imposes duties on the employer for equality of pay between men and women where they are employed on work of 'the same or broadly similar nature'. This has, to some extent, been superseded, though not repealed by the *Sex Discrimination Act 1975* and ensures that where men and women are employed in 'like work' or work 'rated as equivalent', neither sex should be treated 'less favourably' than the other, unless the employer can show a 'material difference' in the work undertaken which justifies a variation in the wage rates. A provision in the Treaty of Rome, by which the UK became a member of the European Community, concerning equal pay for equal work, is also applicable. 'Pay' includes any benefit which the employer receives directly or indirectly in respect of their employment.

Any difference in pay between men and women employed on 'like' work must be due to a genuine material difference other than sex. Listed below are some examples of differences that have been accepted as genuine material differences:

1. greater length of service;
2. distinction in hourly pay of workers based in two different towns, for example, Nottingham and London;
3. different responsibilities, for example, handling more expensive products;
4. men doing 'heavy' work involving lifting and unloading while women do the 'lighter' work of sorting, packing and labelling;
5. extra pay for academic qualifications;
6. difference in hours that is not sex based. This would not be a genuine material difference where men and women doing the same job were working at different times of the day, in such a case if only the men worked at night they could be compensated by night-shift payment.

SAFETY AT WORK

An employer has always been under a common-law duty to provide a safe system of work, safe equipment and safe premises, and breach of that duty will give rise to a claim for compensation. This duty is illustrated by the case of *Mitchell v De Lima*[3] in 1990. Here, Mitchell, a young groom working at the stables of a polo player was seriously injured when she fell off a polo pony while leading two other ponies. Mitchell had not been provided with the correct headgear and the judge found De Lima, her employer, was negligent for not providing the correct headgear and therefore liable for the consequences of the accident.

Where one employee commits a tort against a fellow employee, the employer of both is vicariously liable to the injured party and more likely to be sued, as compensation payments would be more readily available from an employer than an employee! The employer can, however, sue the employee responsible for the damages that had to be paid.

In addition to a common-law duty, statutory duties have also been imposed by a variety of statutes, but this produced fragmented law with legislation concentrating only on particular industries. Although the law had made provision for claiming compensation for injuries suffered at work, it was felt that the law had not been achieving the main objective of securing health and safety for people at work and thus preventing accidents. To rectify this situation the *Health and Safety at Work etc. Act 1974* was passed.

The intention of the 1974 Act is to replace existing legislation with a system of regulations and codes of practice to maintain and improve existing standards of health and safety, applicable to all places of employment. New powers of control are contained in the Act which established the Health and Safety Executive, and transferred the functions of former factories inspectors to health and safety inspectors. The executive operates under the direction of the new Health and Safety Commission, which has the duty of achieving the general purposes of the Act, which are to ensure the health and safety of people at work.

Certain duties relating to particular people are defined in the Act. Employers must now safeguard, as far as is reasonably practicable, the health, safety and welfare of the people who work for them. This applies, in particular, to the provision and maintenance of safe plant and systems of work, and covers all machinery, equipment and appliances used. There is a statutory requirement for the employer of five or more people to prepare a written statement of the employer's general policy, organization and arrangements for health and safety at work, to keep it up to date, and to bring it to the notice of the employees.

It is also the duty of employers to provide any necessary information and training in safe practices, including information on legal requirements. Employers must consider the specific training needs of their organizations, with particular reference to any special hazards.

Self-employed persons also have a duty to avoid danger or risk to the health of other people, or to themselves. Designers, manufacturers, importers or suppliers of articles or substances for use at work must also ensure, as far as is reasonably practicable, that they are safe when used. This duty extends to anyone responsible for articles installed or erected for use at work. Where an article of substance is itself defective the manufacturer will be strictly liable, that is, no proof of fault is necessary, by virtue of the *Consumer Protection Act 1987*.

Employees have a duty under the *Health and Safety at Work etc. Act* to take reasonable care to avoid injury to themselves or to others by their work activities, and to co-operate with employers and others in meeting statutory requirements. The Act also requires employees not to interfere with or misuse anything that has been provided to protect their health, safety or welfare in compliance with the Act.

The Act established the Health and Safety Commission and the Health and Safety Executive, both to publicize the need for safety at work and to instigate prosecutions for breaches of the Act. They can also conduct inquiries into accidents that have occurred at places of employment. This covers accidents, not only to employees themselves, but also to visitors and would therefore include, for example, persons using sports centres and other recreational facilities. Enforcement of this legislation is primarily a matter for inspectorates set up under the Act, and controlled by the Health and Safety Executive. These inspectors have wide powers to enter factories, and examine records and people to check that the Act is being complied with. Inspectors are also authorized to conduct proceedings in the magistrates' courts.

If a health and safety inspector should discover a contravention of one of the provisions of the *Health and Safety at Work etc. Act 1974* or any of the earlier legislation that is still valid, the inspector can take one of several courses. An inspector can issue a prohibition notice if there is a risk of serious personal injury, to stop the activity giving rise to this risk, until remedial action specified in the notice has been taken. This notice can be served either on the person undertaking the activity or the person in control of it.

An alternative measure would be the issue of an improvement notice requiring that the contravention be remedied within a specified time. This notice will be served on the person deemed to be contravening the provision or on any person on whom responsibilities are placed, whether that person is an employer, an employee, or a supplier of equipment or materials.

Finally, a person contravening the Act or regulations made under it, may, instead of, or in addition to, the above measures, be prosecuted. Contravention of some of the requirements can lead to summary prosecution in a magistrates' court. Contravention of the main provisions of the Act could result in prosecution, either summarily or on indictment in the Crown Court.

There is a maximum fine, on summary conviction, for most offences, but there is no limit to the fine on conviction on indictment. Imprisonment for up to two years can also be imposed for certain offences. The court may also make an order requiring the cause of the offence to be remedied. Anyone failing to comply with a prohibition or improvement notice is liable to prosecution. An appeal against the service of such a notice lies to an industrial tribunal.

There are also powers in the Act to seize, render harmless or destroy any substance or article considered to be the cause of imminent danger or serious personal injury.

One particular effect of the 1974 Act is that it brings nearly all 'places of work' within the network of the *Fire Precautions Act 1971*, which means anyone employing staff has to comply with regulations concerning lighting, heating, means of escape and precautions in case of fire. Regulation and enforcement of these provisions is by inspectors, in conjunction with the local fire authority.

Certain employers must, under the *Employers' Liability (Compulsory Insurance) Act 1969*, take out an approved insurance policy to cover personal injury or disease suffered by any of their employees in the course of their employment. Failure to do this may incur penalties imposed by the Act, because the aim is to protect an employee who has a claim against their employer.

DUTIES OF AN EMPLOYEE

There is an implied term in a contract of employment that an employee will act honestly and in good faith. This includes working for the benefit of the employer and not for third parties by taking on part-time employment which harms the employer's business or using an employer's property in a manner against the interests of the employer.

A clause 'in restraint of trade' (page 16) may be written into a contract of employment which provides that an employee cannot enter into competition with their employer by restricting the area within which they may engage in the same sort of work on leaving the employee's present employment. Whether or not such a clause applies depends on its reasonableness, either geographically or in terms of the length of time for which the employee is restricted. Nor must an employee take with them to a new job any confidential information (other than their training), obtained from their previous employment, such as lists of customers and secret formulas.

Another implied duty arising from a contract of employment is that an employee will take reasonable care in performing their duties. Where there is a breach of this duty an employer may be entitled to dismiss the employee. Compensation can be claimed by an employer from an employee causing damage or injury in the course of their employment.

Obedience to an employer is implied, provided orders given are lawful and reasonable. However, a skilled person would be justified in refusing to do unskilled work. Any other refusal may result in dismissal.

Finally, an employee promises to work and, unless the contract provides otherwise, giving notice to strike is notice either to terminate or break the contract. Other activities, such as a work to rule, may amount to a breach, depending on the circumstances. An employee is not expected to cause disruption to the employer's business, in fact it is implied that an employee will promote the commercial interests of the employer.

DISMISSAL

Dramatic changes have occurred in the area of law relating to dismissal, the most significant being the introduction of the concept of 'unfair dismissal' in 1971.

By law an employee who is to be dismissed must be given notice of dismissal, the period of notice required depending on the terms of employment. Every employee who has been employed for at least 4 weeks for more than 16 hours a week is entitled to not less than 1 week's notice for each year of continuous employment, with a maximum of 12 weeks' notice after 12 years' continuous employment.

An employee, however, need only give one week's notice on wishing to end their employment, regardless of the length of time that employee has worked for that employer. These are minimum periods of notice and the parties are free to negotiate longer periods by which they will be bound. Each party can regard the contract of employment as at an end immediately if the behaviour of the other party warrants this, for example, where an employee is guilty of theft. This right is preserved in the *Employment Protection (Consolidation) Act 1978*. This Act also states that either party may waive the need to give notice and either party may accept payment instead of notice.

Merely giving the correct period of notice does not mean that the employer is free from further liability regarding the dismissal. The grounds for dismissal and method of dismissal must also be acceptable in law. The length of notice is one of several factors relating to dismissal. Only certain reasons for dismissal, according to the 1978 Act, will normally be regarded as 'fair'. It has become normal practice for an employer to bring the grounds for a dismissal within one of these reasons or the employer may be found to have dismissed the employee unfairly. Fair grounds for dismissal are discussed below.

Inability to carry out work

An employee was neither able nor qualified to do the work that person was employed to do. 'Ability' includes any assessment by reference to skill, aptitude, health or other physical or mental quality. 'Qualifications' means any degree, diploma or other academic, technical or professional qualification relevant to the position which the employee holds.

Dismissal of any employee for either of these reasons will be fair, provided the employer acts reasonably. That includes a full and proper inquiry into the reasons why the employee cannot do the job adequately and consideration of suitable alternative employment for the employee concerned.

It may be enough that the employer honestly believes, on reasonable grounds, that the employee is incapable or incompetent because an industrial tribunal may not be competent to decide such matters. In *Gray v Grimsby Town Football Club* (1979)[4] the Employment Appeal Tribunal accepted a football club manager's assessment of a player's capabilities in the first team as the industrial tribunal were hardly in a position to review his decision.

Misconduct of employee

Dismissal was justified by the conduct of the employee. Dismissals relating to misconduct may cover many different situations, but for simplicity they can be divided into three main areas: breach of the employer's reasonable orders; breach of the employer's reasonable rules; the commission of a criminal offence. In considering whether or not the conduct of any employee merits dismissal an industrial tribunal will consider matters such as the reasonableness and importance of the orders or rules concerned, and whether any warnings were given and the seriousness of any criminal offence, whether it was committed at work or outside work and the nature of the offence in relation to the employee's work.

Redundancy

A dismissal for redundancy occurs if it is wholly or mainly attributable to:

1. the cessation of business; or
2. the employer moving his place of business; or
3. surplus labour.

Where possible an employer should offer those employees affected by redundancy suitable alternative employment. Refusal of suitable alternative employment will not make the dismissal unfair. Where the employer recognizes an independent trade union that employer must consult with that union as soon as possible regarding such matters as method of selection.

Breach of legal duty

Continuing to employ the employee would have resulted in a breach of a legal duty or restriction either by the employer or the employee, for example, continuing to employ a disqualified driver where driving is essential for the job. In such a situation an employer would still be expected to act reasonably and this may include the transfer of a disqualified driver to a stationary job.

Some other substantial reason

This provision seems to have been included as a 'safety-net' to catch substantial reasons for dismissal which do not fall into the other four categories. Reasons that have been accepted as substantial include: the homosexuality of a man working with small boys; refusal to accept lower wages when all other employees have agreed a reduction; refusal to accept a variation in the terms of the contract of employment where it was necessary in the commercial interests of the company. Whatever the reason given the employer must also be shown to be acting reasonably, and to have made a full investigation of the problem and explored any possible alternatives.

Any reason for dismissal relating to trade union membership is 'inadmissible' according to the Act, although an amendment to the *Employment Protection (Consolidation) Act 1978* by the *Employment Act 1990* states that an employee cannot now complain of unfair dismissal if at the time of that dismissal, the employee was taking part in 'unofficial' industrial action.

Whether or not a dismissal is 'fair' will depend on the facts and circumstances of each case, but all employers should remember that they may be called on, if challenged by a past employee, to justify any dismissal.

In September 1981 a former football club physiotherapist was awarded £5681 compensation for unfair dismissal by an industrial tribunal. The physiotherapist had worked for Bristol City Football Club for three years prior to his dismissal by the manager on the grounds that a new back-up team was to be employed to start the new football season.

An employee who has been employed for 26 weeks, working at least 16 hours each week, may, on request within 14 days of the dismissal, obtain a written statement of reasons for dismissal, which should be received within 14 days of the request. These statements are admissible in any subsequent proceedings brought on the basis that the reasons given are either inadequate or untrue. Where such a statement is unreasonably refused, an action may be brought. Should the tribunal accept the complaint it may make its own declaration of the reasons for dismissal.

Unfair dismissal is not only a dismissal for inadequate reasons, but could also be dismissal by the wrong method. Various Codes of Practice have been issued by the government giving guidance concerning the correct method of dismissing an employee, although failure to comply with the current Code of Conduct does not automatically imply there has been an unfair dismissal.

The last Code of Conduct (in the Code of Practice on Disciplinary Practice and Procedures in Employment of June 1977) included the following broad recommendations.

1. All employees should be given a copy of the employer's rules relating to disciplinary procedures.
2. Any employee against whom a complaint is made should be informed and given an opportunity to state their case. Such an employee should be told there is a right to be accompanied by a trade union representative or a fellow employee.
3. No disciplinary actions should be taken until each case has been fully investigated.
4. Immediate superiors to an employee should not have the power of dismissal without consulting a more senior authority.
5. No employee should be dismissed for a first offence, unless it amounts to 'gross misconduct'.
6. Where any employee is subjected to a penalty, it should be explained what that penalty is and why it has been enforced.
7. There should be a right of appeal following specified procedures available to all employees.
8. Where disciplinary action other than instant dismissal is necessary, then supervisors should give a formal oral warning for minor offences and a written warning for more serious offences.
9. A senior union official must be consulted before disciplinary action beyond an oral warning is taken against a union official.
10. The fact that an employee has committed a criminal offence outside their employment is not an automatic reason for dismissal.

An employee claiming unfair dismissal may bring an action before an industrial tribunal. A successful action usually results in an award of financial compensation based on the period of employment, age, weekly wage before dismissal, expenses incurred as a result of dismissal, loss of any benefits and any contribution on the employee's part to the dismissal. Where an employee contributes to their own dismissal any award made may be reduced. This was so in the case of Gareth Roberts, a former Welsh rugby international, who was compensated for unfair dismissal by his employer, a pharmacist, for taking time off to train and play in a charity match. The award was reduced because Roberts had contributed to his own dismissal.

The tribunal may also, within its powers, order the 'reinstatement' or 're-engagement' of an employee. 'Reinstatement' means an employee returns to their old employment as though they had never been dismissed, and will be paid arrears of salary and benefit. 'Re-engagement' is the return of an employee to their former employment on terms decided by the tribunal. In either case the tribunal will consider the wishes of the employee regarding their return and whether or not an employer can, in practice, comply with such an order. Where an employer fails to comply with either of these orders that employer will be severely punished, although it would appear an employer can avoid taking an employee back by payment of sufficient compensation.

The expiry of a fixed-term contract with no offer of renewal can amount to an unfair dismissal unless, where the contract is for one or more years, the parties to the contract agree to exclude the unfair dismissal rights of the employee.

In 1977 Bishen Bedi, the cricketer, an employee with star international status of Northamptonshire County Cricket Club, was 'dismissed' when his contract was not renewed following deterioration in his bowling over two seasons. In an action for unfair dismissal the tribunal concerned decided that the grounds for his dismissal, the deterioration of his bowling, were reasonable. No warning was given to Bedi in this case and as a general rule failure to follow a fair procedure, whether by giving warnings or allowing an employee an opportunity to be heard, will result in the ensuing dismissal being adjudged unfair. However, in this case the tribunal was satisfied that a warning was not relevant here and that Northamptonshire had acted fairly in dismissing him. Where dismissal concerns loss of ability at a high level rather than misconduct or lack of effort or indiscipline it would seem no warnings are necessary.

REDUNDANCY

Redundancy is another way an employee may lose his job. The *Redundancy Payments Act 1965* introduced a system for payment of compensation for people made redundant. Redundancy occurs when the number of jobs in a place of employment are reduced to save money or change working systems.

An employee is not redundant if someone else replaces that employee to carry out substantially the same work. Genuine redundancy occurs when an employer no longer needs anyone to carry out the work of the employee concerned. This employee will then have a right to redundancy pay.

Provisions for redundancy pay were incorporated in the *Employment Protection (Consolidation) Act 1978*. These provisions only apply to persons who have been in 'continuous' employment for more than 2 years, working at least 16 hours a week, and being over the age of 18, and under the age of 65 (men) or 60 (women). They do not apply where the employee is the husband or wife of the employer.

An employee is not 'redundant' if, when that employee's current work is no longer necessary, the employee is offered suitable alternative employment but refuses it. 'Suitable' means employment very close to the work agreed in the contract of employment and not a 'step down'. Any new employment offered must start within four weeks of termination of the original job.

In doubtful cases concerning redundancy an industrial tribunal will decide the issue. Once it has been determined that an employee is redundant, that employee is entitled to redundancy pay based on the term of employment, the employee's age and weekly wage at the time of redundancy. Initially the employer will pay the whole amount and the employee must be given a written statement explaining how the sum was calculated. Standard forms obtainable from local employment offices may be used. The employer may then claim back 41% of this sum from the redundancy payments funds through health and social security departments. A proportion of national insurance contributions paid by an employer on behalf of the employee goes into this fund. Redundancy payments can also be made directly from this fund, where an employer cannot or will not pay the employee. When this happens legal action may be taken against the employer concerned.

Where an employer recognizes an independent trade union as representative of persons the employer is considering making redundant, that employer should first consult representatives of that union. This should be done in writing, including the reasons for redundancy, the number of workers affected, who they are and the method used to select them.

Entitlement to redundancy payment also arises at the end of a fixed-term contract of more than two years' duration, unless the employee has waived this right in writing before the expiry of the contract.

REFERENCES

Normally an employee on leaving one job will look for suitable alternative employment. Prospective employers will require some form of recommendation or 'reference' before employing someone, and it is usual for an employee to request a reference on leaving a job, whatever the reason for leaving. Where an employee has not been satisfactory a difficult situation could arise, as an employer owes an employee a legal duty to say nothing condemning about them, and yet the employer also owes a legal duty to prospective employers to be honest about the employee. Usually there is no legal obligation to provide a reference, although where an employer is not so obliged agreement may be made to provide a reference as a term of the contract. However, this may be unwise, bearing in mind the legal duties that arise from such an obligation.

First, there is a duty owed to a prospective employer to be honest about the abilities of an employee. Where a flattering reference is relied on by a future employer who suffers loss in consequence, that employer may sue the employer who gave the reference for damages, that is compensation, for the loss incurred. Blame can only be attached to a former employer if the employer knew the employee did not possess the qualities described in the reference, for example an employee was known to be a thief, yet was described as 'honest'.

A duty is also owed to the employee to say nothing about them which may be false or damaging, that is 'defamatory' at law (page 34). Refusal of new employment due to a damaging reference renders the employer concerned liable for an action in damages by an employee claiming that loss has been suffered because of it. However, no action can be brought if the statements are true.

Fulfilling both these duties could create a problem, but the law solves this by providing that, if an employer honestly believed what was written or said was true, there was reasonable cause for this belief and the employer was not acting maliciously, the defence of 'qualified privilege' may be claimed (page 35). Any suggestion of malice or carelessness in making the statement concerned will lose the right to claim this defence.

All references should therefore be worded very carefully and anything said or written should arise from an honest belief on reasonable grounds.

TAXATION AND NATIONAL INSURANCE IN PROFESSIONAL SPORT

The vast majority of true 'employees' in the field of sport and leisure present no problems so far as taxation and national insurance are concerned, since they are classed as 'employees' and dealt with in accordance with the normal rules. Alternatively, those who are fully self-employed can be dealt with under appropriate regulations and procedures. But in specific situations, there have been problems.

First, the income of a professional sportsperson is sometimes derived not only from their employer, but also from the public when benefits or testimonials are held for the sportsperson. This places the professional sportsperson in a unique position regarding the payment of income tax. In the case of *Seymour v Reed* (1927)[5] the House of Lords decided that a professional cricketer was not liable to pay income tax on the gate money from a benefit match held for him as it was a gift, not a profit or prerequisite arising from his employment, nor was it provided for in the contract of employment.

Conversely, in *Moorhouse v Dooland* (1955),[6] the contract of employment of a professional cricketer stated that he would be entitled to certain collections made on his behalf. In this case the Crown claimed successfully that these payments were taxable, as he was entitled to them by virtue of his employment, as illustrated by their inclusion in the contract of employment.

More recently the House of Lords in *Shilton v Wilmshurst* (1991)[7] decided a payment by Nottingham Forest Football Club to its international goalkeeper Peter Shilton to induce him to transfer to Southampton was taxable as an emolument for services to be performed under Shilton's contract of employment with Southampton Football Club.

Evasion of tax is treated severely by the Inland Revenue who will prosecute offenders such as the jockey, Lester Piggott, who was successfully prosecuted and imprisoned in 1987. The football manager, Lou Macari, nearly suffered a similar fate when in 1992 he was found not guilty of being involved in a tax fiddle to attract footballers to his club. This fiddle involved the payment of substantial sums of cash to players without the knowledge of the Football League to avoid taxation. The former chairman of the club and the club's accountant were found guilty for their part in the scheme and, although they claimed that such practices were common throughout the UK, the judge decided it was time someone was made an example of to ensure it did not happen again.

Secondly, there are potential problems when a professional sportsperson is rendered unfit for work by a sporting injury and seeks state benefit under the national insurance system. Social Security Tribunals, with an appeal to the Social Security Commissioners, exist for employed wage earners who have suffered 'personal injury … by accident arising out of and in the course of his employed earner's employment', to claim compensation for that injury, this right being entirely separate from any entitlement to sick pay. This is a provision of the *Social Security Act 1975*, as amended by the *Social Security Act 1980*.

Anyone claiming compensation for injuries incurred as a result of taking part in recreational activities at work must therefore show that engaging in that particular activity was part of their employment. A fine distinction has been drawn between recreational activities recognized as a 'duty' of an employee, and those merely 'encouraged' by an employer or higher authority. The former category has included male nurses involved in recreational activities as part of the treatment of patients in a mental hospital within the hospital grounds; an employee obliged to attend physical training classes as part of an obligatory course; and firefighters, obliged to keep themselves fit, who are injured during recreational activities in recreational periods at work or activities organized between fire brigades. Generally, employees taking part in representative matches cannot be said to be doing so in the course of their employment, but purely for their own recreation, even though this may be 'encouraged' by an employer to the extent of allowing employees to play during a duty period. Nor can employees enjoying recreational activities during a lunch break be said to be in the course of their employment.

The expansion of recreational activities and the increase in the number of persons employed by organizers of recreation, as well as the increase in the number of professional sportspersons, has meant that employment law has become increasingly important to recreation.

NOTES

1. [1977] IRLR 362
2. *British Judo Association v Petty* [1981] ICR 660
3. *The Times*, 5 July 1990
4. [1979] ICR 364
5. [1927] AC 554
6. [1955] 1 Ch 284
7. [1991] 3 All ER 148

The provision and control of recreational facilities through the operation of the law

8

The law not only affects recreation by controlling participants and organizers, but may also directly affect the provision of facilities. This may occur through powers vested in the government and by the establishment of government agencies and statutory bodies responsible for the provision of or to control the use of facilities.

Powers in relation to the provision of facilities of recreation have been conferred on all tiers of government from central government departments to local authorities, that is district and county councils and parish councils.

CENTRAL GOVERNMENT POWERS

In central government departments recreation is often a by-product of a primary function such as education, and the department concerned with the primary function will decide where that function is located and which Secretary of State or Minister is responsible. Under the present departmental structure outdoor recreation and water naturally fall within the Department of the Environment; the Forestry Commission and fisheries fall within the Department of Agriculture, Fisheries and Food; while schools and colleges are inseparable from the Department of Education and Science.

Ministerial powers were conferred on the Minister of Education in the *Physical Training and Recreation Act 1937* to make grants towards the expenses of local voluntary organizations in providing or in aiding the provision of facilities for physical training and recreation, including the provision and equipment of gymnasiums, playing fields, swimming baths, bathing places, holiday camps and camping sites, and other buildings and premises for physical training and recreation, and for the training and supply of teachers and leaders by such organizations. The Minister can also make grants to the funds of any national voluntary organization providing facilities for physical training and recreation. A 'voluntary organization' is any non-profit-making person or body of persons.

In 1964 a Minister for Sport was established in the Department of the Environment. The responsibilities of this Minister included exercising, on behalf of the Secretary of State, responsibility for the co-ordination of policies and the promotion of research into the field of active recreation. The diversity of this office was illustrated by the intervention of the Minister for Sport in a dispute between rival bodies to preserve sponsorship in the motor-racing world in 1980. This arrangement involved no change in the functions and departmental responsibilities of other ministers, for example, the Secretary of State for the Environment continued to exercise many functions in relation to the countryside, national parks and areas of outstanding natural beauty.

In 1992 the Ministry of National Heritage was established to embrace sport, the arts, broadcasting and heritage. This department is the responsibility of the Secretary of State for National Heritage and includes a Minister for Heritage with responsibility for sport. At the same time English Heritage, a government quango which provides a major source of public funds for the preservation of historic buildings and monuments, was introduced.

The early 1990s has also seen central government becoming more involved in the funding of recreational activities. In 1991 the three major pools companies which make up the Pools Promoters Association were asked to contribute £40 million a year to provide funding for sport and the arts. In return the government was to further reduce the pools betting duty. This money was used to establish the Foundation for Sports and the Arts, and around two-thirds of the foundation's revenue is to be used for the benefit of 'athletic sports or athletic games'. The remaining one-third will be used to benefit the arts. The foundation handed out its first cheques in September 1991. The Scottish Rugby Union gained the lion's share of the grants awarded by the foundation when they were given £2 million to help with the estimated £37 million cost of converting Murrayfield to an all-seat stadium by 1994. At the other end of the scale £50 was given to a Shinboko karate club in Blyth to help with the purchase of mats. This foundation was set up in addition to the £19 million a year that the major pools firms were already paying to the Football Trust set up to improve stadium facilities. Pools betting duty was reduced in 1991 on condition this benefit was passed to the trust.

Central government has also revived its plans to introduce a national lottery, despite opposition from pools promoters, clubs that run their own lotteries and the Jockey Club because of the possible threat to their incomes. In December 1991 an attempt was made to introduce a state lottery for sport, the arts and heritage schemes through a Private Member's Bill, but the bill failed at its first reading when the government announced it would not vote for it at its second reading in January 1992. Increasing pressure subsequently led to the government reviewing its plans for a lottery. A contributing factor was that European legislation may soon permit the selling of lottery tickets from other countries which is illegal within the UK at the moment. It was felt the UK should have its own lottery rather than supporting those of other countries. An operating national lottery has been promised for April 1994, following the introduction in Parliament of the National Lottery Bill in December 1992. This lottery is to be under the auspices of the Department of National Heritage and the operation of the lottery will be handled by a private sector firm, probably a consortium of firms with experience of similar ventures such as football pools. The distribution of the money will be handled by a separate body, independent of the government but answerable to Parliament. The UK will be the last European country to introduce a lottery. Proceeds of the lottery (after tax it seems) are to be split equally five ways between charities, arts, sports, national heritage and the Millennium Fund. This latter will support local and national restoration schemes of buildings and the countryside, looking towards the year 2000. It will also organize an international trade fair in one of Britain's cities to celebrate the millennium and support Manchester's bid to hold the Olympic Games in 2000. The new Sports Commission (page 158) will be given some of the sports money along with the national sports councils.

POWERS OF LOCAL AUTHORITIES

General powers

As a result of local government reorganization in 1974, the functions conferred on local planning authorities by the *National Parks and Access to the Countryside Act 1949* and the *Countryside Act 1968* are now exercisable in accordance with the provisions of the *Local Government Act 1972*, amended by the *Local Government Planning and Land Act 1980*. These functions are exercisable either by the county planning authority or in certain circumstances by both the county planning and district planning authority. These Acts concern the provision of recreational facilities in the countryside. Under these Acts, local planning authorities have powers to provide facilities in national parks (page 168) and country parks (page 171), and may acquire land compulsorily for these purposes. These powers extend to facilitating the use by the public of any waterway in these areas, provided nothing is done which affects waterways in which any other person has an interest. The *Wildlife and Countryside Act 1981* extended the powers of local authorities in relation to conservation of the countryside.

Local planning authorities also have powers under the Acts mentioned above to plant trees to preserve and enhance the natural beauty of the land, and to carry out such work as appears necessary to enable land to be brought into use or improve its appearance. To preserve order, prevent damage and avoid undue interference with facilities under the aforementioned Acts, local authorities also have the power to make by-laws and are under a general duty to do anything necessary to preserve and enhance the natural beauty of their area.

County planning authorities have powers under the *National Parks and Access to the Countryside Act 1949*, the *Countryside Act 1968* and the *Local Government Act 1972*, to appoint wardens to enforce by-laws, advise and assist the public, and perform such duties in relation to facilities provided by the authority in a manner determined by the authority. A county council may also make traffic regulation orders concerning roads in, or forming part of, or adjacent to, or contiguous with, facilities provided by the authority, an area where the Countryside Commission (page 160) is conducting a project or scheme, or land held by the National Trust (page 159) for the purpose of conserving or enhancing the natural beauty of the area, or improving the enjoyment of the area by the public. These powers are embodied in the *Road Traffic Regulation Act 1967* and the *Transport Act 1968*.

Financial assistance in relation to the powers of local authorities outlined above, may be given in the form of supplementary grants made by the Secretary of State for the Environment. To qualify for a grant for the reclamation and improvement of land under the *Local Government Act 1966* the land concerned must be derelict, neglected or unsightly and requiring reclamation or improvement.

Local authorities also have powers in relation to nature conservation, as they can establish nature reserves under powers conferred by the *National Parks and Access to the Countryside Act 1949*, and the *Local Government Act 1972*, on any land in their area not already held or managed by the Nature Conservancy Council (now English Nature). Local authorities have powers to acquire land and make by-laws in relation to such nature reserves. In *Evans v Godber* (1974)[1] a local authority successfully enforced a by-law that forbade mooring in a nature reserve which they managed.

Therefore local authorities have many and varied powers in relation to recreation and a few more of these will be mentioned briefly to conclude this section. The *Rights of Way Act 1990* introduced the toughest measures yet to force farmers and landowners to identify and keep open rights of way, and gave local authorities powers to ensure public footpaths and bridleways on farmland were kept clear. They can grant planning permission to anyone wishing to build recreational facilities and also, in some cases for a particular activity to take place, for example, if land is to be used for clay-pigeon shooting on more than 14 days a year planning permission must be applied for. Such permission may also impose conditions, as was the case when permission was granted to race at Donnington Park. These conditions were challenged unsuccessfully in court. However, a successful challenge to a local authority decision was made when Leicester City Council banned Leicester Rugby Club from using a council-owned ground because it had not stopped three of its stars from playing for England in South Africa.[2]

Powers concerning access to the countryside

The objects of the *National Parks and Access to the Countryside Act 1949* and the *Countryside Act 1968* are to enable the public to have certain rights of access to open country for open-air recreation. These may be achieved by making an agreement called an access agreement with any person having an interest in the land, making an order known as an access order in respect of the land, or by the compulsory acquisition of the land by the local authority concerned or the Secretary of State for the Environment. These powers are subject to an overriding duty to conserve the natural beauty of the countryside, to protect local agriculture, forestry and social interests, and to avoid pollution.

Access agreements may, in some cases, be made only after prior consultation with the Countryside Commission or a water authority where the land is adjacent to a river or canal coming within its jurisdiction. An access agreement may either be irrevocable, or subject to provisions for revocation or variation, and may provide for payment to be made in relation to the agreement. An access order should not be made unless it is impracticable to make an access agreement. A local planning authority, the authority empowered to make an access order, must submit the access order to the Secretary of State for the Environment and it does not become effective until confirmed by him.

An access order or agreement may contain all the expedient provisions for securing sufficient means of access to the land by the public. This may be effected by the improvement or repair of the existing means of access, constructing a new access or imposing restrictions concerning any interference with the present means of access. Access orders must contain a map prescribing the land comprised in the order. Any access order may be varied or revoked by a subsequent order made in the same manner. Rights of access are not available over land used or about to be used for the growing of timber if it would prejudice that use.

Where works are necessary concerning access the local planning authority may reach an agreement with the owner/occupier of the land concerning these works. If no agreement can be reached the local planning authority may take steps to ensure the work is carried out. A person whose land is affected by an access agreement or order must not carry out any work which would result in the area of land to which the public have access being substantially reduced. Should the value of land be reduced because it has become subject to an access order the local authority may pay compensation to the owner.

Certain areas are 'excepted' from access orders and agreements; these include land covered by buildings, agricultural land other than rough pasture, land managed as a nature reserve and land currently being, or about to be, developed for purposes which would exempt it.

Every local planning authority having land within its area, subject to an access order or agreement, must prepare and keep up to date a map showing the access area, and make these maps available for public inspection. A local authority may also, if it thinks fit, display notices at places where the public obtain access to any land to which a right-of-access map relates, specifying any restrictions on rights of access to the land or any part of that land.

The Wildlife and Countryside Act 1981 was introduced with the general aim of conserving the countryside. This Act gives local planning authorities the power to make management agreements with anyone having an interest in land which allows them to manage that land during a specified term or for an unlimited period.

Powers in relation to public open spaces, parks and recreation grounds

Local authorities also have many statutory powers in relation to public open spaces, parks and recreation grounds. A public open space is any open space on which building is prohibited or restricted, and over which the public has rights and access to for purposes of recreation. A local authority may be authorized by the Secretary of State for the Environment to acquire compulsorily any land in its area in connection with development and other planning purposes, including use as an open space under the *Acquisition of Land (Authorisation Procedure) Act 1946* and the *Town and Country Planning Act 1971*, as amended by the *Local Government Planning and Land Act 1980*. The appropriation of any land forming part of a common, open space or allotments is subject to the approval of the Secretary of State. Local authorities have powers to provide allotments through the *Smallholdings and Allotments Act 1908*.

Parish and community councils may, subject to obtaining the necessary consent, provide and maintain seats and shelters for the use of the public on any land abutting on any road within the parish or community. They may also appropriate a limited part of certain open spaces and recreation grounds under its control, for the purpose of providing public parking spaces for bicycles and motor cycles. These powers are found in the *Parish Councils Act 1957*, the *Local Government Act 1972* and the *Road Traffic Regulation Act 1967*.

Open spaces include village greens, the essential characteristic of which was that inhabitants of a particular locality had an immemorial customary right to use it for exercise and recreation, including the playing of lawful games as defined in the *Commons Registration Act 1965*. The term village green now covers any land which has been allotted by or under any Act for the exercise of recreation by the inhabitants of any locality or on which the inhabitants of any locality have had a customary right to indulge in lawful sports and pastimes for not less than 20 years.

Open spaces may be created under the *Open Spaces Act 1906* which gives local authorities the power to acquire and maintain open spaces, to make by-laws and to pay compensation in relation to the exercise of these powers. Any two or more local authorities may jointly carry out the provisions of the Act. County councils may purchase or take on a lease, lay out, plant, improve and maintain land for the purpose of being used as public walks or pleasure grounds, and they may support, or contribute to the support of public walks or pleasure grounds provided by any person.

Public walks and pleasure grounds

Local authorities are also empowered to provide public walks or pleasure grounds under the *Public Health Act 1925*. These powers extend to county, district, parish or community councils, London borough councils and the Common Council of the City of London. These authorities may purchase, or take on lease, and may maintain, improve or support, or contribute to the support of, public walks or pleasure grounds, and may make by-laws for the regulation of such grounds. Successful enforcement of such by-laws occurred in *Burnley Borough Council v England* (1978)[3] where a local authority was granted an injunction to prevent people exercising their dogs on a pleasure ground in defiance of a by-law.

A local authority may not itself use its public walks or pleasure grounds, or allow them to be used, for any purpose inconsistent with public recreation, although pleasure grounds that are suitable for use as a country park may be converted to this use through powers conferred by the *Countryside Act 1968*.

Any piece of land bought, but not required immediately, by a local authority may be used temporarily as a public pleasure ground, but it must not be diverted permanently from the purpose for which it was originally acquired.

A local authority has no general power to charge admission to, or to close, any public walk or pleasure ground, but limited powers of closure and charging for admission may be obtained, for example, if the ground is enclosed, with entry only through a gate, then closure at night may be provided for by by-laws.

Provision of facilities for recreation

Under the *Local Government (Miscellaneous Provisions) Act 1976*, local authorities may provide in their areas such recreational facilities as they think fit. Included in these provisions are the powers to provide indoor facilities for games and swimming, and facilities for boating, water-skiing and fishing. These powers also extend to the provision of premises for the use of clubs or societies having athletic, social or recreational objects. This includes the provision of buildings, equipment, supplies and assistance of any kind. The authority concerned may make charges for the provision of facilities.

A local authority may also, under powers contained in the *Public Health Acts Amendment Act 1907*, the *Public Health Act 1961*, the *London Government Act 1963* and the *Local Government Act 1972*, set aside part of a park for the purposes of games and exclude the public from any part so set aside while it is in actual use for such purposes. It may also permit the exclusive use of that part by a club or other body of persons. Any such area must not be more than one-third of the total area of the park, or of any pavilion or building provided by the authority.

Local authorities have powers, under the *Public Health Act 1961* and the *Local Government Act 1972*, to provide a boating pool in any park or pleasure ground provided by them or under their management or control, where there is a lake or other water in that park. In addition, they may provide pleasure boats or may license persons to let boats for hire and may make by-laws regulating the control of any such boats on any waters other than those managed by the British Waterways Board.

There is also a general power conferred, mainly in the *Public Health Acts*, on local authorities to provide, in any public park or pleasure ground established or managed by them, apparatus for games and recreation, chairs or seats, reading rooms, pavilions or other buildings and conveniences, and refreshment rooms. Where such facilities are provided, charges may be made for their use. Authorities may also employ officers to ensure observance of regulations in their parks and pleasure grounds.

All parks, gardens, recreation grounds, open spaces and other land for the time being vested in or under the control of the Secretary of State for the Environment or the Minister of Agriculture, Fisheries and Food are subject to powers conferred by the *Parks Regulations Acts 1872-1974*. 'Parks', in this context, includes royal parks over which the Secretary of State and Minister of Agriculture, Fisheries and Food have supervisory functions.

As well as conferring powers on local authorities relating to the provision of facilities in country parks (page 149), the *Countryside Act 1968* also gives local planning authorities and district councils powers concerning the provision of camping and picnic sites. These authorities have power to provide, in the countryside within their areas, camping sites for holiday and recreational purposes, to be used primarily as places for setting up tents, and picnic sites for motorists and others using the roads. Sites of this nature may have space for parking vehicles, and a means of access to and from the road. A local authority may acquire compulsorily any land required by it to carry out these functions and may make by-laws controlling the use of these sites. Reasonable charges may be made for the use of any camping site, picnic site or parking place.

The *National Parks and Access to the Countryside Act 1949*, the *Countryside Act 1968* and the *Local Government Act 1972* also conferred special powers over common land on local authorities to be exercised in the interests of persons resorting to the land for open-air recreation. This includes the compulsory acquisition of land in the neighbourhood of common land to secure its use for open-air recreation. A local authority has power to do anything appearing to it desirable for the purposes of providing or improving opportunities for public enjoyment of the countryside and in the interests of persons resorting to the common land. In particular, it may provide facilities and services for the enjoyment and convenience of the public, erect buildings, carry out works and make by-laws in respect of that land.

Powers of local education authorities

Local education authorities also have duties in relation to the provision of recreational facilities. The *Education Act 1944* states that the duty to provide education includes a duty to provide adequate facilities for recreation, and social and physical training. For this purpose, with the approval of the Secretary of State for Education and Science, a local education authority may establish, maintain and manage, or assist in the establishment, maintenance and management of camps, holiday classes, playing fields, play centres and other places. Other places includes playgrounds, gymnasiums and swimming baths not appropriated to any school or college at which facilities for recreation and for physical training are available for persons receiving primary, secondary or further education, and may organize games, expeditions and other activities for such persons.

In making arrangements for the provision of such facilities, or the organization of such activities, a local education authority must have regard to the expediency of co-operating with any voluntary societies or bodies whose objects include the provision of facilities or the organization of activities of a similar character.

Additional to their powers relating to the provision of facilities, local education authorities may, under the *Local Government (Miscellaneous Provisions) Act 1976*, contribute towards the cost of facilities provided by voluntary organizations. They also have powers relating to the making of grants for the acquisition of land for public open space, under the *Local Government Act 1966*.

Effective use of the powers of local authorities

Legally, therefore, local authorities are able to provide a multitude of facilities themselves or offer financial assistance for their provision by other bodies. However, availability of finance, not the law, has curtailed their activities in this area. In fact, a survey in 1991 suggests that local authorities, including local education authorities, are actually selling off existing playing fields in order to realize some capital assets to find money for capital programmes. Despite the Environment Department advising against such sales and the development of a co-ordinated policy against these sales by the Playing Fields Association and the Central Council for Physical Recreation, the councils themselves feel they have no alternatives available to them.

One method of encouraging provision of facilities is the granting of rate relief, a power available to local authorities. Rate relief is available in relation to the facilities of non-profit-making organizations and could be used to encourage the provision of facilities which relieves the pressure on local authorities to provide facilities. This may also induce organizations to open their facilities to the public. Unfortunately, not all local authorities are prepared to grant such relief.

In an effort to make local authorities use their powers and facilities as economically as possible the *Local Government Act 1988* introduced competitive tenders into the provision of local government services. Leisure was not included until 1990 when it was formally incorporated into the Act. Local authorities are now required to submit their leisure management and catering functions to tender. Although many authorities were already operating some form of tender, especially catering, the Act now requires tendering on a much larger scale. The principle of tendering is that the operation of the service is undertaken by the person who wins the tender by offering the best bid (which could, of course, be the authority itself). Ownership is unchanged.

The Act will therefore ensure that the public sector takes a more commercial attitude to leisure management and will seek to maximize income wherever possible. The tenders may be for a total service, such as a leisure centre or swimming pool or for a part service, for example catering within a leisure centre. Local authorities are now required by law to advertise for competent persons to tender for their leisure management operations. Recreational facilities in schools and colleges are exempt and councils will still be able to control admission fees and opening hours if they wish.

Local authorities must advertise for and find competent persons interested in tendering for their leisure management operations. At the time the advertisement appears copies of the specification stating how the leisure facilities are to be managed must be freely available for purchase or to be read at the local authority office.

There are basically five stages in the tendering procedure:

1. the intention to let a leisure management contract is advertised and interested persons invited to contact the local authority;
2. the local authority assesses the relative abilities of those applying;
3. a short list of competent contractors is compiled;
4. those on the short list are invited to tender for the contract, that is, to outline how they would manage the facility and what it would cost;
5. on receipt of tenders the local authority decides which is the best bid (not necessarily the lowest) and awards the contract.

The local authority prepares all the documents concerning the tendering procedure and the subsequent contract.

GOVERNMENT AGENCIES AND STATUTORY BODIES CONCERNED WITH RECREATION

Various government agencies and statutory bodies concerned with the promotion of recreation include bodies established by Royal Charter, which is a Charter granted by the Crown, setting out the aims and powers of the organization concerned. In this manner the Nature Conservancy Council was originally established in 1949, although it has since become a statutory body through the *Nature Conservancy Council Act 1973* and subsequently became English Nature. The Sports Council has also been granted a Royal Charter. In 1972 the Sports Council, originally established as an advisory and consultative body in 1965, was granted executive functions by the Charter, with a government Minister as an independent chairman.

Sports Council

The objects of the Sports Council, set out in the Charter, are to foster the knowledge and practice of sport and recreation among the public at large, and to assist in the provision of facilities. Powers granted to the Sports Council include the provision of facilities, carrying out research, co-operating with foreign and international bodies, making grants and loans, advising and co-operating with government departments, local authorities, governing bodies of sport, and other relevant bodies and acting as trustee of any charitable bodies whose objects are the same as those of the Sports Council.

Functions of regional sports councils established by the Sports Council were revised and extended in 1972, so that they became responsible for the development of sport in their regions. They also advise the Sports Council on matters relating to grant aid for both major schemes to local authorities and other public bodies, and for minor schemes of an exceptional character. Regional sports councils are supported nationally by the Technical Unit for Sport, the Information Centre and the Press and Publicity Council.

When, in 1991, the Amateur Boxing Association (ABA) were apparently not using their grant from the Sports Council to follow an agreed four-year development plan the Sports Council withheld payment of grant aid until satisfied the money was not going to be used to settle debts incurred from an industrial tribunal award of £16 000 to a sacked former executive. The ABA administration and spending plans were subsequently reviewed by the Sports Council who provide the largest single contribution, more than £130 000 a year, to the ABA.

In a government sports policy statement launched in December 1991, 'Sport and Active Recreation', it was announced that in order to improve the present structure of sports administration the Sports Council of Great Britain had agreed to surrender its Royal Charter so that two successor bodies could be established, a UK Sports Commission and a Sports Council for England. The main functions of the Sports Council for England will, in common with other home country sports councils, be the promotion of participation and the development of sports foundation skills, and the promotion of higher standards of performance and excellence. It will also contribute to performance and excellence programmes throughout the UK in accordance with work commissioned by the Sports Commission to foster and support the provision of sports facilities, to promote active recreation and to provide grant aid to implement these objectives.

Sports Commission

The main functions of this body will include long-term planning in relation to the interests of the UK as a whole, co-ordination of efforts to promote participation, the development and co-ordination of initiatives to promote higher standards of performance and excellence in sport at UK level, collaboration with foreign and international bodies to further UK sport and active recreation interests abroad, and the administration of grants or loans to implement these objectives.

Central Council for Physical Recreation

In 1972 the Sports Council took over the staff and assets of the Central Council for Physical Recreation (CCPR), a body established in 1935 by organizers and teachers of physical education, which was re-established as the representative body of sport and physical recreation with the status of consultative body to the Sports Council. The CCPR is the collective voice of the governing bodies of sport and recreation, the forum for debating and the springboard for action, and is divided into six sections which have regular meetings. The CCPR is an effective lobby for the promotion of sport and recreation, and has organized action in Parliament, industry and local authorities.

A Sports Arbitration Panel was set up by the CCPR in 1992 to provide sport with an arbitration service for final resolution of disputes relating to, for example, disciplinary rules and procedures. This independent panel comprises an equal number of lawyers with expertise on sports matters and non-lawyers experienced in sports administration. Reference to this panel to solve disputes concerning the contracts of employment of sportspersons can be included as a term of these contracts in accordance with the *Arbitration Act 1950*.

National Playing Fields Association

Another organization with a Royal Charter is the National Playing Fields Association. This association is a registered charity which has, for over 50 years, been concerned with the provision of playing fields, playgrounds and recreation space where they are most needed, and for those whose needs are greatest. Over the years it has pioneered many new ideas, both in the general technical sphere, and in various aspects of play and recreation for children and young people, including the handicapped. The activities of the association are supported by a technical advisory service, a special department for the promotion of play and recreation for children and youth, grant and low interest aid, a wide range of technical books and drawings, and a comprehensive information centre. In 1986 Rochford in Essex made history when it gave recreational land to the association to protect it from developers.

Unfortunately, not all local authorities are so aware of the recreational needs of their communities and many local authorities are selling off playing fields to developers as they are seen as being surplus to requirements. Local authorities are, of course, free and able to give themselves planning permission. The National Playing Fields Association and the Central Council for Physical Recreation have developed a co-ordinated policy against such sales to protect playgrounds and playing fields on the grounds that 'sales should be considered in the context of educational and community need now and for the future, as opposed to the purely educational use of the day'. One problem is that no one knows how much land has been sold already, but the government is to create a register of playing field land. Councils regard as surplus any land over minimum levels required by law.

Provision of recreational facilities is also the duty of statutory bodies established specifically for that purpose or having such powers conferred on them in conjunction with their main purpose, for example the water authorities, whose primary function is the supply of water. These bodies are established by Act of Parliament, which defines their powers and duties. Such powers and duties may be extended or limited by later Acts of Parliament. Such bodies generally operate in conjunction with the relevant government departments and have been given the general label of quangos (quasiautonomous non-governmental organizations). The increasing importance of these bodies to recreation has been recognized by successive governments through the creation of new ones or the extension of the powers of existing bodies to include recreational functions.

National Trust

One of the first of these bodies was the National Trust, established by the *National Trust Act 1907*, from which it derives its powers and authority, which were extended by Acts of the same name in 1937, 1939, 1953 and 1971. The purposes of the National Trust are to promote the preservation of buildings of national interest and places of national interest or beauty, and to provide access to and the enjoyment of such buildings and places by the public. In *Re Verrall* (1916)[4] the purposes of the National Trust were found to be charitable.

In 1990 the National Trust adopted a members' resolution to ban deer hunting on their land although it was subject to consideration by the ruling council who do not have to accept resolutions passed by the members. A working party considered the effect of such a ban and reported in early 1993 to the effect that culling deer was a necessity. The ruling council therefore decided not to accept the resolution to ban deer hunting. Disquiet had been voiced on the basis that such a ban would be outside the remit of the National Trust as set out in the *National Trust Acts*, because it is ultimately responsible to the nation, not to its paying membership. During 1991 there were attempts to widen the ban to all forms of hunting and shooting for sport, which could have created problems where landowners had given property on the understanding that hunting would continue. However, in 1991 a resolution was passed giving the ruling council of the National Trust the power not to debate the issue again for five years. Although this introduced a fundamental change in National Trust procedures it was intended to stop groups using it for their own purposes and creating an arena for sectional interests. The resolution gives the council an option, not an obligation, to stop discussion of any issue if it has been debated within the last five years.

In November 1991 the Quorn hunt was banned from hunting over National Trust land in Derbyshire and Leicestershire after admitting to the breaking of rules governing the treatment of foxes intended to prevent cruelty. This is the first time the Trust has revoked a hunting licence and the licence was not renewed until the person responsible had been suitably punished. These licences are issued by the Trust to all hunts that wish to use its land and are renewed annually.

English Nature

English Nature developed from the Nature Conservancy Council. The Nature Conservancy Council, originally established by Royal Charter in 1949, was eventually established, after existing for a short period as the Natural Environmental Research Council, as a statutory body by the *Nature Conservancy Council Act 1973*. The Nature Conservancy Council establishes, maintains and manages national nature reserves, advises generally on nature conservation, advises the government on nature conservation policies and on how policies may affect nature conservation, and finally supports, commissions and undertakes relevant research. In 1991 English Nature became the successor to the Nature Conservancy Council and will work alongside conservancy councils for Scotland, Wales and Northern Ireland on the Joint Nature Conservation Committee.

Countryside Commission

Another body established for recreational purposes is the Countryside Commission. Originally set up as the National Parks Commission by the *National Parks and Access to the Countryside Act 1949*, it was renamed, and its powers and functions redefined, by the *Countryside Act 1968*. The Countryside Commission is responsible for the conservation and enhancement of the natural beauty and amenity of the countryside as a whole, for encouraging the provision and improvement of facilities for the enjoyment of the countryside and to encourage open-air recreation in the countryside.

The exercise of the functions and responsibilities of the commission inevitably impinges on a number of central and local government responsibilities in certain fields, including planning, forestry, agriculture, tourism, sport, water-based recreation and nature conservation. Where the commission is involved in these areas, its aims are to develop liaison arrangements with the organizations concerned, in order to promote understanding and to co-ordinate action, and to concentrate on work directly relating to the particular responsibilities of the Commission for the protection and management of the countryside and its use for recreation.

One duty of the Countryside Commission is to review continually the provision of facilities for the enjoyment of the countryside, the conservation and enhancement of natural beauty, and the need for public access to the countryside. Persuading other public authorities to take action rather than to act itself, is the policy of the commission, but it does have the power to provide technical assistance, to carry out experimental projects and to make grants and loans to non-public bodies, including the National Trust, for approved schemes.

The Countryside Commission was given powers in the *Local Government Act 1974* to make grants for country parks, picnic sites and other countryside facilities. The commission also advises ministers and local planning authorities about the effect of proposed development likely to be prejudicial to the natural beauty or amenity of the countryside. Provision of interpretive services for the public is also within the powers of the commission. The duties of the Countryside Commission were extended by the *Wildlife and Countryside Act 1981*.

When a new chairperson was appointed in 1991 he stated his belief that the future of England's landscape depended on building a bond of confidence between landowners, farmers and other country users, and that priorities should be better access to the countryside, management agreements with farmers and the creation of very long walks. The new chairperson was also intending to introduce a new countryside stewardship scheme whereby farmers in particular areas would be offered about £50 an acre to retain or manage specific elements of their land. Some farmers would be offered money simply to create picnic areas, particularly where their land ran alongside rights of way.

The Countryside Commission is also proposing new legislation that would permit walking over all open countryside, but with restrictions on access in wilder areas where farming may be banned. The commission is also calling for a new Countryside Act to reconcile the conflicting pressures of tourism, development and conservation. Pressure for less intensive agriculture offers an opportunity to pay farmers a modest amount to manage the country with conservation as a priority. The commission is currently committed to creating 12 new long walks, 12 community forests and a national forest in the Midlands.

Countryside Recreation Research Advisory Group

The Countryside Commission services the Countryside Recreation Research Advisory Group (CRRAG), a group established in 1968 to ensure that the powers of the various government agencies undertaking research into aspects of countryside recreation are used as effectively as possible. CRRAG keeps in touch with other official and semi-official organizations concerned with countryside recreation. Aims of this organization include harmonizing the research efforts of member agencies, promoting countryside recreation research and providing information for public and private agencies on countryside recreation research studies and techniques.

Forestry Commission

Forestry management and water management are two areas which have been extended to include recreational functions. Forestry management is the concern of the Forestry Commission which operates as the managers of the national forest authority. As managers they are charged primarily with the production of timber and secondly they are responsible for allowing reasonable access to the forests, the provision of recreational facilities there, wildlife management in the woodlands and for paying due regard to the beauty of the countryside in its afforestation activities. The primary activities of the Forestry Commission, originally established by the *Forestry Act 1919*, are now governed by the *Forestry Act 1967*. Recreational functions were added to the duties of the commission by the *Countryside Act 1968*. A Ministerial statement in 1974 declared that 'the Forestry Commission ... will give still further emphasis to providing recreational facilities'. The Forestry Commission initiated the concept of national forest parks, now referred to as forest parks. There are currently seven of these, which are generally of a relative wilderness character. In 1970 a headquarters branch, responsible solely for conservation and recreation, was set up and this did much to implement the recreation policy of the Forestry Commission.

In 1992 the Forestry Commission was divided into the Forestry Enterprise, responsible for managing the nation's woodland estate, and the Forestry Authority, to advise the government on policy. The Forestry Authority and the Forestry Enterprise will still be answerable to the Forestry Commission whose future plans include planting national forests in the Midlands and establishing community forests around conurbations.

The National Rivers Authority

Facilities for water-based recreation are provided by a number of bodies responsible for the provision of the water supply in England and Wales. The main responsibility for providing a water supply is that of the water authorities, who were first charged with a duty to preserve amenity and rights of access by the *Water Resources Act 1963*.

In 1974 the management of water resources was reorganized as a result of the *Water Act 1973*. This Act conferred a duty on the Secretary of State for the Environment, the Secretary of State for Wales and the Minister of Agriculture, Fisheries and Food to promote jointly a national policy for water in England

and Wales. This policy was to relate to, among other matters, the use of inland waters for recreation, the enhancement and preservation of amenity in connection with inland water and the use of inland water for navigation.

As a result of the *Water Act 1973* 10 regional water authorities were created, nine for England and one for Wales. These authorities were charged with a general duty concerning the promotion of recreation, and the enhancement and preservation of amenity. This duty was extended by the *Wildlife and Countryside Act 1981*.

New legislation in 1989, the *Water Act 1989*, has had a profound effect upon the law and administration of the water management in England and Wales. The Act introduced a division of responsibility whereby new, privatized water companies, responsible for the same areas as the original 10 water authorities, undertook the 'utility' functions of water supply and sewerage services. The 'regulatory' functions relating to the protection of the aquatic environment were entrusted to a new public body, the National Rivers Authority.

The range of functions with which the authority is entrusted include control of pollution; water resources; flood defences; salmon and freshwater fisheries; navigation, conservancy and harbour functions; along with various supplementary provisions and powers in relation to land and works. These particular functions arc to be exercised subject to broadly worded general environmental and recreational duties. A balance must therefore be drawn between the execution of the authority's specific functions and adherence to its general environmental and recreational duties. This general environmental duty requires the authority to exercise its powers, as far as possible in relation to its other functions, so as to further the conservation and enhancement of natural beauty and the conservation of flora, fauna and geological or physiographical features of special interest; to have regard to the desirability of protecting and conserving buildings, sites and objects of archaeological, architectural or historic interest; and to take account of any effect which proposals would have on the beauty or amenity of any rural or urban area or on any flora, fauna, features, buildings, sites or objects. A general recreational duty requires the authority to have regard to the desirability of preserving public freedom of access to areas of woodland, mountain, moor, heath, down, cliff or foreshore and other places of natural beauty; to maintain public facilities for visiting or inspecting any building, site or object of archaeological, architectural or historic interest; and to take account of public freedom of access or the availability of facilities of this kind.

The broad wording of the general environmental and recreational duties leaves a lot of scope for deciding the way in which these obligations of the authority should be applied in relation to particular projects or proposals. Some of the detail in this respect is filled in by means of the power of the Minister of Agriculture, Fisheries and Food or the Secretary of State to approve a code of practice giving practical guidance as to desirable practices in relation to conservation and recreation. The Ministers have issued the Code of Practice on

Conservation, Access and Recreation providing more detailed guidance as to what is entailed in respect of consultation, integrated land use and management plans, training and research, and publicity.

Failure to comply with any provision of this code will not incur any criminal or civil liability, but the Ministers are bound to take into account any contravention in determining how to exercise their powers under the *Water Act 1989*. Therefore it is possible that any serious failure to comply with the code would prompt the Ministers to exercise their power to give general or specific directions to the Authority with which the Authority must comply.

British Waterways Board; Inland Waterways Amenity Advisory Council

The British Waterways Board was established by the *Transport Act 1962* and given responsibility for the 2000 miles of canals and river navigations it controls in the *Transport Act 1968*. This Act also designated 340 miles as commercial waterways, principally for the carriage of freight, but recreation was not banned from these waterways. There were 1100 miles designated as cruising waterways and the remainder, about 600 miles were to be maintained only to the standards of health and safety, but local authorities were given powers to make funds available for their restoration for amenity use.

The *Transport Act 1968* also established the Inland Waterways Amenity Advisory Council to plan and bring about recreational use and development on the board's waterways involving the board, local authorities and private enterprise, and to advise the public on such matters as the setting up of boating stations and the landscaping of water-side frontages and fisheries. The council is also responsible for craft licensing and recreational research, as well as the running of two hire-cruiser fleets.

British Tourist Authority

Finally, mention should be made of the British Tourist Authority, established by the *Development of Tourism Act 1969* which also established the English Tourist Board, the Welsh Tourist Board and the Scottish Tourist Board. Although the tourist boards are mainly concerned with the provision of facilities for tourists, this may result in the provision of a wider range of facilities for the local population. Co-ordination is important regionally in relation to plans for developing and improving recreational facilities, and the national tourist boards work closely with local authorities, both directly and through regional tourist boards, in continually reviewing and encouraging provision of recreational facilities.

ENCOURAGING RECREATION THROUGH LEGISLATION

Although legislation exists in England and Wales conferring powers to provide recreational facilities or make grants available to assist their provision, there is no enforceable duty to do so. Nor is there any legislation positively encouraging participation in recreation or providing for assistance to be given to participants. Other countries have introduced much more positive legislation, several countries having legislated to provide subsidies for amateur sports persons.

Legislation of a similar nature would, it seems, be welcomed by governing bodies of recreational activities in England and Wales, both to encourage amateur participation in recreation generally and to assist the training of talented performers. Such legislation has become even more necessary following dramatic cutbacks in local authority spending on recreation and the current trend of selling off playing fields.

NOTES

1. [1974] 3 All ER 341
2. *Wheeler and Others v Leicester City Council* [1985] 2 All ER 1106
3. (1978) 76 LGR 393
4. [1916] 1 Ch 100

<table>
<tr><td>

Outdoor recreational facilities available through the operation of the law

</td><td>

9

</td></tr>
</table>

RECREATION IN THE COUNTRYSIDE

There is no right of access as such to the countryside, because most land is in private ownership, therefore access must be through some formal arrangement recognized by the law, which means it must be created by legislation or established at common law. In the countryside the majority of recreational facilities were originally provided by owners of country estates and the National Trust (page 159), who have opened country houses and their adjoining land to the public. Members of the public were also richly endowed with rights of access to commons, fells and footpaths, and many landowners and farmers allow access over their land. Comparatively recently local authorities have become increasingly important as providers of facilities through powers granted to them by various Acts of Parliament, mentioned earlier.

Apart from statutory provisions, members of the public have no general right to wander at will in the countryside or to resort to particular sites. In *Attorney-General v Antrobus* (1905)[1] it was decided that a right to resort to particular sites was unknown to English law. The site in question was Stonehenge and the plaintiff argued that the public had acquired a right to resort to this ancient monument and that this right could not be interfered with by the owner of the land. However, the court decided that such a right was incapable of being acquired, either by long use or any other method at common law. Inhabitants of a particular locality may, however, acquire such a right through establishing a custom. *Fitch v Rawlings* (1795)[2] decided that the inhabitants of Steeple Bumpstead in Essex were entitled by ancient custom to play cricket on private land in the village. In *Re Ellenborough Park* (1956)[3] it was held that the right to use a private pleasure ground was an easement recognized by law.

Should a person wish to give land to the public to be used for recreation purposes, the gift was liable to be held invalid by the courts, unless the gift was charitable. According to *Re Haddon* (1932)[4] this means that the main object of the gift must be the health and welfare of the working classes, through the provision of healthy recreation mainly in the open air, and in particular by providing playing fields, parks and gymnasiums. Such provision of the means for public recreation could amount to a charitable object.

However, as early as 1859, Parliament passed the *Recreation Grounds Act* which enabled land to be conveyed to trustees to be used as playgrounds and places of public resort. Should a local authority acquire land to be used as a public park under any of the powers available to it, it cannot use it later for some other purpose. This was decided in *Attorney-General v Sunderland Corporation* (1876)[5] where the corporation had acquired land under the public health legislation (page 153) to use for a recreation ground and later decided to build on it. The court held that they were entitled to build a museum, library and conservatory, as these buildings were ancillary to the use of land as a park, but they were forbidden to build council offices and a school there. However, in *Attorney-General v Poole Corporation* (1936)[6] the corporation was allowed to build a caretaker's cottage in a park.

Facilities provided by local authorities also include those contained in the *National Parks and Access to the Countryside Act 1949*, which provided for the designation of extensive areas of the countryside as national parks and areas of outstanding natural beauty, the establishment of nature reserves, the making of access orders and agreements, and the carrying out of a survey of public paths, including powers to create, divert or close public paths.

National parks

National parks are intended to preserve and enhance the natural beauty of an area and promote enjoyment of that area by the public. It must be an area affording opportunities for open-air recreation and situated within a reasonable distance of populated areas. Local planning authorities were made responsible for seeing that these objects were carried out. This was to be achieved by strict control over development, ensuring that the national parks were not exclusively for the enjoyment of the public and allowing the life of the area to continue without hindrance, having regard to the needs of agriculture and forestry. Essentially, a national park is an area subject to special controls in which amenity considerations are predominant, but not exclusive to everything else.

Due to the *Local Government Act 1972*, from 1974 national parks became the responsibility of new National Park Committees or, in the case of the Lake District, a new special or joint planning board. It became the duty of county councils to establish a new National Park Committee for each national park. Where a park covered two or more counties, a multi-county park, the committee was to be established by one of the councils by agreement or, in the absence of such agreement, jointly by the councils concerned. In all cases, with the approval of the Secretary of State for the Environment following consultation with the Countryside Commission, the new park authority could be given responsibilities in respect of land outside the area of the national park.

Following a report produced by the National Parks Review Panel, which was set up by the Countryside Commission, it was decided in 1991 that all national parks should be free from local authority control. At that time only the Peak District and the Lake District, the first to be set up in 1951, were independent. It is likely that the parks will have direct access to funding from central government and county councils which will guarantee their independence. The new independent committees that run the parks will consist of one-third of members from district councils, one-third from county councils and one-third nominated by the Environment Secretary to ensure that people who live and work in the parks will be fully represented.

The members of staff of the National Park Committees are headed by a national park officer. It is the responsibility of these authorities to conserve and enhance the natural beauty and amenity of the parks, and to promote their enjoyment by the public. Special supplementary block grants are paid in accordance with the provisions of the *Local Government Act 1974* towards the total costs of administering the parks for the national benefit. National parks are not publicly owned and designation does not confer on the public a right of access. Much of the land in national parks, for example the farm land, is in private ownership. Rights of access in national parks are the same as in other parts of the countryside and any additional access facilities have to be specially negotiated by agreements with the owner or, failing agreement, by an access order.

By 1992 there were 11 national parks. Proposals to make the New Forest a national park were abandoned and instead a new statutory body to co-ordinate the interests of a wider New Forest area has been proposed because it has been accepted that the area requires special protection through its international importance, equal in status with national parks and the Broads. The new body would have overall responsibility for 'conserving and enhancing' the area, maintaining present grazing and management regimes, and promoting quiet enjoyment and understanding of the area by the public. Currently the New Forest comes under the responsibility of a number of organizations which include Hampshire and Wiltshire county councils, three district councils, the Verderers (the body responsible for the management of grazing and commoning), the Forestry Commission and English Nature which has responsibility for the substantial areas of the forest which are designated as sites of special scientific interest (SSSIs). There is also the New Forest Committee, a non-statutory body, which, at present, has a co-ordinating role. The intention is to apply a planning regime to the proposed 'designated area' akin to that operating in the national parks. Major development will not be allowed, save in exceptional circumstances, and rigorous environmental assessments will be applied.

The functions of this new body will include employing staff and entering into agency agreements. It will work through the existing organizations rather than replace their functions. It will also prepare a New Forest Plan in order to establish and advertise its strategic plan. Local planning authorities will, however, continue to be responsible for the preparation of statutory development plans for the area. The government is proposing that the new body will have a membership of 17, comprising 8 local authority representatives, 5 representing organizations involved and their ministerial appointees.

Extended government grants are available through the 1949 Act to encourage local authorities to use the powers contained in that Act and the *Town and Country Planning Act 1971* to achieve its purposes.

Areas of outstanding natural beauty

Many areas of outstanding natural beauty are not suitable for designation as national parks, possibly because they are too small or too remote. Such areas may be designated as areas of outstanding natural beauty under the *National Parks and Access to the Countryside Act 1949*. Local planning authorities can do anything that appears necessary to preserve and enhance the natural beauty of such areas, and special grants are available, but there is no power to provide facilities for the public. Responsibility for designation of such areas lies with the Countryside Commission (page 160). These areas tend to be smaller and perhaps less spectacular, though hardly less beautiful, than national parks. There are no special statutory administrative arrangements for these areas, but planning authorities are encouraged to protect them through appropriate policies for planning or controlling development. The Countryside Commission supports them by advice and grants.

Nature reserves

The *National Parks and Access to the Countryside Act 1949* also enlarged the powers originally given to local planning authorities in the *Town and Country Planning Act 1947* to define sites for nature reserves in the development plan. Normally the establishment of a nature reserve would be undertaken by the Nature Conservancy Council (now English Nature), who may either enter into agreements with the landowners or compulsorily purchase the land. The council has established and manages over 100 national nature reserves in Great Britain, many of which have interpretative facilities for the public, although their primary purpose is to safeguard wildlife and physical features. Local authorities have the power to establish, in consultation with English Nature, local nature reserves, of which there are over 80 in Great Britain. There are also approximately 39 county nature conservation trusts in England and Wales, which are registered as charities, and some independent companies limited by guarantee that own or manage nature reserves.

Access orders and agreements

Both the *National Parks and Access to the Countryside Act 1949* and the *Countryside Act 1968* provide that all local authorities ought to consider what action they should take to secure a public right of access to the countryside, for example, by purchase and access agreements or orders (page 170). Under the Acts, access agreements or orders can only be secured over land defined as 'open country' in the Acts. 'Open country' is defined in the 1949 Act as any area consisting 'wholly or predominantly of mountain, moor, heath, down, cliff or foreshore (including bank, barrier, dune, beach, flat or other land adjacent to the foreshore)'. This definition was extended in the 1968 Act to include woodlands, rivers, canals and lakes. When a local authority has opened a particular area of land for access, any members of the public may enter it for open-air recreation and, provided they comply with certain conditions, they may not be treated as trespassers. Where there is a public access to water, the right extends to the bank and areas for picnic and boating facilities, as well as to reasonable access from the highway.

Country parks

In 1968 the *National Parks and Access to the Countryside Act 1949* was extended by the *Countryside Act;* this provided for the establishment of country parks which would be the responsibility of local authorities.

A country park established under the 1968 Act is very different from the national parks introduced in the 1949 Act. Country parks are suitable or adaptable sites made into parks or pleasure grounds by the local authority for the purpose of providing or improving opportunities for the enjoyment of the countryside by the public. Once a site has been selected for a country park the local authority has powers under the Act to purchase the land, prepare the site and provide facilities. Country parks provide not only access to the countryside, but also car parks and public lavatories, and sometimes refreshment facilities. A number of parks also offer facilities for sailing or riding, nature reserves and footpaths or forest trails, as local authorities are empowered to provide facilities and services for open-air recreation. The Countryside Commission provides grant assistance to approved schemes for the acquisition and laying out of the land, these grants being available to private bodies as well as local authorities. Similar grants are available for the provision of picnic sites, camping sites and other outdoor facilities.

Country parks are administered by local authorities or other bodies who have agreed to act as administrators in their respective areas. Local authorities may make by-laws for the preservation of order, prevention of damage to the land or anything on it and for securing that persons resorting to it will so behave themselves as to avoid undue interference with the enjoyment of land by others. These powers are exercisable on land belonging to the local authority or on such terms as may be agreed with the owners on other land.

There is a general duty in the *Countryside Act 1968* that all authorities, when exercising their powers, should do so with regard to the amenity and natural beauty of the countryside, although there is no provision for the enforcement of this duty.

Unfortunately, the availability of government finance is essential to the provision of such facilities, and may be the governing factor concerning the number and extent of parks and other amenities that are provided within these statutory powers. Although the powers exist for the provision of a wide range of recreational facilities by local authorities, there are no means of ensuring these powers are actually used.

Forest parks

Forest parks, which are established by the Forestry Commission (page 162), offer a wider range of recreational facilities than do other forest areas. The Forestry Commission is not the only owner of forests and woodlands in the UK; substantial areas are controlled by the National Trust (page 159) and English Nature (page 160). Access is also available to some of the privately-owned forests on payment of an annual subscription.

Regional parks

Regional parks are a comparatively recent development in the provision of leisure facilities. The first regional park in Britain, the Lee Valley Regional Park, was established by a private Act of Parliament in 1967, the *Lee Valley Regional Park Act 1967,* and is administered by an independent statutory authority. The Colne Valley Park, a similar project, is administered by a standing conference and working party, whose members are drawn from the local authorities within whose boundaries the park lies.

The Lee Valley Regional Park introduced an entirely new concept in recreation. It is a unique collection of recreational facilities stretching along the valley of the River Lee, between Ware in Hertfordshire and Bromley-by-Bow in London's East End. Already many different facilities have been provided to meet the recreational needs of London, Essex and Hertfordshire. These facilities include two sports centres, three boatyards, a riding school, a custom-built cycle circuit, a dairy and arable farm open to the public, and a lido. Altogether nearly 3000 acres of formerly derelict land and water were reclaimed and opened to the public, with the possibility of this area being extended as additional facilities are created.

Sites of special scientific interest and heritage coasts

'Natural' recreational facilities include SSSIs and heritage coasts. Areas which are of special significance for their flora, fauna or geology can be designated as

SSSIs by English Nature (formerly the Nature Conservancy Council). In due course some of these sites may become national nature reserves. Special protection was afforded to these sites by the *Wildlife and Countryside Act 1981*. Heritage Coasts are a relatively new concept, proposed to the government by the Countryside Commission in an attempt to resolve the conflicts concerning the use of the coastline between those interested in conservation and those interested in the provision of facilities for more active recreation, for example, beach huts. The government endorsed the suggestion of the commission which is now taking action to identify the finest lengths of unspoilt coastline.

In 1991 the first grant system specifically for encouraging landowners to look after SSSIs was introduced under the auspices of English Nature. Under the Wildlife Enhancement Scheme landowners in two pilot areas will be paid a specified sum per acre to manage their designated sites in agreed ways. This scheme represents an attempt to stop those who own SSSIs from viewing the designation as a burden. Owners and occupiers will agree management plans with English Nature and keep records.

Wildlife parks and zoos

Finally, mention should be made of wildlife parks and zoos. Zoological gardens have long played an important part in the provision of recreational facilities, and they have become more important with the establishment of the 'safari' parks and similar facilities. Some of these are owned and run by private individuals or private companies, and others by zoological societies or local authorities.

Commons

Members of the public also have certain rights of access to common land recognized by common law. The history and law relating to commons is very complex. Some commons can claim to have survived since before the advent of William the Conqueror in 1066. Commons were mainly areas of grazing or farm land over which groups of people, such as the inhabitants of a particular locality, had certain rights. The *Law of Property Act 1925* gave members of the public a right of access for air and exercise to all metropolitan commons, to all commons situated partly or wholly in a borough or urban district and to any other common originally designated for that purpose by the lord of the manor.

Public paths: footpaths and bridleways

A mixture of legislation and common law governs rights concerning footpaths and bridleways. There are some 103 000 miles of paths in England and Wales over which every citizen has a legal right to pass. Historically, these were routes habitually used by local country people. Many such paths have become overgrown, neglected or even obstructed. The manner in which these footpaths evolved represented a compromise between the competing claims of private landowners and public walkers in relation to the use of land, and they remain subject to the same competing claims. Footpaths may be very inconvenient to a farmer when they cross the farmer's land and may cause real problems when land is being ploughed. The elimination of a footpath may represent an extra acre under crop production. Neglect may force footpaths to fall into disuse, although many people would use them if they were free from obstruction. Enshrined as they are in the law of the land and history, footpaths and bridleways have acquired a new and enhanced importance as a facility for country recreation.

The law, in very general terms, puts an obligation on owners of land, over which a right of way passes, not to obstruct that right of way with obstacles or cultivation and makes it a duty of the local highway authority to maintain rights of way. Should a landowner obstruct a path, the local authority can clear away the obstruction and charge the landowner for the work. However, where paths have fallen generally into disuse, both these obligations have been widely neglected, not due to a deliberate disregard of the law, but mainly due to lethargy over the expenditure of money, time and effort by the farmers and councils on the upkeep of rights of way for which there has apparently been little demand. However, where there is a demand local authorities should enforce a law often ignored with impunity.

Legislation has attempted to clarify the law relating to footpaths and bridleways, particularly relating to their use for recreation purposes. The *National Parks and Access to the Countryside Act 1949* required local authorities to survey, with a view to preparation of definitive maps, all footpaths and bridleways in their area. This requirement was modified by the *Wildlife and Countryside Act 1981*. These definitive maps are designed to provide conclusive evidence of the existence of a footpath or bridleway, and of its position or width, and of any limitations or conditions affecting the public right of way over it at the relevant date shown on the map. In *Suffolk County Council v Mason* (1978)[7] the plaintiff successfully prevented the defendants from using a lane for vehicular access as the lane was shown on a definitive map as a footpath with a right of way on foot only.

There are provisions in the *National Parks and Access to the Countryside Act 1949* concerning rights of way which apply to the whole of England and Wales, and not only to areas such as national parks designated under the Act. Local authorities have the power to make agreements with landowners for the creation of new public paths and, if necessary, to make compulsory orders in order to create such paths. Powers to make diversions and close existing paths, and to replace them with new paths, have also been conferred on local authorities. Where a path is no longer needed a local authority may make an extinguishment order, without having to provide an alternative path. These powers are now exercised in accordance with the *Wildlife and Countryside Act 1981*.

The *National Parks and Access to the Countryside Act 1949* also set up the machinery for establishing long-distance footpaths. Responsibility for planning these paths lies with the Countryside Commission which submits proposals to the Secretary of State for the Environment. Local authorities negotiate with landowners the agreements necessary to open those parts of the proposed footpath which are not already rights of way. These routes, which are usually over 70 miles long, establish continuous rights of way along which the public may make long journeys on foot or, where the route is a bridleway, on horseback or bicycle. Negotiations of agreements to join those sections of a long-distance path, that are already rights of way, fall to the local authorities, but the Countryside Commission helps and advises as problems arise; it also meets the costs involved and continually reviews this network of footpaths.

The *Countryside Act 1968* was intended to clarify and afford greater precision to the previously uncertain position of the law relating to footpaths and bridleways, for example, in relation to the signposting of footpaths, and liability regarding the maintenance of gates and stiles. The 1968 Act places an obligation on highway authorities to signpost or mark footpaths and bridleways wherever they leave a metalled road, subject to the agreement of the local parish council or chairperson of the parish meeting that signs were not necessary. The Act makes landowners responsible for maintaining stiles and gates across footpaths and bridleways, but requires the highway authorities to contribute 25% of the cost, with powers to make further contributions of an amount they consider reasonable.

New provisions regarding the ploughing up of public footpaths were also contained in the 1968 Act, additional to those provided in the *Highways Act 1959*, recently replaced by the *Highways Act 1980*, as amended by the *Wildlife and Countryside Act 1981*. A farmer wishing to plough across the line of a public footpath or bridleway must give at least seven days' notice to the highway authority and reinstate the path within two weeks of starting ploughing. Where a farmer is prevented from doing so by exceptional weather the path must be reinstated as soon as reasonably practicable. The *Highways Act 1980* was amended and strengthened in 1990 by the *Rights of Way Act* which introduced offences relating to the disturbance and blocking of rights of way unlawfully and increased the powers of local highway authorities to ensure rights of way were kept open.

In 1991 the Ramblers' Association set up a legal department to bring legal action against farmers who persistently block public footpaths and bridleways, and any other offending landowners. The association is also planning to take legal action against county councils who do not use their statutory powers to force persistent offenders to repair paths and bridges. The Ramblers' Association also suggested in February 1993 that landowners and walkers should try and meet halfway by walkers accepting a statutory code of behaviour, warden services and suspensions of access in return for a legal presumption against trespass. Although landowners have welcomed this conciliatory approach they are still likely to campaign for voluntary agreements as opposed to the statutory rights the Rambers' Association wants.

Footpaths and bridleways, as well as metalled roads, are defined as 'highways'. A highway is a way over which all members of the public have a right of passage. This right does not extend to activities such as standing still on a highway and flapping an umbrella to interfere with grouse shooting,[8] or timing racehorses with a stop watch,[9] although it is permissible to rest on a highway for a reasonable period.[10] Pursuers of recreation are entitled to use highways in the same way as other members of the public, for passing and repassing. Organizing any recreational activity on a highway, such as motor racing or cycling is illegal, unless proper authority has been obtained.

The mode of passage depends on the type of highway. A public footpath is a highway over which the public can go on foot only. Bridleways are highways over which passage can be by foot, horseback or leading a horse. Cycling is not permitted on a footpath, but a bicycle, though not a motor vehicle, may now be ridden on a bridleway, provided the cyclist gives way to pedestrians and horse-riders. No race or trial of speed between bicycles or tricycles may be authorized on a bridleway, but may be authorized on a public road by regulations under the *Road Traffic Act 1960*.

The *Wildlife and Countryside Act 1981* extended the duties and powers of local authorities in relation to public rights of way, for example, they may appoint wardens for them and they must publicize dedication of public rights of way in at least one local newspaper.

This Act also defined a 'byway'. A byway is open to all traffic, that is, it is a highway over which the public have a right of way for vehicular and all other kinds of traffic, but which is used by the public mainly for the purposes for which footpaths and bridleways are used. Local authorities must signpost byways open to all traffic.

RECREATION ON RIVERS AND CANALS

Historically, the rights to use water highways are older than the rights to use highways on land; because civilizations grew up around river basins and most forms of early travel were by water, a free right of navigation was established. Where the basic right of navigation existed for the public benefit it was never really lost.

Public rights of navigation, which include rights incidental to navigation such as temporary mooring, in addition to those existing on the high seas, still exist in the majority of the estuaries in England and Wales, and on many of the natural rivers, particularly the four great rivers, the Thames, the Severn, the Trent and the Yorkshire Ouse. In some cases these rights may have been defined, limited or organized by legislation, notably on the Thames which has, through the Thames Conservancy, one of the best recreational navigations in Europe. The underlying right of public navigation still exists, however.

The necessity of linking navigable rivers caused a boom in canal construction, and between 1760 and 1820 about 4000 miles of waterway were made navigable within England and Wales, and of which there are still some 3000 miles. Following the advent of the railway and its increasing use for freight, to cut down the cost of maintenance as canals fell into disuse, closure Acts were passed, and many waterways would have been lost but for a voluntary body, the Inland Waterways Association which, in 1946, started a public campaign for the preservation of these rights of way, an aim supported and helped by the National Trust. When the *Transport Act 1968* was passed it gave the British Waterways Board, established in 1962 (page 164), new and wide-ranging powers concerning the canals, but it removed the public right of navigation on canals granted earlier by the *Regulations of Railways Act 1873*.

There now exists a mixture of navigation rights on the waterways. Public rights exist over most estuaries and many rivers, although rights related to use by commercial traffic have lapsed with the passing of time, particularly where pleasure cruising did not immediately follow commercial use and there may have been periods of closure. In such circumstances there may be difficulty in re-establishing the public right of navigation. Private navigation rights exist, over which there may also be public navigation rights, particularly where they are held by public bodies or private trusts. However, the nationalized network under the British Waterways Board does not generally still have a right of public navigation on it. The right to use the waterway is a right controlled by the Board who try to exercise that right in the public interest.

For members of the public wishing to cruise on the waterways the present position is the result of compromise. The need to work together to maintain these waterways has led to the growth of voluntary organizations trying to keep this facility available for the public. Generally anglers have come to accept that where a right of navigation exists, this takes precedence over any fishing; whatever the legal position, sportspersons have to exist together and compromise can avoid conflict.

One modern difficulty concerns the growth of the use of the canoe, mainly because of its mobility, and the reluctance of canoeists to be confined to one stretch of water. Most canoeists want the excitement of 'white water', rapid-like stretches of rivers. As it has not been possible to navigate these waters in the past, most of them have no right of navigation and have come under the control of private individuals, often forming valuable fisheries. Where a riverbed is owned by a person, known as the riparian owner, persons travelling on the water above that riverbed are technically trespassers. In English law a trespasser may be taken to court, whether or not that person has caused any actual damage by trespassing.

It is well established in law that, where rights of navigation can be proved to exist, no one may impede the passage of a boat, provided it complies with any statutory rules or regulations, or appropriate payments regarding that stretch of water. Where no rights of navigation exist, anyone navigating that water without the permission of the riparian owner is technically a trespasser and the person who suffers the trespass may take reasonable steps to prevent a trespasser from using that water.

The law concerning the rights of navigation is still confused in relation to canoeists who have had to establish rights in legal battles which have resulted in differing interpretations. In one such case, *Rawson v Peters* (1972),[11] the plaintiffs were suing as trustees of the Bradford Waltonians Angling Club who owned the fishing rights on a stretch of the River Wharfe, and brought an action in trespass against a canoeist who had used that stretch of water. Even though no one had been fishing that stretch of water at the time, the plaintiffs were successful because canoes disturb fish which may affect fishing later on. Lord Denning said in his judgment:

> There are many cases where people with canoes have a right to take their canoes up and down a river. They certainly have such a right in tidal waters. They also often have such a right in non-tidal waters. They may acquire it by long user, as where the public have passed up and down in boats for a long time. Where the public have a right of user, the owners of the fishing rights must allow the canoes and boats unrestricted passage. … But, unless a person with a canoe has some such right, he must not interfere with the fishing rights.[12]

The banks of navigable rivers are in private ownership and are not subject to a general common law right of the public to use for towing, although a right of towing may exist through custom, usage or prescription, dedication or statute. A towpath by a canal may be either a private path or a public right of way for towing. Unless a towpath is a public right of way, no one is responsible for maintaining it and, even where there is a duty to maintain such a path, this may cease if support for the path is washed away.

RESERVOIRS

Legislation may also play a part in the availability of facilities other than rivers and canals for water-based recreation. The responsibility for the provision of recreational facilities on reservoirs rests with the water authorities and the British Waterways Board, according to ownership. Their duties and powers are derived mainly from the *Water Act 1989* and the *Transport Act 1968,* respectively. Access to reservoirs and gathering grounds may be denied for health reasons, although water authorities are under a general duty to provide facilities for recreation in connection with their reservoirs.

Rutland Water, a 3000-acre man-made reservoir in Leicestershire was declared a specially protected area under European Community rules. This designation was announced by the Department of Environment in 1991 following a European Directive giving the reservoir and wetlands Special Protection Area status. The reservoir is already an SSSI (page 172) but this will give the site extra protection as the Directive has to be complied with and is binding on the UK government.

FISHERIES

Another form of water-based recreation, angling, is also based on common-law rights and legislation. Common-law fisheries arise from the right to fish in one's own or another person's water. The public have a common-law right to fish tidal waters, but cannot obtain, by prescription or otherwise, a right to fish non-tidal waters.[13] Since Magna Charta in 1215 Parliament has taken an interest in salmon fisheries which it has controlled by Acts of Parliament, the latest being the *Salmon and Freshwater Fisheries Act 1975* (amended by the *Salmon Act 1986*). Over the years control over salmon fisheries has been extended to trout, eel and freshwater fisheries. The 1975 Act transferred the functions of fisheries previously exercised by river authorities to the water authorities established by the *Water Act 1973*. These functions were subsequently transferred to the National Rivers Authority (page 162) by the *Water Act 1989*.

The National Rivers Authority is now responsible for the enforcement of the *Salmon and Freshwater Fisheries Act 1975*, as amended by the *Salmon Act 1986*. The general responsibility which this legislation entails is to maintain, improve and develop salmon, trout, freshwater and eel fisheries, and to establish and maintain advisory committees of persons interested in fisheries in different parts of the fisheries area of the authority. Powers available to the authority include granting fishing and general licences on payment of licence duties, making and enforcing by-laws to protect, preserve and improve fisheries, purchase or lease obstructions for use for fishing purposes, and to construct and maintain fish passes in dams.

Provision has been made for the Minister to make an order, on the application of the authority, for the imposition on owners and occupiers of fisheries of requirements to pay contributions to the authority in respect of its functions. Increasing pressure upon salmon and sea trout as a sporting resource may soon necessitate a general review of this area of fishery legislation, along with the motley collection of local fishery by-laws acquired by the authority from the former regional water authorities. As a stop-gap measure, the Salmon Act 1986 showed some promise in curbing trade in unlawfully taken salmon in order to remove the commercial incentive that was causing serious problems affecting salmon fisheries.

THE SEASHORE

The seashore may be used for recreation, and limited rights of access to the foreshore and seashore are enjoyed by the public at common law. The use made of beaches is often in excess of these rights and is only by acquiescence of the owners. The seashore is the portion of land which lies between high and low watermark at ordinary tides, 'ordinary' tides being measured by the average tides throughout the year.[14] Generally the soil of the seashore, and the bed of arms and estuaries of the sea and of tidal navigable rivers, as far as the tide ebbs and flows, are owned by the Crown, unless there is a stronger claim to ownership or the Crown has parted with ownership, for example, to a local authority or private individual.

Public rights at common law over the seashore are limited to fishing, navigation and ancillary rights;[15] walking, bathing and beachcombing, though tolerated by the Crown, give no legal rights to the public. The right to use the seashore for bathing may be claimed by custom or prescription, but such a right must be exercised 'decently'. A local authority may make by-laws regulating sea bathing under the *Public Health Act 1936* or by means of a private Act.

Access to the seashore for open-air recreation can be secured through powers conferred on local authorities in the *National Parks and Access to the Countryside Act 1949.* Also in some cases the public are admitted to portions of the seashore vested in local authorities, subject to any local regulations or by-laws in force which may be made through powers given by local Acts. A district council which owns the seashore may make by-laws under the *Public Health Act 1875*, the *Open Spaces Act 1906* or the *Public Health Acts Amendment Act 1907*. By-laws to regulate the speed and use of pleasure boats can be made under the *Public Health Act 1961,* as amended by the *Local Government (Miscellaneous Provisions) Act 1976.*

The general rule is that the natural products of the sea found on the seashore, such as seaweed, shells, gravel and sand, belong to the owner of the seashore and can only be removed with the owner's permission, as the public have no general right to enter on the seashore for such purposes. A right to take sand, shells, shingle and seaweed may, however, exist under statute or be claimed by prescription.

THE USE OF AIRSPACE FOR RECREATION

Airspace is also a facility used for recreation and one becoming increasingly important with the advent and growing popularity of activities such as hang-gliding. Ownership of land includes ownership of the airspace above that land and invasion of that airspace is a trespass unless allowed by agreement or permitted by statute. The extent of the ownership of airspace towards the sky is not unlimited[16] and 'sailing through the air over a person's freehold in a balloon', it was thought in *Saunders v Smith* (1838),[17] would not be a trespass. Landing on private land without permission is, however, unlawful.

The *Civil Aviation Act 1982* provides that no action for trespass or nuisance would arise from aircraft flying over property at a height which, having regard to the wind, weather and all other circumstances, is reasonable as long as the Act is complied with. 'Aircraft' is not defined in the Act, but references in the Air Navigation Orders suggest that it includes balloons, gliders, kites and possibly hang-gliders. Where loss or damage to persons or property is caused by aircraft, the people in them, or articles or persons falling from them, absolute liability is incurred through the *Civil Aviation Act 1982*.

As this chapter has illustrated there are many facilities that may be available for outdoor recreation through the operation of the law. However, opportunities to increase such facilities are limited by lack of finance, the absence of any means of enforcing the use of statutory powers conferred on the various bodies concerned or lack of resources to establish rights of use through legal actions.

NOTES

1. [1905] 2 Ch 188
2. (1795) 2 HyBl 393
3. [1956] Ch 131
4. [1932] 1 Ch 133
5. (1876) 2 Ch 634
6. [1936] 3 All ER 852
7. [1978] 1 WLR 716
8. *Harrison v Duke of Rutland* [1892] 1 QB 142
9. *Hickman v Maisey* [1900] 1 QB 752
10. *Hadwell v Righton* [1907] 2 KB 345
11. Unreported case heard in the Court of Appeal on 1 November 1972
12. See also the Scottish case *Wills' Trustees v Cairngorm* [1976] SLT 162
13. *Smith v Andrews* [1981] 2 Ch 678
14. *Attorney-General v Chambers* (1854) 23 LJ Ch 662
15. *Lord Fitzhardinge v Purcell* [1908] 2 Ch 139
16. *Lord Bernstein of Leigh v Skyways and General Ltd* [1977] 2 All ER 902
17. (1838) 2 Jur 491

Index